D1290103

Post-Christendom

'For people in exile, messages of hope are vital. This book draws a clear road map of where we have come from and where we are headed. It beckons with hope.'
Ian Coffey, Spring Harvest Leadership Team

'Stuart Murray's is a distinctive and important voice in debates about the future of the church in these islands. His latest book shows us why the model of church of the last millennium and a half has run its course and what kinds of options there are for the emerging church. This is not just speculation as it is rooted in the experience of thousands of Christians in the UK who are experimenting with new ways of being church and following Jesus Christ in the contemporary world.'
Christopher Rowland, Dean Ireland's Professor, Queen's College, Oxford

'How are we to make an impact on society in the twenty-first century? With the marginalisation of the church to the sidelines, we need to think of creative ways of presenting the church and mission. *Post-Christendom* does just that. It arms us with the necessary weapons to combat and challenge the increasing secularization, and offers a rare glimpse of hope in this strange new world. Read it and renew your vision for the church C21.'
David Coffey, Moderator of the Free Churches and General Secretary of the Baptist Union

'If you like challenging questions then this is a book that you must read! As in his earlier book *Church Planting*, Stuart Murray approaches the topic of post-Christendom with thoroughness, outside-the-box thinking, and with a wide range of comments reflecting his widely read mind. This is not just a book for reading, but for discussing and wrestling with and trying to work out what are the best ways of using the many insights given in it for changing contemporary church culture. Stuart Murray has no doubts that it must be changed, and seeks to encourage leadership to change it authentically, fashioned less on our traditional understanding of the Scriptures and more on the new life that is in Christ. This is likely to be a formative book for the twenty-first-century church, and we simply HAVE to answer some of the questions that he raises if we are to survive.'
Peter Brierley, Executive Director, Christian Research

'The journey into Post-Christendom is already upon us. Stuart Murray is a reliable guide for the journey. Most unusually, Murray combines wide-ranging scholarship with extensive hands-on experience in urban mission. So he is ideally equipped to help Christians understand where we have come from and to think about where we are going. A special gift that Murray brings is his discerning assessment of what in the Christian past is provision for our journey, and what is baggage that weighs us down. Murray's instincts are imaginative; his passions are practical and mission-centred; his perspective is faith-filled and rooted in Jesus. *Post-Christendom* is superbly written and will be significant for all who care about the future of Christianity in the West.'
Alan Kreider, Associated Mennonite Biblical Seminary, Elkhart, Indiana, USA

Post-Christendom

Stuart Murray

PATERNOSTER

First published in 2004 by Paternoster Press
Reprinted 2005

11 10 09 08 07 06 05   8 7 6 5 4 3 2

Paternoster Press is an imprint of Authentic Media,
9 Holdom Avenue, Bletchley, Milton Keynes, Bucks., MK1 1QR, UK
and 129 Mobilization Drive, Waynesboro, GA 30830-4575, USA
www.authenticmedia.co.uk

British Library Cataloguing in Publication Data
A catalogue record for this book is available from the British Library

ISBN 1-84227-261-6

Cover Design by fourninezero design.
Typeset by WestKey Ltd., Falmouth, Cornwall
Printed and Bound by J.H. Haynes and Co. Ltd., Sparkford
Print Management by Adare Carwin

Dedicated to friends and colleagues in the
Anabaptist Network

Contents

Contents

Foreword

The recognition that we are living 'after Christendom' has been around for some time. Christian scholars and thinkers in the West, and particularly missiologists, have now turned their attention to the question of what it means to be the church at a time when the church no longer 'possesses' the culture in which it is set. A few seem to hanker after what used to be and imagine in their theologies how it may be recovered. Others, understandably, lament what has been lost but gird up their loins anyway for the new missionary task. Yet others see the loss of Christendom as an opportunity for the church to discover itself, to shake off the shackles of compromise and live as the church should always have lived – as a faithful community of disciples of Jesus Christ who have no continuing city here but who look forward 'to the city that has foundations, whose architect and builder is God' (Heb. 11:10). Dr Stuart Murray and this excellent book belong to this last category.

In endorsing this book I am commending first of all its author as a tried and trusted scholar and commentator whose insights and gifts are recognised across the world. Stuart Murray is well known as a leading writer and thinker on Anabaptism, biblical hermeneutics, church planting and new ways of being church. Before turning to theology he studied law, which explains why in all his writings there is clear and rigorous argument and analysis, bolstered by relevant evidence and issuing in a case that has to be answered. In this book that case includes the telling of a 'grand narrative' describing the rise and fall of Christendom and the emergence of post-Christendom, but it also takes in many incidental details of Christian practice. Whether readers agree or disagree with the overall argument or the individual details presented here, all will profit by considering the way the case for welcoming the onset of post-Christendom is developed.

This is a time when many parts of the church are giving thought to the relationships between faith and society. Interestingly the discussion is echoed by secular thinkers and 'devout sceptics' who, at their best, take seriously the presence of faith communities and value the transcendent perspectives they bring, even while not endorsing them. The fact is that none of us have ever been this way before. It is indeed a strange new world. This book should help us all to think that bit more clearly about issues of enormous significance both for the Christian communities and the wider communities in which they are set.

Dr Nigel G. Wright
Principal, Spurgeon's College, London

Preface

Writing *Post-Christendom* has been daunting. It has meant surveying 1700 years of European church history and delving into missiological, sociological and theological studies. I am grateful to scholars whose research I have learned from, indicating in footnotes where their insights can be accessed. But I realise complex subjects and periods have often been summarised in a single paragraph or sentence. In a survey, broad brush-strokes do not permit many nuances or discussion of disputed issues.

I hope *Post-Christendom* contains few factual errors or irresponsible judgements, but it engages in what Alan Kreider calls 'bunking'. Some books engage in 'debunking' – critical studies that examine previous research and offer new interpretations of details or challenge unreliable conclusions. These are important and helpful books, providing secure foundations for those who rely on their careful work. But 'bunking' is valid too – describing the big picture, presenting a framework, identifying recurrent themes and exploring implications.

Post-Christendom suggests we are experiencing cultural turbulence as the long era of Christendom comes to an end. It argues that to negotiate this we need to understand Christendom, why it is collapsing and how we reconfigure discipleship, mission and church for a new era. It looks at familiar issues from unfamiliar angles, using the lens of post-Christendom. It offers perspectives and resources for Christians and churches no longer at the centre of society but on the margins. It invites a realistic and hopeful response to challenges and opportunities awaiting us in the twenty-first century.

The transition from modernity to postmodernity (whatever this means) has received a huge amount of attention. The shift from Christendom to post-Christendom is at least as significant for church and society, but the issues and implications have not yet been explored to anything like the same extent. This book is an introduction, a journey into the past, an interpretation of the present and an invitation to ask what following Jesus might mean in the strange new world of post-Christendom.

Post-Christendom has benefited from the critique of friends who read various chapters and whose feedback was helpful (though I am responsible for errors and shortcomings that remain). I am grateful to Jonathan Bartley, David Norrington, Dave Nussbaum and Rosemary Pearse for their comments and to Jared Diener for help with research. Alan Kreider read the entire manuscript and I am deeply grateful for his friendship, encouragement and insights. The other person who read the book chapter by chapter as first drafts appeared and helped me see issues in fresh ways was my wife, Sian, whose love and affirmation continues to sustain and humble me.

Many issues and perspectives in this book were first explored in conversations with friends and colleagues in the Anabaptist Network – including Nigel Wright, from whose writings on related themes I have learned much, and who kindly agreed to write the foreword. To them this book is gratefully dedicated.

Stuart Murray
Oxford, July 2003

1

The End of Christendom

Snapshots of Post-Christendom

In a London school a teenager with no church connections hears the Christmas story for the first time. His teacher tells it well and he is fascinated by this amazing story. Risking his friends' mockery, after the lesson he thanks her for the story. One thing had disturbed him, so he asks: 'Why did they give the baby a swear word for his name?'

One Sunday in Oxford a man visits a church building to collect something for his partner who works during the week in a creative-arts project the church runs. He arrives as the morning congregation is leaving and recognises the minister, whom he knows. Surprised, he asks: 'What are all these people doing here? I didn't know churches were open on Sundays!'

Two snapshots of 'post-Christendom' – a culture in which central features of the Christian story are unknown and churches are alien institutions whose rhythms do not normally impinge on most members of society. Only a few years ago, neither would have been credible, but today there are numerous signs that the 'Christendom' era in Western culture is fading.

In these snapshots, an unknown story and alien institution provoke surprise not hostility, curiosity not indifference. The story fascinates; the institution is intriguing. Total ignorance of church and Christianity may not yet be widespread, but it is becoming more common, especially in our inner cities. Over the coming decades, as the last generation who are familiar with the Christian story and for whom churches still have cultural significance dies, the change of epoch from Christendom to post-Christendom will be complete.

Then, for the first time in many centuries, Christians in Western culture will be able to tell the Christian story to people for whom it is entirely unknown – a challenging scenario but full of opportunities we have not had for generations. This was the early Christians' experience as they carried the story across the Mediterranean basin and Central Asia. It has been the task of pioneer missionaries throughout the centuries as they have translated the story into diverse cultures. But it is new to us.

In Western culture, until recently, the story was known and church was a familiar institution. Evangelism meant encouraging those who already knew the story to live by it and inviting those already familiar with church to participate actively. Many were 'de-churched', but hardly anyone was 'unchurched' (neither term is appropriate in a post-Christendom culture where church is marginal and abnormal, but they help us understand the transitional phase we are experiencing). But our culture is changing. Adult churchgoing continues to decline and only four per cent of children are involved in churches.[1] Ignorance of Christianity is increasing and church buildings are becoming as alien as mosques or gurudwaras. Some residual knowledge and belief will persist, though this will become

---

[1] More attend church schools.

attenuated and syncretistic, and church buildings will still provide vital community space. But we will no longer be able to assume we are in a 'Christian society' where most are latent Christians and lapsed churchgoers.

The end of Christendom will require radical changes in our understanding of mission and church. We have already discovered through the disappointments of the Decade of Evangelism in Britain in the 1990s that 'exhortation and invitation' evangelism is becoming obsolete. This has stimulated a widespread search for more authentic and contextual ways of being church and engaging in mission. But important attempts to reconfigure church and mission, rooted in theological reflection on contemporary cultural shifts, are often hampered by limited understanding of the significance of the shift from Christendom to post-Christendom. It is *this* shift that is the subject of this book.

We are not quite there yet. We are in a lengthy transitional phase. Christendom took centuries to develop and will not collapse overnight. In this interim period, some still know the story and memories of faith may still draw some into the churches, but this era is fading. We must prepare for change. New expressions of church and mission will be needed, new ways of thinking on ethics, politics and evangelism. Anything proposed at this stage must be experimental, tentative and modest, since we cannot yet see more than the outlines of the emerging culture. But post-Christendom is coming and we cannot continue as if Christendom will endure forever.

What Post-Christendom Is Not

Understanding and engaging with post-Christendom will occupy us throughout this book, but we need a working definition of post-Christendom.[2] It may be helpful to clarify what post-Christendom is not.

Post-Christendom does not comprehensively describe the culture that will replace Christendom. It is one of many 'post-' words in contemporary society signalling a time of cultural turbulence, of transition from the known to the unknown. The prefix means 'after' and indicates something familiar is passing. It says nothing about what is replacing it. We know things are not how they used to be and sense change in the air, but we are unsure what is approaching. 'Post-' words are backward facing, indicating something is disappearing. If we could describe the new reality taking shape, we would not use 'post-' language but would name it. Used appropriately, this terminology displays humility: we do not have a full and accurate understanding of what is happening, but we know previous assumptions, structures and responses are now inadequate. Christendom is dying: we are entering a new culture that is 'after Christendom' and we realise we will need time to find our bearings in this new landscape.

Post-Christendom does not mean post-Christian. Some use these concepts interchangeably, arguing that post-Christendom will result inevitably in a post-Christian culture. But conflating these terms causes confusion and prejudges debatable issues.

The demise of Christendom does mean the Christian story is becoming unfamiliar. The proportion of the British population with any church connection (measured by usage

---

[2] 'Post-Christendom' will be used rather than 'post-Constantinian': this is less focused on the influence of Constantine at the start of the Christendom era and allows consideration of developments that owe nothing to him. Christendom was the term its advocates used approvingly; 'Constantinian' is normally associated with its critics.

of rites of passage, occasional attendance, regular participation or membership) has declined steadily over the past half-century. The influence of Christianity on public debate and personal belief and behaviour has diminished. As Callum Brown concludes in *The Death of Christian Britain*, 'what emerges is a story not merely of church decline, but of the end of Christianity as a means by which men and women, as individuals, construct their identities and their sense of "self"'.[3] He catalogues the changes in the late twentieth century:

> In unprecedented numbers, the British people since the 1960s have stopped going to church, have allowed their church membership to lapse, have stopped marrying in church and have neglected to baptise their children. Meanwhile, their children, the two generations who grew to maturity in the last thirty years of the twentieth century, stopped going to Sunday school, stopped entering confirmation or communicant classes, and rarely, if ever, stepped inside a church to worship in their entire lives. The cycle of inter-generational renewal of Christian affiliation, a cycle which had for so many centuries tied the people however closely or loosely to the churches, and to Christian moral benchmarks, was permanently disrupted in the 'swinging sixties'.[4]

Some dispute Brown's explanation of the causes of this collapse, but this sustained decline in almost all aspects of 'Christian affiliation' since 1960 is unprecedented. The demise of Christendom might mean the virtual extinction of the church in Britain. Some trends and statistical projections point in this direction. Some denominations are facing

---

[3] Callum Brown, *The Death of Christian Britain: Understanding Secularisation 1800–2000* (London: Routledge, 2001), 2.
[4] Brown, *Death*, 1.

not just the continuing attrition of declining numbers but also the possibility of meltdown:

- If the current rate of decline is not arrested, the Methodist Church will have zero membership by 2037.[5]
- If it continues to shrink at the present rate, the Church of Scotland will close its last congregation in 2033.[6]
- Unless something happens to reverse the decline it is experiencing, the Church in Wales will be unsustainable by 2020.[7]
- The Salvation Army and United Reformed Church face similar prospects.

Although we should treat such projections with caution, recognising that wipe-out is unlikely, denominational non-viability is looking increasingly probable for these groups of churches.

Larger denominations are suffering drastic decline that will make it difficult for them to continue as normal. Attendance at Mass in Catholic churches fell from nearly two million to just over one million between 1965 and 1996.[8] Almost all indicators in the period 1980–2000 show accelerating decline in the Church of England, with Sunday attendance figures below one million for the first time.

---

[5] Philip Richter and Leslie Francis, *Gone but not Forgotten* (London: Darton, Longman & Todd, 1998), 1.

[6] Brown, *Death*, 4.

[7] Heather Wraight, *Strategic Thinking from a Christian Perspective* (London: Christian Research Association, 2002), 11.

[8] Kenneth Leech, *Through Our Long Exile: Contextual Theology and the Urban Experience* (London: Darton, Longman & Todd, 2001), 141.

However, few churches are closing, suggesting increasingly desperate efforts to maintain the national coverage Anglicans regard as crucial to their self-identity.[9] Chronic shortages of Catholic and Anglican ordinands exacerbate the problem; it unlikely the present parish system and ubiquity of a national church can be sustained for much longer.

There are signs of hope and growing congregations in most denominations (one in five churches reports growth), and some denominations are holding their own or even growing slowly,[10] but John and Olive Drane summarise the seriousness of the situation:

> For the last forty years, the statistics have reflected an accelerating crisis in church life, and we are now faced with the serious possibility – likelihood, even – that the Christian faith might disappear entirely from our culture within the first half of this century ... Our churches are in incredibly bad shape. Moreover, the decline is affecting all Christian traditions. Every denomination faces the same issues, and they extend right across the theological spectrum.[11]

Due to our inability to recruit new members and our failure to retain existing members or their children, church attendance could be down to four per cent within the next twenty years.[12] Currently about 1500 people each week are leaving

[9] Bob Jackson, *Hope for the Church: Contemporary Strategies for Growth* (London: Church House, 2002), 1-14.
[10] Baptists, Orthodox churches and some Pentecostal and newer church networks.
[11] John and Olive Drane, 'Breaking into Dynamic Ways of being Church', in *Breaking New Ground : The First Scottish Ecumenical Assembly 2001*(Dunblane: Action of Churches Together in Scotland, 2001), 142.
[12] Extrapolating information from the English Church Attendance Survey indicates this level could be attained by 2016.

the churches (excluding deaths and transfers).[13] Christian values and perspectives will no longer have the limited influence they currently have when Christians are one among many marginal communities. This prospect is unthinkable to many Christians. They note surveys indicating greater interest in Christianity and greater resilience in church attendance than headline figures indicate, enthuse about 'emerging forms of church', suggest others emulate growing churches, hope and pray for revival, or assume God will intervene. But Christianity has been eradicated before in places (the Middle East and North Africa) that were once Christian heartlands. It could happen in Western Europe.

But post-Christendom need not mean post-Christian. The near future will be difficult for Christians in a society that has rejected institutional Christianity and is familiar enough with the Christian story not to want to hear it again. Inherited assumptions and Christendom models will not help us respond creatively to the challenges ahead. But perhaps – if we have the courage to face into this future rather than hankering after a fading past, if we resist short-term strategies and pre-packaged answers, if we learn to be cross-cultural missionaries in our own society, and if we can negotiate the next forty years – whatever culture emerges from the ruins of Christendom might offer tremendous opportunities for telling and living out the Christian story in a society where this is largely unknown. Whether post-Christendom is post-Christian will depend on whether we can re-imagine Christianity in a world we no longer control. Christendom is dying, but a new and dynamic Christianity could arise from its ashes.

There is another reason for avoiding the term 'post-Christian': it assumes Christendom was Christian, Europe was a Christian civilisation and Britain was a

---

[13] Richter and Francis, *Gone*, 2.

Christian nation. But persistent voices throughout previous centuries queried whether Christendom was as Christian as was generally believed and suggested its Christianity was little more than a veneer. If this is so, calling the emerging culture 'post-Christian' and proclaiming the 'death of Christian Britain' is unhelpful. Using the term 'post-Christendom' does not prejudge these issues, which will be investigated in the following chapters.

Post-Christendom is not the same as pre-Christendom. Although telling the Christian story to those who have never heard it has similarities to the pre-Christendom context of early Christians and pioneer missionaries, we should distinguish carefully between pre-Christendom and post-Christendom. Vestiges of Christendom will be scattered across post-Christendom. Even when obvious anachronisms are removed (with or without the church's approval) its Christendom past will haunt post-Christendom. Mediated through literature, historical studies, architecture, coinage, art, music and other aspects of culture will be powerful memories of the all-pervasive Christendom culture that shaped Western society. Even movements that are antagonistic towards Christianity are shaped by it: the ideology of neo-paganism, for example, owes as much to the Christendom era it dismisses as an extended deviation from indigenous European pagan religion as to the ancient paganism it claims to be recovering.

In the twilight zone between the demise of Christendom and the full development of post-Christendom, these memories will in the churches often be tinged with nostalgia. This may discourage the reappraisal of Christendom attitudes, priorities, structures and practices that we must undertake to thrive, or even survive, in post-Christendom. Elsewhere, such memories may dissuade those who associate the Christian story with what they dismiss as an oppressive and failed culture from listening afresh to this story. Renewal within the church and evangelisation beyond it are both problematic in this interim period. We have neither of two advantages: the freshness of the story in pre-Christendom nor its familiarity in Christendom.

Forty years on, both renewal and evangelisation may be easier. As memories of Christendom fade, as the generation of church members dies for whom the final years of Christendom were disappointing, and as the snapshots with which this chapter opened become commonplace, resistance to change may be less, post-Christendom forms of church and mission may be emerging and there may be greater openness to a story that is quite unknown. But, even then, we will be in post-Christendom, not pre-Christendom. As heirs of Christendom we must decide what to discard as baggage that weighs us down and what precious resources for the ongoing journey into post-Christendom we should carry with us.

Post-Christendom does not mean secular. During the second half of the twentieth century the demise of Christendom in Western culture was generally assumed to be a cause or consequence of secularisation. Decline in Christian belief and abandonment of a Christian worldview were linked with the mid-eighteenth century Enlightenment. Transition from the medieval world to the modern world, growing reliance on reason rather than revelation, the disenchantment of nature and the processes of urbanisation and industrialisation were all cited as factors in the marginalising of Christianity and development of a secular society.

Religious warfare between supposedly Christian nations in Europe preceded and provoked the emergence of a secular worldview that undermined Christendom. This involved a philosophical shift towards a society based on reason and science rather than dogma and religious intolerance. The political disintegration of Christendom can thus be perceived as a *cause* of secularisation. As this secular

approach gained sway, the societal, psychological and institutional disintegration of Christendom can be interpreted
as a *consequence* of secularisation. Some versions of the
'secularisation thesis' describe a slow process of
marginalising Christianity over two or three centuries and
resulting in the gradual demise of Christendom.[14] Brown
proposes a catastrophic collapse of Christendom in the past
fifty years, as pent-up pressures were released in the single
generation that experienced the revolutions of the 1960s.[15]

However, whether the process was gradual or sudden
and whether secularisation was a cause or consequence of
the demise of Christendom, confident assertions in the
1960s and 1970s about the emergence of a secular culture
now seem strangely dated. Secularisation has continued
apace: secular assumptions rule contemporary society and
guide political, economic and social decision-making. But
the expectation that religious beliefs would wither has
proved false. Spirituality and religious beliefs, in remarkably diverse forms, have flourished and we can now identify
a counter-process of desecularisation challenging secular
assumptions. Neopaganism, westernised oriental religions,
'new age' ideas, Islam, new religious movements, interest in
the occult and other expressions of spirituality and religion
are undermining any claim that post-Christendom is secular. Some may be 'designer spirituality', resistant to
institutional expression and eschewing truth claims. Much
of it is privatised and unconnected with public life or daily

---

[14] Steve Bruce (ed.), *Religion and Modernization: Sociologists
and Historians Debate the Secularization Thesis* (Oxford: Oxford University Press, 1992); and his *Religion in Modern Britain*
(Oxford: Oxford University Press, 1995); Grace Davie, *Europe:
The Exceptional Case* (London: Darton, Longman & Todd,
2002).
[15] Brown, *Death*, 1.

work, where economism and consumerism maintain the dominance of the secular worldview. But it suggests human beings are incurably religious and that secularism is an inadequate basis for any society.

In post-Christendom, however, renewed interest in spirituality is generally not related to Christianity, which is associated with oppressive dogmatism and seen as spiritually inhibiting. The fervent hopes many Christians express that resurgent spirituality might represent new opportunities for the churches have not yet been realised. Most people interested in spirituality in post-Christendom are looking elsewhere for insights and resources. Post-Christendom is not secular, but neither is it Christian.

Post-Christendom is not the same as postmodernity. The most familiar 'post-' words in descriptions of contemporary culture are postmodernism (a philosophical stance) and postmodernity (a cultural shift). But post-Christendom should not be confused with postmodernism or postmodernity.[16] There are significant connections between these concepts, but they are different. Many Christians are investigating this aspect of culture, examining postmodern challenges to theology, developing postmodern ways to communicate the gospel and designing postmodern churches. This is valuable (though we must beware becoming locked into what may be a passing phase), but the transition from Christendom to post-Christendom should neither be marginalised nor subsumed within discussions about postmodernity.

Postmodernism represents a critique of modernism and is variously hailed as the most significant philosophical shift since the Enlightenment or a minor adjustment within a

---

[16] In books, articles, websites and conversations 'post-Christendom' and 'postmodernity' are often used inter-changeably: this confusion is unhelpful.

worldview that will continue to be dominant for centuries. Postmodernism enhances the process of desecularisation: it endorses the resurgence of spirituality, reflects loss of confidence in rationalism and science and urges pursuit of authentic humanity. It regards all meta-narratives (overarching explanations and truth claims) as inherently oppressive. Uninterested in coherent systems or consistency, it is relativistic, playful, pessimistic and sceptical.

Some use the term to catalogue criticisms of modernism, some to signal a vacuum as modernity collapses, and some to greet an emerging worldview shaping our culture. Many are weary of the term and whatever it signifies – mid-course correction in the onward march of modernity, a cultural dead-end, or a philosophy replacing modernism as the dominant Western worldview. Its critique of modernity is often apt (though it is also governed by unacknowledged meta-narratives) and its recovery of marginalised dimensions of human and social life is welcome. Some hail its liberating potential. Others find it too fragmentary, self-indulgent and incoherent to offer a sustainable foundation for society or human flourishing: debunking is temporarily exciting, but a more integrative and inspiring philosophical basis is needed for personal and societal values. But, even if postmodernism is merely a short-lived burst of deconstructive pessimism, reconstructing modernity will require substantial redesigning and greater humility. Whatever we think of postmodernism, we inhabit postmodernity.

As with secularisation, both causes and consequences are involved in the relationship between the demise of Christendom and the development of postmodernism. One of the meta-narratives postmodernists reject is the Christian story, especially in the way this was told during Christendom. The demise of Christendom and widespread loss of confidence in the Christian story led first to the new meta-narrative of modernity and then to the ambivalent plurality of postmodernity. Postmodern values – suspicion of dogma, distaste for institutions and acceptance of multiple and contradictory stories and expressions of spirituality – have so far frustrated Christians' attempts to seize the opportunities presented by its critique of modernity and accelerated the demise of Christendom. Postmodernity represents a challenging component of the new mission frontier in Western culture.

Our concern, however, is with post-Christendom. Although this term also represents a transitional phase, the prospect of Christendom recovering its former influence is less likely than modernity absorbing postmodernity and recovering the centre ground. The demise of Christendom will surely continue. And the opportunities and challenges associated with this deserve as much attention from Christians concerned about God's mission in contemporary culture as those associated with postmodernity. Indeed, the shift from modernity to postmodernity may be quite minor in missiological terms by comparison with the shift from Christendom to post-Christendom. But this latter shift has received far less attention.

Post-Christendom is not the experience of all Christians. It is the experience of Christians in Western Europe and other societies with roots in this culture.[17] The term 'post-Christendom' is less familiar in some places than others, but once understood it is widely accepted as a framework for explaining changes many have perceived but not analysed, and for interpreting strong but confusing feelings. Using this language on recent visits to Australia, New Zealand, Canada and several European nations has

---

[17] The story of the Orthodox Christendom that developed in the Eastern Roman Empire is different and will not be examined in detail in this book.

provoked vigorous nods of confirmation from those already aware of the issues and excited or tearful responses from others who can suddenly understand their context. Historical, socio-political and cultural differences have produced different forms of Christendom in different nations and have resulted in variations in the pace of its demise and the shape of the emerging post-Christendom. But transition to post-Christendom is the shared experience of most Christians in Western culture.[18]

It is not, however, the experience of Christians in many other societies. Some belong to ancient churches in regions where there was no Christendom era. Early Christian missionaries went east as well as west, planting churches across central Asia and reaching India and China. In the medieval period there were probably more Christians in Asia than in Europe. But, because church history is usually told from a Eurocentric perspective, only recently has the story of Asian Christianity become better known.[19] Asian Christianity spread, flourished and struggled in a different environment, facing not ageing European paganism but major religious alternatives – Zoroastrianism in Persia, Hinduism in India, Buddhism in China and Islam in the Middle East and Central Asia. It never experienced Christendom (although on occasions this suddenly seemed possible). The history of Asian Christianity may offer insights to Christians in post-Christendom faced with a plural religious context for which Christendom has not prepared us.

Nor is post-Christendom the experience of Christians in nations, especially in Africa, Asia and Latin America, where

---

[18] The critique of Christendom and language of post-Christendom is not a thinly veiled assault on established churches. Issues explored in this book concern *all* churches in Western culture.
[19] An excellent introduction is Samuel Moffett, *A History of Christianity in Asia* Volume I (Maryknoll: Orbis, 1998).

Christianity is growing exponentially in cultures that can be described as pre-Christendom or still-Christendom. The decline of Christianity in Western societies is more than matched by its expansion in these areas. Christians in post-Christendom are abnormal: our wealth, whiteness, declining numbers, experience of secularisation and postmodernity, weariness and struggle to adjust to marginality are exceptional within the global church. During the twentieth century Christianity's centre of gravity moved south, even if our denominational and institutional structures have not yet acknowledged this. If post-Christendom does spell the virtual extinction of Christianity in Europe, this will not be terminal for God's global mission – any more than God's mission was thwarted by similar geographical shifts in previous generations. Indeed, missionaries from the former 'mission fields' of Asia, Africa and Latin America are arriving in Europe in increasing numbers to evangelise the former 'sending nations': their impact on post-Christendom culture may be as significant as any response Western churches make.

But, as we celebrate the extraordinary growth of the global church and redefine mission as 'from everywhere to everywhere', we should heed some notes of caution. Missionaries from Christendom exported their culture, assumptions and structures as they preached the gospel in Africa, Latin America and Asia. New Christendoms may be established in these continents, with consequences that are scarcely imaginable but that may also be profoundly disturbing.[20] Can painful stories from European Christendom

---

[20]   Philip Jenkins, *The Next Christendom: The Coming of Global Christianity* (New York: Oxford University Press, 2002). For a different perspective, based on a more restrictive interpretation of Christendom, see Andrew Walls, *The Cross-Cultural Process in Christian History: Studies in the Transmission and Appropriation of Faith* (Edinburgh: T. & T. Clark, 2002), 34.

be shared, humbly but urgently, with these emerging 'Christian societies' before they are repeated with devastating consequences? Furthermore, adopting southern hemisphere patterns of church or mission for post-Christendom, hoping missionaries from these regions will re-evangelise Europe and tailoring our expectations to growth rates in other cultures will exacerbate the crisis we face. Partnership and mutual learning across different cultures offers more than dependence or plagiarism.

Missing from the list of Western societies experiencing the shift to post-Christendom was the United States of America. Some places in America and aspects of American society have all the hallmarks of post-Christendom, so the language and issues are recognisable. But the form, status and experience of American Christendom has been significantly different from other Western societies. How this will affect the transition to post-Christendom is unclear. In some parts of America, despite constitutional separation between church and state, an unofficial but deeply entrenched form of Christendom continues to thrive. This kind of Christendom may persist far longer in America than in other Western nations, or a renegotiated form of Christendom might even succeed in capturing the heart of American society. Some predict America will buck the trend of declining church attendance and the marginalising of Christianity (though in the northwest attendance is already at European levels). But the shift to post-Christendom, already evident in many urban areas across America, may occur a generation or two after Europe but with similar consequences.[21] Either way, uncritical reliance on American models of church, techniques of evangelism and approaches to mission will be of little help to Christians in

---

[21] Again Jenkins and Walls offer divergent interpretations. See also Brown, *Death*, 196–7 and Davie, *Europe*, passim.

post-Christendom. Recent experience of imported American programmes and strategies suggest these often raise illegitimate expectations and distract us from what needs to be done.[22]

This section has flagged up important (and contentious) issues that later chapters will revisit. But, just as the meaning and implications of postmodernity cannot be understood without reference to modernity, so the significance of post-Christendom cannot be understood without Christendom. For, as well as being *post*-Christendom, our context is also post-*Christendom*. Christendom is passing, but it is Christendom that has shaped our culture and from which post-Christendom is a development. As Robert Jensen writes, 'Western civilization is still defined by Christianity, but as the civilization that *used* to be Christian.'[23]

So the following chapters will begin in the fourth century and examine the birth of the culture that is now dying; trace its territorial and ideological development and identify the main ingredients of Christendom; and chart its gradual

---

[22] What follows will concentrate on the European context, as engagement with the American context would complicate the discussion and require additional space. To explore the post-Christendom scene in America, see Loren Mead, *The Once and Future Church* (Washington: Alban, 1991); Rodney Clapp, *A Peculiar People: The Church as Culture in a Post-Christian Society* (Downers Grove: InterVarsity Press, 1996); Stanley Hauerwas, *After Christendom?: How the church is to behave if freedom, justice, and a Christian nation are bad ideas* (Nashville: Abingdon, 1991) and Stanley Hauerwas and William Willimon, *Resident Aliens: A provocative Christian assessment of culture and ministry for people who know that something is wrong* (Nashville: Abingdon, 1991).

[23] Cited in Rodney Clapp, *Border Crossings: Christian Trespasses On Popular Culture And Public Affairs* (Grand Rapids: Brazos Press, 2000), 91.

demise and the emergence of post-Christendom. This study of Christendom will set the scene for missiological engagement with post-Christendom.

The Meaning of Post-Christendom

Having explored what post-Christendom does not mean, this may suffice as a working definition:

> Post-Christendom is the culture that emerges as the Christian faith loses coherence within a society that has been definitively shaped by the Christian story and as the institutions that have been developed to express Christian convictions decline in influence.

Post-Christendom makes no sense without a knowledge of the past. In societies where churches have flourished and declined, where the Christian story has been told and has influenced individuals and even the culture as a whole, but where other stories have had a definitive or equivalent influence alongside the Christian story, post-Christendom is not an appropriate term to describe the diminished influence of the churches or the story they tell.

The demise of Christendom may be sudden or gradual. It involves both institutional and philosophical changes, for Christendom is both a power structure and a mindset. Sustained persecution may lead to the demise of Christendom (as in some parts of the former Soviet Union and Eastern Europe), or it may result from the official choice of another story (as in the transition from Christianity to Islam in North Africa). The demise of Christendom in Western culture is the first instance of such a cultural shift occurring without the pressure of persecution or the adoption of a different story. Here the Christian story has not been replaced by another story but by scepticism about all explanatory and culture-shaping stories. In this sense, post-Christendom in Western culture is different from earlier versions: we really have not been here before.

Post-Christendom includes the following transitions:

- *From the centre to margins*: in Christendom the Christian story and the churches were central, but in post-Christendom these are marginal.
- *From majority to minority*: in Christendom Christians comprised the (often overwhelming) majority, but in post-Christendom we are a minority.
- *From settlers to sojourners*: in Christendom Christians felt at home in a culture shaped by their story, but in post-Christendom we are aliens, exiles and pilgrims in a culture where we no longer feel at home.
- *From privilege to plurality*: in Christendom Christians enjoyed many privileges, but in post-Christendom we are one community among many in a plural society.
- *From control to witness*: in Christendom churches could exert control over society, but in post-Christendom we exercise influence only through witnessing to our story and its implications.
- *From maintenance to mission*: in Christendom the emphasis was on maintaining a supposedly Christian status quo, but in post-Christendom it is on mission within a contested environment.
- *From institution to movement*: in Christendom churches operated mainly in institutional mode, but in post-Christendom we must become again a Christian movement.

Post-Christendom can easily be perceived as a threat and associated with failure and decline. Our response to the challenges it presents may be to burrow ostrich-like into the remaining sand of familiar church culture, scan the horizon for growing churches that claim we can continue doing what we have always done, or clutch desperately at promises of revival or programmes that promise to restore our fortunes. Indeed, the more we understand post-Christendom, the greater may be the temptation to respond in such ways: post-Christendom is not an easy environment for discipleship, mission or church.

The perspective from which this book is written is different. It celebrates the end of Christendom and the distorting influence of power, wealth and status on the Christian story. It grieves the violence, corruption, folly and arrogance of Christendom. It rejoices that all who choose to become followers of Jesus today do so freely without pressure or inducements. It revels in a context where the Christian story is becoming unknown and can be rediscovered (by Christians and others). It welcomes the freedom to look afresh at many issues seen for so long only through the lens of Christendom. It anticipates new and liberating discoveries as Christians explore what it means to be a church on the margins that operates as a movement rather than an institution. And it trusts that history will turn out how God intends with or without Christians attempting to control it.

Some may find this a very odd perspective, but it is not new. Ever since its birth in the fourth century, not all Christians approved of Christendom. There was a price to pay for Christendom and some considered this too high, protesting that it was corrupt, that excessive wealth and the use of coercion were contrary to the gospel. Others asked if Christendom was real: was Western Europe Christian or was its Christianity a veneer over a culture that remained

essentially pagan?[24] Around the edges of Christendom were
marginal communities, persecuted as heretics and subversives, who dissented from Christendom and dared to
imagine Christianity without it. Their courageous witness is
receiving fresh attention, as increasing numbers find their
insights inspiring and helpful for marginal churches in
post-Christendom.

So you are invited to journey back to the dawn of Christendom, then forward through the centuries during which
the Christian story was dominant in Europe, and on to the
twilight zone that is our present context as Christendom
dies and post-Christendom awaits its proper name. One
word of warning: if you are hoping for easy answers to the
challenges ahead, you will not find them here. In this transitional period there are more questions than answers and
our primary task is to discover which questions are worth
asking. Hopefully, the journey ahead will at least offer some
clues.

---

[24] Anton Wessels, *Europe: Was it ever Really Christian?: The Interaction Between Gospel and Culture* (London: SCM Press,
1994).

2

The Coming of Christendom

The Achievement of Christendom

Although the term 'Christendom' was coined in ninth-century England, the story begins in fourth-century Rome. Some of its distinctive elements were new and would have been surprising – and disconcerting – to earlier Christians; others were developments of trends already apparent in previous decades. Christendom advanced both through startlingly rapid changes and gradual evolution.

Historical circumstances produced several versions of Christendom in different eras and regions, but the flourishing of this culture amidst political disintegration, social turbulence and economic upheaval is impressive. The transition from Late Antiquity through the 'Dark Ages' to the medieval world is incomprehensible without the contribution of Christendom. Its achievements are remarkable, as is its cultural, literary and religious heritage.

However, the 'Christendom shift' was seismic, resulting in profound changes in how the church understood itself, its theology and its social responsibility. Its structures, values, priorities, language, relationships and ethos underwent revolutionary change, the effects of which are still with us. To understand post-Christendom, we must first investigate the dying culture of Christendom that formed us. Alan Kreider insists:

We will not fully understand the current malaise of Western
Christianity until we come to terms with the phenomenon of
Christendom in its many dimensions. Our Christian past
shapes our Christian present; decisions taken in the past shape
our current predicaments and possibilities. And yet, although
many people realise this, there has been little attempt to define
Christendom as a term or to discuss it systematically as a phenomenon.'[1]

Defining and discussing the Christendom shift requires
examination of the coming of Christendom and its progress
through many centuries. There are several detailed
accounts of this, from which we can discern the outlines of a
complex and fascinating story. Evidence for particular incidents is often inconclusive, resulting in divergent
interpretations, but the main developments are clear
enough for our purpose, which is to understand how our
past has shaped our present – and may jeopardise our future
unless we come to terms with it.

The traditional starting point is the man whose name has
often been synonymous with Christendom, the Roman
emperor whose decision to make Christianity the imperially
favoured religion brought about the 'Constantinian revolution' that dramatically changed the fortunes of
fourth-century churches and ushered in Christendom.

Constantine

Constantine was born at Naissus in 272 or 273. His father,
Constantius I, was a Caesar (junior emperor) from 293 and
an Augustus (senior emperor) from 305 until his death the

---

[1] Alan Kreider, *The Change of Conversion and the Origin of
Christendom* (Harrisburg: Trinity Press, 1999), xiv.

following year. Attempting to bring order to a sprawling Empire under assault on several frontiers, the emperor Diocletian had formed an imperial college, consisting of a senior and junior emperor in the East and their counterparts in the West. This had advantages but resulted in frequent conflicts between emperors, ambitious for greater power. Constantine served in Diocletian's army in the East but was in York when his father died, and his troops hailed him as Constantius' successor.

Before long Constantine was master of the Western Provinces and strong enough to attack Rome, where, in 312, he defeated Maxentius to become sole emperor in the West. Four years later he marched east, where Licinius had removed his own imperial colleague, and defeated his adversary; but only in 324 did Licinius' abdication and subsequent death mean Constantine ruled the whole Empire until his death in 337.

The power politics and shifting fortunes of the imperial claimants are the background to Constantine's momentous decision, following his victory over Maxentius, to adopt Christianity as his favoured religion. The Edict of Milan in 313 represented a joint declaration by Licinius and Constantine guaranteeing Christians freedom from persecution throughout the Empire.[2] During the remaining twenty-four years of his reign, Constantine introduced measures designed gradually to replace paganism with Christianity as the imperial religion. He issued laws favouring the churches, lavished privileges and resources on them, sought the counsel of bishops and built a new city, Constantinople, as his own memorial and a new 'Christian' establishment.

Constantine is an enigmatic character, whose motives have been assessed and actions interpreted in widely

---

[2] The precise nature of this 'edict' is disputed but its symbolic significance is not.

differing ways. Buried in the Church of the Twelve Apostles in Constantinople and regarded by some as a thirteenth apostle, canonised by the Eastern churches, vilified by pagan writers as a brutal thug, regarded by historians as a gifted soldier and administrator, lauded by Eusebius as the church's saviour, Constantine must be understood in the context of his family, culture and imperial concerns. Our information, apart from official documents, comes mainly from two Christian writers, Lactantius and Constantine's biographer, Eusebius. Given their pro-Constantine bias, doubts have been cast on their reliability, but their writings can be used, with caution, alongside less favourable presentations in pagan writers.

Why was Constantine attracted to Christianity?

There are indications Constantine was sympathetic to Christianity and well disposed towards Christians several years before 313. He named his daughter Anastasia (a distinctively Christian name) and granted Christians in Britain, Gaul and Spain freedom from persecution, restoration of confiscated property and liberty to worship in 306, shortly after succeeding his father, whose policy appears to have been passive toleration.[3] However, the family's patron deity, to whom devotion was expected, was *Sol Invictus* (the Unconquered Sun).

The popular account of Constantine's encounter with Christianity – and with Christ himself – focuses on the period prior to the decisive Battle of the Milvian Bridge, where he defeated Maxentius. Both Eusebius and Lactantius report Constantine seeing a vision that persuaded him the God of the Christians was on his side and

---

[3] Timothy Barnes, *Constantine and Eusebius* (Cambridge: Harvard University Press, 1981), 14, 28.

would give him victory. Details of the vision and its timing vary. Eusebius claims he received the story directly from Constantine years later and describes an incident that occurred before the army approached Rome:

> About the time of the midday sun, when day was just turning, he said he saw with his own eyes, up in the sky and resting over the sun, a cross-shaped trophy formed from light, and a text attached to it which said, 'By this conquer'. Amazement at the spectacle seized both him and the whole company of soldiers which was then accompanying him on a campaign he was conducting somewhere, and witnessed the miracle. He was, he said, wondering to himself what the manifestation might mean; then, while he meditated, and thought long and hard, night overtook him. Thereupon, as he slept, the Christ of God appeared to him with the sign which had appeared in the sky, and urged him to make a copy of the sign which had appeared in the sky, and to use this as protection against the attacks of the enemy.[4]

Lactantius describes a dream on the eve of the battle:

> Constantine, with steady courage and a mind prepared for every event, led his whole forces to the neighbourhood of Rome, and encamped them opposite to the Milvian Bridge ... Constantine was directed in a dream to cause *the heavenly sign* to be delineated on the shields of his soldiers, and so to proceed to battle.[5]

Both accounts agree Constantine fought then, and subsequently, under a sign he regarded as Christian. His triumph over the superior forces of Maxentius, who surprisingly

---

[4] Eusebius: *Life of Constantine* I.28(2)-29.
[5] Lactantius: *On the Deaths of the Persecutors* XLIV.

risked battle rather than sheltering behind the city walls, encouraged the new master of Rome to believe the God of the Christians was both powerful and favourably disposed towards him. Whether any such vision occurred or whether these reports amount to no more than a stylised conversion story or conventional piece of religious propaganda is impossible to judge. A pagan account of the battle, describing the ominous appearance of owls on the city walls, was probably intended to counter these Christian claims.[6]

Constantine's interest in Christianity should not be regarded as surprising or requiring the stimulus of a heavenly vision. The early fourth-century church was no longer an insignificant community scattered across the Mediterranean basin. From its origins in Jerusalem, despite setbacks and opposition, it had grown rapidly and spread widely: there were congregations in all the cities and towns of the Empire and some villages were almost entirely Christian. Although persecution was a recent memory and still a threat, Christians were becoming respected members of society and their ideas were increasingly influential. Reliable estimates of the size of the Christian community are difficult to achieve, but a figure of 10 per cent of the population (more in the East than the West) is widely accepted.[7] This may represent 40 per cent growth per decade over 250 years[8] – an astonishing growth rate – and exponential

---

[6] Zosimus: *New History* II.16.2. See further Samuel Lieu and Dominic Montserrat, *From Constantine to Julian: Pagan and Byzantine Views* (London: Routledge, 1996).

[7] See, for example, Kreider, *Change*, 10; Peter Brown, *The Rise of Western Christendom: Triumph and Diversity, AD 200–1000* (Oxford: Blackwell, 2003), 73.

[8] The sociological evidence is presented in Rodney Stark, *The Rise of Christianity: A Sociologist Reconsiders History* (San Francisco: HarperCollins, 1997).

increase during the second half of the third century. Christian ideas and imagery were now familiar throughout society.

Furthermore, as traditional multi-faceted paganism was losing its religious hold on the Empire, if not yet its cultural significance, many intellectuals welcomed Christianity's ethical monotheism. Political leaders were keenly aware of the potential of religious ideas for shaping the Empire, undergirding its institutions and uniting its citizens, especially in the face of threats of disintegration. If the influence of paganism was waning, new religious options might be required. So Constantine could be expected to show interest in Christianity – especially if, as he seems to have assumed, accepting Christianity implied no disrespect to the Unconquered Sun.

Was Constantine a Christian?

Whether Constantine's adoption of Christianity resulted in him becoming a Christian (however defined) has provoked vigorous debate. Reviewing the evidence will not enable us to reach a firm conclusion but will shed light on his character, policies and influence on the church. It will also highlight theological and ecclesiological issues that would be re-negotiated during the fourth and fifth centuries and would shape the culture of Christendom.

We might ask what Constantine *believed*. He evidently regarded worshipping the God of the Christians as an appropriate way to honour the god he had previously identified as the Unconquered Sun. His recent experience convinced him that this god was effective in winning battles, so prayer for victory was offered during military campaigns. How much theology he knew or understood is uncertain: he seems not to have received the systematic instruction normally provided for converts but was evi-

dently interested in theology and participated actively in
contemporary debates. The terminology used in his public
pronouncements and Eusebius' reports of the emperor's
speeches suggest he might be understood as a philosophical
monotheist rather than a Christian, since he usually seems
averse to referring explicitly to Jesus or Christ.[9]

From 312 Constantine consistently identified himself
with Christianity, but what this meant to him or how it
related to his previous religious ideas is unclear. He retained
the title *Pontifex Maximus*, the pagan high priesthood, but
this was largely ceremonial in the fourth century. *Soli
Invicto* on his coinage expressed his continuing devotion to
the Unconquered Sun, as did his designation as a holiday of
the first day of the week (Sun-day), which fortuitously coincided with the day of Christ's resurrection. The choice of 25
December, the day on which the Unconquered Sun was
honoured, as the date for celebrating Christ's birth and the
'Christus-Helios' image in a fourth-century fresco, with
Christ superimposed on a traditional sun-god design, are
further examples of efforts to combine sun-worship and
Christianity.[10] Constantine undoubtedly saw Christianity
as the most effective way of obtaining divine favour, but did
not regard this as incompatible with other religious loyalties. Historians have variously assessed Constantine as a
deeply religious if poorly instructed Christian, a credulous
buffoon, a political manipulator using religion for his own
ends or a syncretist trying to graft Christianity onto solar
monotheism.

---

[9] Alister Kee, *Constantine versus Christ: The Triumph of Ideology* (London: SCM, 1982), 96. For a contrary interpretation, see
Barnes, *Constantine*, 253–4.
[10] H.A. Drake, *Constantine and the Bishops: The Politics of Intolerance* (Baltimore: John Hopkins University Press, 2000),
130–2.

We might enquire how Constantine *behaved*. He was not the saint Eusebius presents in his biography. Epithets used to describe him include: brutal, hardly squeamish, dictatorial, ruthless, bloodthirsty, violent, prone to irrational anger, suspicious, hungry for power, greedy for praise, severe, cruel, mean, petty-minded and profligate. He was widely regarded as responsible for murdering his son, Crispus, his wife, Fausta, and his father-in-law. During his reign the use of torture increased and the number of crimes subject to capital punishment multiplied.[11] His behaviour may have been no worse than his predecessors, and some aspects of his life appear more attractive, but his allegiance to Christianity appears to have tempered neither his own baser instincts nor the practices customarily associated with the imperial position. One reason given for Constantine delaying the decision to become a catechumen (someone receiving instruction in the Christian faith) and be baptised until shortly before his death was his awareness that theologians taught that those who sinned grievously after baptism would lose their salvation: Constantine did not want to risk this, but neither did he want his behaviour circumscribed.

We might consider whether Constantine and others felt he *belonged* to the church. As an unbaptised person, he was excluded from its central acts of worship.[12] So, in 325 he presided somewhat irregularly over the ecumenical council at Nicaea that produced the first great creed of Christendom. There are indications he regarded himself as an outsider and interpreted this positively, on occasions describing himself as a kind of lay bishop. Only at the very

---

[11] Ramsay MacMullen, 'Judicial Savagery in the Roman Empire', in Ramsay MacMullen: *Changes in the Roman Empire: Essays in the Ordinary* (Princeton: Princeton University Press, 1990), 204–17.

[12] Kreider, *Change*, 21–42.

end of his life did he submit to the normal process of instruction and baptism, thereby dying as a member of the church even if he had not lived as such. If Constantine was converted, perhaps we should locate this at the end of his life rather than associating it with a vision en route to Rome.

Church leaders undoubtedly struggled to know how to respond to Constantine. They had never had an emperor as a potential catechumen! Their whole-hearted embracing of him as the church's saviour from persecution, their appreciation of favours he was determined to lavish on them, their conviction that this sea change in their fortunes was divinely ordained and their recognition that emperors faced different challenges than ordinary people jostled with traditional requirements that those wanting to follow Christ should be instructed and baptised. They reached an accommodation, whereby Constantine was not regarded as a full church member but was welcomed into its councils and lauded as its defender.

Why did Constantine adopt Christianity as the imperial religion?

Whether or not Christians thought Constantine belonged to the church, their pagan contemporaries were convinced he was an adherent of the Christian faith because he demonstrated in numerous ways that he no longer subscribed to traditional religious views. His discouragement of pagan worship and sponsorship of the church left them in no doubt Constantine had adopted Christianity as the imperial religion. Christianity was not merely tolerated but endorsed, and on the way to becoming dominant.

It is, in fact, difficult to envisage a Roman emperor considering any alternative policy. Emperors were responsible for ensuring divine favour rested on the Empire, bringing economic prosperity and military success. If Constantine believed honouring the God of the Christians was the best way to achieve these ends, this must be imperial policy rather than merely personal conviction. Some of his predecessors attempted to repress Christianity in order to gain divine favour. Constantine promoted Christianity for the same reason: imperial policy was unchanged but was applied differently.

The above discussion of the nature of Constantine's conversion considered reasons for the imperial adoption of Christianity: an expression of his deeply-held conviction that Christianity was true and so should be promoted; a sense of divine calling and mission to convert the Empire to Christianity; political opportunism that recognised the potential of Christianity to replace paganism as the ideological glue to unite an Empire in danger of fragmentation; or political calculation that realised the church's growth rate and increasing influence precluded further repression and made imperial endorsement sensible. Although the proportion of Christians, especially in the Western Provinces, was still quite small, there was no comparable Empire-wide organisation; Constantine recognised its significance in the multicultural Empire he was struggling to govern.

Peter Brown concludes:

> Constantine's 'conversion' was a very 'Roman' conversion ... Worship of the Christian God had brought prosperity upon himself and would bring prosperity upon the empire ... He was over 40 and an experienced politician when he finally declared himself a Christian. He had had time to take the measure of the new religion and the difficulties which emperors had experienced in suppressing it. He decided that Christianity was a religion fit for a new empire.[13]

---

[13] Brown, *Rise*, 60–1.

Whatever Constantine's motives for adopting Christianity as the imperial religion, his predominant concern was to encourage progress towards a united church. He was impatient with theological disputes, not only because of his limited understanding of the issues at stake, but mainly because he wanted a united religious organisation to bring harmony to his realm. He showed no inclination to pressurise pagans to become Christians – though he discouraged public ceremonies that might undermine the sense of religious unity in the Empire – but he was as intolerant of dissent *within* the church as his pagan predecessors had been *of* the church as a dissenting element within the Empire.[14] Sadly, his legacy was a church deeply divided over theological and cultural issues, unconvinced by his attempt to impose a unifying creed on it.

How did Constantine promote Christianity?

Constantine concentrated on favouring Christianity rather than suppressing paganism. As Christians represented only a small, though expanding, minority in his Empire, this was the only feasible strategy. His actions proclaimed – sometimes by omission and non-participation, sometimes more positively – that he had scant regard for traditional religious ideas and was committed to a new cause. He closed some prominent temples – especially those associated with sexually immoral cults – and forbade divination and magic practices, even in private. And his pronouncements, especially as sole emperor, became increasingly dismissive of pagan practices. But he counselled Christians to exercise restraint, so there were no pagan martyrs in his reign. Pagans could practise their faith unmolested and even build

---

[14] W.H.C Frend, *The Early Church: From the Beginnings to 461* (London: SCM Press, 1991), 132, 150.

new temples, provided they did not publicly parade their beliefs or draw attention to their sacrifices.

With regard to the Jews Constantine acted more vigorously. Sensitive to Christian prejudice against Jews and a long history of mutual distrust, he issued laws forbidding Jews from owning Christian slaves or accepting Christian converts and also instituted the death penalty for anyone attempting to prevent Jews converting to Christianity (conversion in either direction was evidently still plausible).

But his main strategy involved favouring Christianity by providing financial resources for the churches, conveying status and power on the bishops and offering inducements to any considering becoming Christians. Kenneth Scott Latourette lists some of his measures:

> Constantine exempted the Christian clergy from all contributions to the state ... Laws which had forbidden celibates and the childless to receive inheritances were annulled, possibly out of consideration for the clergy. Wills in favour of the Church were permitted. The manumission of slaves in churches in the presence of the bishop and clergy was legalized. A litigant was permitted to bring suit before a bishop and the latter's decision was to be accepted by civil officials. The Christian Sunday was placed in the same position as the pagan holidays by the suspension of the courts and of urban labour. Constantine ordered the provincial governors to respect the days in memory of the martyrs and to honour the festivals of the churches. He kept about him Christian ecclesiastics and had his children educated in the Christian faith. He erected, enlarged and embellished churches. He encouraged the bishops to do likewise and authorized them to call on the civil officials for assistance.[15]

---

[15] Kenneth Scott Latourette, *The First Five Centuries* (Grand Rapids: Zondervan, 1970), 173–4.

The impact of Christianity on the criminal law reflected the views of fourth-century Christian leaders on immorality. Reforms humanised punishments for some crimes, but severe penalties were imposed on (especially sexual) offences that church leaders regarded as especially corrupt or dangerous. And these leaders were now honoured and powerful imperial officials, dispensing justice and speaking with authority. Ramsay MacMullen reports:

> Bishops now actually dined with Constantine himself ... They were seen riding along provincial highways in state convey-ances, bent on their high affairs, as guests of the government. All the world could behold what fantastic changes had come about in the repute and position of ecclesiastical officials.[16]

Constantine's most obvious contribution to the church's growing prestige, however, was the proliferation of church buildings and construction of basilicas in major cities of the Empire. Many were accompanied by huge, tax-exempt endowments of land and food allowances for church employees. Constantine also underwrote the magnificent decoration and ornamentation of these buildings and funded copies of the Scriptures to be placed in them.

The climax of this building project was the establishment of Constantinople, a 'new Rome', dedicated in 330 and henceforth Constantine's capital. A surprising feature of this supposedly Christian city was the presence within it of pagan statues plundered from temples across the Empire: did this demonstrate the triumph of Christianity that had transformed idols into an open-air art museum (as Eusebius argues[17]), or did it symbolise the combination of

---

[16] Ramsay MacMullen, *Christianizing the Roman Empire (AD 100–400)* (New Haven: Yale University Press, 1984), 113–14. On the bishops, see further Drake, *Constantine*, passim.
[17] Eusebius: *Life*, III.54 (1)–(3).

paganism and Christianity that would characterise Christendom?

From Pre-Christendom to Christendom

However we interpret Constantine, his adoption of Christianity as the imperially favoured religion was a turning point in Christian and European history. His reign was long enough to ensure no successor could simply rescind Christianity's new status; and the dramatic increase in the number of Christians and their morale galvanised the church in its advance against paganism and its mission to establish Christianity throughout the Empire. Although Christendom emerged gradually over the decades and even centuries ahead, its foundations were laid in the first half of the fourth century.

The church was taken by surprise when Constantine chose to identify himself with Christianity. Achieving toleration was not unexpected – though very welcome after Diocletian's recent persecution – for there had been earlier edicts of toleration and the church was harder to persecute as it grew and became respectable. But Constantine's patronage was more than most can have dreamed of, and the prospect of Christianity becoming the imperial religion required nifty theological footwork. What should a Christian Empire look like? What adjustments or accommodation might be necessary? What aspects of pre-Christendom Christianity must be reinterpreted for Christendom? How should the church induct the many thousands who followed the emperor into Christianity?

This was a time of rapid, exciting and unsettling transition. Very few church leaders objected to Constantine's championing of the church and the favours he bestowed on it. Not all were as uncritically effusive about Constantine as

Eusebius, but almost all assumed this was God's doing and represented the triumph of the gospel over the Empire after centuries of marginality, struggle and opposition. If adjustments were necessary, these were a small price to pay for the opportunities that the church now had.

Furthermore, some of these adjustments were already underway. The church had grown rapidly during the past sixty years and was already making the transition from socially insignificant cult to mainstream religious community. In some places, mainly in the East, Christians comprised half the population and met for worship in publicly recognised church buildings. Church structures had become more complex, its liturgy more developed, its leadership more hierarchical, its practices more fixed. As they became socially respectable, churches attracted adherents with greater wealth and higher status; adjustments were already being made for such influential converts. The churches were better prepared for the transition to Christendom than they would have been if an emperor had adopted Christianity even half a century earlier. And the mood was buoyant, despite the pressure of persecution, anticipating further progress with or without a favourable emperor. But the church's gradual transition from marginality to respectability during the second half of the third century was eclipsed by its fourth-century transformation as pre-Christendom evolved into Christendom.

Constantine's Successors

Constantine intended on his death in 337 to restore the imperial college instituted by Diocletian, dividing the Empire between his three surviving sons and a nephew, but the army refused to be governed by anyone except a son of Constantine. A period of violence and confusion resulted in a division between the three sons, Constantine II, Constantius and Constans. In 340, following the defeat and death of Constantine II, Constans ruled the West and Constantius the East. In 350, after the death of Constans and a brief uprising in Gaul, Constantius became sole emperor until his death in 361.

Constans and Constantius continued their father's policy of favouring the church and marginalising paganism. Bishops used Constantius' palace as their headquarters and the partnership between church and state flourished. This was a period of intense theological controversy: divisions in the pre-Christendom churches paled beside the vitriolic debates of the early Christendom years. Constantine's longed-for unity seemed a distant prospect. But the church was expanding rapidly in numbers and influence. Imperial endorsement conveyed social advantages on church members and the churches struggled to incorporate many thousands of newcomers. The long and demanding initiation process that led to baptism and membership was truncated to avoid them being swamped by the flood of those wanting to become Christians.

In 361, this seemingly unstoppable advance received a sharp jolt. The new emperor, Julian, though raised as a Christian, rejected Christianity and tried to restore paganism as the imperial religion. However, his reign lasted only eighteen months; his death in 363 ended the attempt to revive paganism. Some have queried whether, if he had reigned as long as Constantine, he might have succeeded, but the momentum was surely too great for the advance of Christianity to be stopped. Indeed, Julian himself despaired of making progress: paganism did not have either the infrastructure, moral fibre or social care qualities needed to resist Christianity now.

Four emperors who reigned only a few years (or months) succeeded Julian: Jovian, Valentinian I, Valens and

Gratian. All embraced Christianity – though not always the Nicene version that would eventually be accepted as orthodox – but they did not restore to the churches all the favours Julian had removed. They were far from neutral in matters of religion, but tolerated paganism and were more concerned about dissent within the church than converting pagans. Gratian took some symbolic steps signalling the demise of paganism: he renounced the title *Pontifex Maximus*, had the famous Altar of Victory removed from the Roman senate and abolished all remaining privileges of pagan temples and priests.

But Theodosius I, who reigned alongside Gratian from 378 and as sole emperor from 383 until 395, introduced several measures that would result in the establishment of Christendom. In an edict of 380, he defined the church as those 'in communion with the bishops of Rome and Alexandria': unity within church and Empire was secured by legislation penalising Christian groups unwilling to accept this definition. Expulsion, seizure of goods and property, inability to inherit or bequeath and other restrictions increased the pressure to conform. In 391 and 392, further measures banned pagan sacrifices and other cultic practices and closed pagan temples. 'Together, these measures established Christianity, legally defined, as the official religion of the empire.'[18]

The church's journey from illegality and susceptibility to persecution, via toleration and preferential treatment, to official status as the imperial religion had taken only eighty years. Christendom had arrived. The church was now firmly established – but in an Empire only a few years away from invasions that would result in its fragmentation and ultimate demise.

---

[18] S.L. Greenslade, *Church and State from Constantine to Theodosius* (London: SCM Press, 1954), 29.

Converting the Empire

Before following the story into the fifth and sixth centuries, however, pondering the means the church employed to convert fourth-century pagans raises concerns. This was the task of the church rather than the emperors, who provided financial resources, inducements and favourable conditions, but expected bishops to develop strategies for incorporating others into the church. The influx of increasing numbers attracted by its new wealth and status, the promise of imperial favour and enhanced career prospects began in Constantine's reign. Such inducements grew throughout the fourth century until Theodosius could assume 'that people, at any rate some people, could be turned into coreligionists with his party and himself simply because it would cost them too much to refuse'.[19]

But not all were induced to convert through the hope of material or social gain. We should not underestimate the intellectual and religious appeal of Christianity in an Empire riddled with insecurity and fearful about the future. There was substantial common ground between Christianity and a monotheistic impulse that was already attracting many away from traditional religion. The church's exemplary care for the poor and its compassionate response in times of epidemic were further incentives: Julian cited its care for the poor, including poor pagans, as the main reason for the failure of his campaign to restore paganism. As in previous centuries, the attractive lives of Christians and their communities, the appeal of Christian theology and ethics in a culture reaching towards monotheism and the church's capacity to transcend socio-economic and gender barriers were all factors in the appeal of fourth-century Christianity, even if it now attracted converts for more mundane and questionable reasons.

---

[19] MacMullen, *Christianizing*, 56.

There were other fourth-century religious options, including the Egyptian mystery religion of Serapis and the Persian cult of Mithras, both of which were popular, and Judaism, which was numerically strong and appealed to many, including Christians. Transition from minority cult to the overwhelming majority that constituted Christendom was not a foregone conclusion, even with sustained imperial support. But the time seemed right to proceed towards the total evangelisation of the Empire. Many church leaders realised this would require vigorous missionary strategies, some of which were only feasible now the threat of persecution had been lifted and they could operate openly. But what forms would mission take in this new context?

The mood of Christians towards the end of Constantine's reign was surprised but buoyant. Other, less noble, attitudes and aspirations were also present: intolerance towards pagans, Jews and all who dissented from the faith regarded as orthodox; a crusading mentality towards paganism that perceived an opportunity to crush all resistance; and even ill disguised desires for revenge on former persecutors. Despite the church's historic plea for religious liberty and its own experience (within living memory) of persecution, intolerance and oppression marred the response of fourth-century churches to their new freedom to engage in mission.

The use of physical force was limited, though after 380 bishops in their sermons more often advocated coercion as they strove to complete the task of converting the Empire. Incidents of idol-smashing and temple desecration were uncommon but not absent in the first half of the century. By the end of the century such incidents were reported in several locations, especially in Gaul – where Martin, bishop of Tours, razed pagan shrines and built churches on their sites – and in North Africa. Synagogues were also vulnerable, as an infamous example at Callinicum in 388 demonstrates. Theodosius, angered by the pillaging of a synagogue at the instigation of the local bishop, ordered it rebuilt, incurring the wrath of Ambrose, bishop of Milan, who by threatening excommunication bullied the emperor into rescinding this order.

This incident reveals the church's growing arrogance, readiness to use violence and ability on occasions to dominate the state/church partnership. What can explain this developing intolerance? Two influential factors may have been the shock of Julian's attempt to revive paganism, convincing church leaders that more rigorous action was needed to buttress the church's position, and the application to pagans of coercive methods first used against heretics.[20] More common than such destruction, however, was widespread expectation that pressure would be exerted within families and through employment ties. It was assumed landowners would require workers on their estates to become Christians and that heads of households would insist the household shared a common faith.

Alongside such imposition the fourth century witnessed a revival of public preaching and individual missionary work, evident in the New Testament but too dangerous in the second and third centuries.[21] This would be a sporadic but persistent feature of the advance of Christendom over the coming centuries, though most converts were won by other means.

But effective catechesis was uncommon. Thousands wanted to join the churches but were unenthusiastic about the demanding traditional induction process. Those

---

[20] Drake, *Constantine*, 409, 416. Drake suggests this ensured the triumph over the moderates of a militant faction in the churches.
[21] On pre-Christendom evangelism, see Alan Kreider, *Worship and Evangelism in Pre-Christendom* (Cambridge: Grove, 1995).

responsible for instructing converts concentrated on avoiding heresy and did little to encourage ethical transformation or spiritual growth. Most bishops were concerned not with instructing converts but with the seemingly interminable theological debates that dominated ecumenical conferences and produced bitterness and division.

What progress, then, did the church make in the fourth century towards converting the Empire? Its rapid expansion in the second half of the third century, impressive though that was, was dwarfed by growth in the fourth century. A five-fold increase to thirty million Christians has been suggested.[22]

Christendom was by no means fully formed at the end of the fourth century, but the past eighty years had witnessed remarkable advances in the numerical strength, status and influence of the church. The level of resistance was amazingly low. Few protested openly about the diminished status of the Empire's traditional religion, though there was private disquiet and occasional representations to one or other of the emperors. Few expressed concern about the missionary methods used or the increasingly nominal Christianity within the churches. The Christendom shift took place largely unopposed.

Some Questions

But was this the triumphant period subsequent generations celebrated as the beginning of Christendom? Had Christianity conquered the Empire or had the Empire co-opted and domesticated Christianity? What price did the church pay for imperial patronage? The gains were obvious, but what were the losses?

---

[22] MacMullen, *Christianizing*, 86.

We will be better placed to consider these issues once we have traced the spread of Christendom into other parts of Europe and into the medieval world that replaced the Empire into which Christianity was born. It may be helpful here, however, to record some questions that arise from the story so far:

- What impact on the theology and worship of the church did the identification of the God of the Christians with the Unconquered Sun have?
- How significant was Constantine's reticence about Jesus or Christ in his presentation of Christianity?
- What were the long-term pastoral consequences of the precedent Constantine set by delaying baptism and not receiving proper instruction?
- How were the creeds written in the fourth century and so influential through subsequent centuries affected by the Christendom shift?
- Why was the church's commitment to religious liberty and non-violence so quickly forgotten when it became powerful?
- How corrupting was the acquisition of enormous wealth and high status by the churches and their leaders?
- What were the implications for community and discipleship of the growth of huge congregations and magnificent buildings?
- How did the addition to the church of millions of largely nominal believers help or hinder the church's mission?
- How important is theological agreement in the search for unity and as a basis for the church's mission?
- Why was there so little resistance to – or even questioning of – the massive changes involved in the Christendom shift?

Undergirding all these issues is the question of contemporary significance: how did these fourth-century changes shape the Christendom church, and what relevance do they have for us as we negotiate the transition to post-Christendom? Are these issues only of historical interest or do they represent an agenda that needs to be addressed if we are to discover how to be church and engage in mission in a world where we no longer enjoy the patronage of Constantine and his successors?

3

The Expansion of Christendom

From the Margins to the Centre

As the fifth century dawned, Christians were not yet in the majority throughout the Empire, but they were a privileged minority and their numerical strength and influence were increasing daily. Changes from a century earlier were more marked in some regions than others. Different experiences in the churches and deep political enmity between Eastern and Western Provinces created a divide that would grow more painful and entrenched until a final rupture produced Eastern Orthodox and Western Catholic versions of Christendom.

Already in the fourth century protracted theological wrangling had produced several competing creeds,[1] replete with anathemas[2] on any who disagreed with the party in the

---

[1] The major issue was the nature of Christ and his relationship with the Father. Arius, an Alexandrian presbyter, seemed to suggest Christ was less than fully God, but many bishops and some emperors endorsed creeds expressing variants of his position. Arianism was eventually rejected but survived for centuries, especially among tribes evangelised by Arian missionaries. Significant theological issues were at stake, but linguistic confusion hindered agreement.

[2] Theological curses!

ascendancy. Some issues divided Greek-speaking and
Latin-speaking Christians and some 'ecumenical councils'
were overwhelmingly attended by Eastern bishops, where
churches were numerous and deeply embedded in the surrounding culture. Eastern (or Byzantine) Christendom
flourished for centuries with fewer fluctuations than the
Western version. But the following chapters concentrate on
the Christendom that survived the collapse of the Western
Empire and spectacularly reinvented itself in Western
Europe.

In the fifth century, the church was no longer on the margins of society but at the centre. Not long ago it had been
dangerous to join this illegal organisation, but now not
belonging was disadvantageous. Previously pagans had
sporadically persecuted Christians, but now Christians
were persecuting pagans and, more frequently, those they
regarded as heretics within their own ranks (though theologians insisted the term 'persecution' was inappropriate!).
Once, being a Christian and joining the army had seemed
incompatible, but now a Christian army was being assem-
bled to defend an Empire that was becoming Christian;
soon, *only* Christians would be allowed to enlist.

These were remarkable changes requiring theological
dexterity to explain how the church now at the centre was
in continuity with the church on the margins of the first
three centuries. So much looked different from the centre.
The burgeoning churches at the heart of society and feeling
increasingly responsible for the fortunes of the Empire
needed able and creative theologians to chart a course
through this exhilarating but confusing period. But, before
considering the most influential of these theologians, it will
be helpful to pick up the story from the point when Christianity was recognised as the official imperial religion and
follow it through the next few centuries.

From the Centre to the Margins

Less than twenty years after Christianity's achievement of official status, in 410, Alaric, the Christian Visigoth, sacked Rome. Although he stayed for only three days, this symbolised shifting power dynamics. The Empire would struggle on and brief periods of renaissance would promise restoration of the old order, but a new world was taking shape. Augustine's *The City of God* pointed anxious Christians to the true city (imperfectly identified with the church) that was their hope now the vulnerability of the 'eternal city' of Rome was evident to all.

The map of Western Europe was redrawn often during the next four centuries. The enforced stability of the Roman Empire was replaced by complex migrations of tribal groups pillaging, conquering, settling, inter-marrying, assimilating and facing the next wave of tribal movements. By the fifth century, imperial borders had been permeable for many years; around the Empire were semi-Romanised communities (such as the Visigoths). The Empire's demise did not mean the end of Roman civilisation but its diffusion and the development of hybrid cultures blending Roman and tribal values, structures and practices. Historians, using Roman terminology, call the kingdoms that flourished during this period 'barbarian'; but they were not uncouth, devoid of culture or entirely different from the disintegrating Empire. Nevertheless, this was an era of economic stagnation, political instability, urban decline and regression into regional loyalties and very local community life.

These changes impacted the network of churches scattered across Europe, but there is evidence of continuing communication, exchange of personnel and a cohesive infrastructure outstripping other organisations. Constantine hoped Christianity would provide the glue to

hold together his Empire: instead, it provided the framework and interpretive story on which medieval Europe
would eventually be constructed. The collapse of the
Empire presented the churches with a challenge and an
opportunity: Christendom was their response. Christianity,
concludes Judith Herrin, 'permeated and transformed the
inherited culture of Greece and Rome, providing a crucial
link in the transmission of the ancient past to a medieval
future ... the Christian faith, rather than the barbarian
kingdoms, constituted the successor of the Roman Empire
in the West.'[3]

The story of how Christianity spread from its heartlands
in southern Europe and North Africa to the farthest reaches
of Western and Northern Europe is complex,[4] heroic and
troubling. Missionaries travelled enormous distances,
planting thousands of churches; the gospel was translated
into many languages and cultures; monasteries proliferated
as centres of learning and mission; and whole societies
accepted Christianity. But the missionary methods, the
church's role in society and the Christian story that was
received all require examination.

Having come in from the margins to the centre during the
fourth century, in the next four centuries Christianity
spread from the centre to the margins – downwards and
outwards. Even where the church was well established, the
conversion of the rural population was not accomplished
quickly and required pressure from landowners and the
admonition of bishops – top-down evangelisation. Not all

---

[3] Judith Herrin, *The Formation of Christendom* (Princeton:
Princeton University Press, 1997), 21, 126.
[4] For comprehensive accounts, see Richard Fletcher, *The Bar-
barian Conversion: From Paganism to Christianity* (Berkeley &
Los Angeles: University of California Press, 1999) and Brown,
Rise.

were enthusiastic about the conversion of barbarians who settled in former Roman areas, but gradually they were incorporated into the churches. The outward spread involved re-evangelising outlying regions of the former Empire (including Britain), which Christianity had penetrated earlier but where its influence had faded, and evangelising areas (such as Frisia and Scandinavia) that had escaped both Roman and Christian influence. This was accomplished by political and military pressure, cultural influence and individual missionary work. This also was top-down evangelisation: progress depended largely on the receptivity of kings, chieftains, warlords and wealthy landowners.

Strengthening the Centre

Following an unsuccessful protest by aristocratic pagan families in Theodosius' reign, the fifth and sixth centuries witnessed inexorable increase in the proportion of those in the imperial provinces who accepted Christianity. This was mostly unremarkable and unenthusiastic: a 'drift into a respectable Christianity'.[5] Paganism did not die quickly or entirely, particularly in rural areas,[6] but it no longer threatened the official status of Christianity, even if it held enduring appeal for many supposed now to be Christians. Some church leaders wanted the task of converting the Empire completed and urged action, but many were already oriented towards maintenance rather than mission and more interested in theological conformity within the church

---

[5] R.A. Markus, *The End of Ancient Christianity* (Cambridge: Cambridge University Press, 1990), 27.

[6] 'Pagan' originally meant 'rustic'; 'heathen' derived from 'people of the heath'.

than evangelising those outside it. Those they designated
heretics and schismatics, who were disturbing the peace of
the church,[7] and the popularity of Manichaeism,[8] provoked
greater concern than those who adhered to the old gods.

Consequently, though top-down pressure was exerted
through families, employers and landowners, there was little actual violence against pagans, nor were there legal
penalties for remaining pagan. Conversion owed more to
inducement than coercion. Many avenues for advancement
were open only to Christians: from 416 employment in the
civil service and the army was restricted to Christians. As
catechetical and liturgical hurdles were lowered, many
understandably chose to convert to avoid discrimination.
Furthermore, there were substantial benefits, in status and
financial rewards, for those choosing to become members
of the clergy – tax exemptions, pension provision and other
privileges, together with civic authority and positions of
respect in the community.

Changes in the status and responsibilities of bishops
reflected the church's increasing influence and central role
in society. They adopted the lifestyles and attitudes of other
civic leaders and acted like an additional department of the
secular administration. They continued to guide the
churches and engage in theological debate, but now also
exercised widespread jurisdiction over the cities where they
were based. Their tasks included ensuring implementation
of imperial decrees, disbursing resources to those in need,
education, hospitality for travellers, providing public enter-
tainment, judging legal cases, negotiating with invading

---

[7] As early as 385, Priscillian was executed as a heretic.
[8] A syncretistic and ascetic religion presenting itself as the successor of Zoroastrianism, Buddhism and Christianity. Founded
in Persia by Mani (216–277), it penetrated the Roman Empire until checked by vicious persecution.

armies, ransoming prisoners of war, organising military forces, accompanying them on campaigns or even leading them into battle, and other civil, economic and military duties.[9] In the chaos of disintegrating Roman administration, bishops were often the only remaining symbols of stability and order. Many were drawn to Christianity and its impressive leaders, whether hoping to benefit from their wealth and influence or to achieve similar status.

Other factors had more in common with the pre-Christendom spread of Christianity: the inherent power of the gospel and its attractiveness to those for whom paganism was losing its appeal; healings and exorcisms (though miracles were waning); the church's compassionate service and practical aid; and the testimonies of Christians living distinctively (although pagans were now also repelled by the inconsistent lives of professing Christians and their use of coercion).[10] The influential witness of the martyrs was missing, but ascetic holy men and women inherited their exemplary role. More significant now was regular preaching in the basilicas and church buildings that were becoming central in the cities. But as miracles decreased and the gap diminished between the lifestyles of Christians and pagans, the influence of inducements and top-down pressure grew.

During the fifth century, pressure increased on the remaining pagans. They had to attend church services to receive instruction, their children were to be baptised and they could be exiled and their property confiscated if they resisted baptism. In 438, the *Theodosian Code*, a chronological collection of imperial edicts from Constantine to Theodosius II, included a book on religion that indicated decreasing toleration for pagans, Jews and schismatics and

---

[9] Herrin, *Formation*, 49, 72–3; Fletcher, *Barbarian*, 50–1.
[10] Kreider, *Change*, 56.

heretics (who did not 'follow this rule' or 'embrace the name of Catholic Christians'). More consistent pressure was applied to pagans to embrace Christianity than had previously been used on Christians to revert to paganism, although violence against those who resisted was sporadic. Less obvious but more significant in the long run was the psychological pressure of the continuing growth of the Christian majority and the stability the churches offered in a time of social disintegration. Year by year it became more normal for Romans to be Christians. *Not* being a Christian was becoming an act of courageous nonconformity.

Eventually, Justinian, who preferred things neat, codified and well ordered, issued an edict in 529 making conversion compulsory.[11] Only the Jewish community was allowed to practise its own religion, though there were periodic attempts to convert Jews by forcibly baptising them. For all others, religious allegiance was no longer a matter of choice but of law: all babies were baptised to mark their entry into Christian society. Christianity was mandatory. Christendom was becoming all embracing. By the end of the sixth century, almost all the barbarian kingdoms in the area Rome once ruled had officially accepted Christianity. One exception was Anglo-Saxon England.[12]

Extending the Boundaries

As indicated above, many fifth- and sixth-century Christians regarded as inappropriate evangelising barbarians beyond the imperial boundaries (or what remained of them). So complete was the identification of Christianity with Roman culture that it was not self-evident

---

[11] Code of Justinian 1.11.10.
[12] Fletcher, *Barbarian*, 114.

that others could or should be Christians. As Richard Fletcher writes, 'If *Romanitas* and *Christianitas* are co-terminous, then the faith is for all dwellers within the ring fence of the Empire, but not for those outside.'[13] Identifying Christianity with Roman or, later, European culture would have an enduring impact on whether and how European Christians engaged in mission beyond the boundaries of Christendom.

Nevertheless, Kenneth Scott Latourette concludes that early in the sixth century:

> Christianity was numerically many times stronger than when Constantine came to power. From being a minority cult, it had become the professed faith of the vast majority in what was still the most important civilized area of the human race, and had won minorities in some regions where other cultures were dominant.[14]

There were now churches over much of Western Europe, beyond as well as within the old imperial boundaries, linked together loosely but effectively by travellers, creeds and liturgical practices. In some regions Christians were still a small minority; in others they were members of the official religion of their society. How had this been accomplished?

The spread of Christianity and, inevitably, of the Christendom system occurred partly through *osmosis*. The boundaries between Christendom and the world beyond were open; ideas travelled through conquest, trade and cultural exchange. Mixed marriages, diplomatic connections and barbarians returning home after serving in the imperial army facilitated the spread of Christianity. Those who

---

13 Fletcher, *Barbarian*, 25.
14 Latourette, *First*, 173.

pillaged lands where churches were already established carried back with them Christian slaves and ecclesiastical goods, importing Christian influence and symbols into their homelands. Apparently, Danish traders were baptised annually when they visited the ports of Christendom in order to smooth trading arrangements![15] Those who settled within the boundaries of Christendom gradually adopted the religious beliefs of their conquered communities whose culture increasingly infiltrated their own. The association of Christianity with the wealth, power and heritage of fading but still impressive Roman culture meant Christendom extended its boundaries without intentional missionary work.

There were *missionary enterprises*, however, such as one pope Gregory despatched to England at the end of the sixth century. These had organised strategies and presented themselves to local rulers effectively as embassies from Christendom. Royal support was crucial for the success of such enterprises: not only did this provide protection for the missionaries but, if the king were converted, his people would soon follow. Reports of royal conversions indicate similar factors to those noted in relation to Constantine. A responsible ruler, considering transferring his allegiance to a new deity, assessed the advantages and disadvantages. Would this new god offer enhanced prospects of military success and economic progress? How much support was there for a change of allegiance? The attitude of the war bands and aristocracy was crucial in the king's decision. An account of the conversion of Clovis, king of the Franks, at the end of the fifth century, demonstrates the importance of such considerations.[16]

Aware such factors would determine the response of local rulers and, therefore, their success or failure, mission-

---

[15]   Fletcher, *Barbarian*, 225.
[16]   Fletcher, *Barbarian*, 103-6.

aries learned to present the gospel in ways that connected with these issues. Fletcher notes:

> We observe the repeated assurance that acceptance of Christianity will bring victory, wide dominion, fame and riches. This was what Germanic kings wanted to hear, because their primary activity was war ... Nor would it have profited them to dwell upon facets of Christian teaching which kings might have found unappealing. The injunction to turn the other cheek would surely have fallen on deaf ears.[17]

Once the king and his supporters decided to accept Christianity, which might take time and depended on the new faith fulfilling the missionaries' promises, there was considerable pressure on the rest of that society to embrace the faith. The combined impact of coercion and inducement that ensured the establishment of Christianity in the centre of Christendom was influential also on its fringes. Bede's frank account of the conversion of Kent after King Ethelbert's acceptance of Christianity reports that, although there was no compulsion, many converted 'through fear of the king or to win his favour'.[18] As in fourth-century Rome, so in various barbarian kingdoms between the fifth and eighth centuries, political support and economic resources ensured the widespread acceptance of Christianity.

The boundaries of Christendom were also extended through the activities of *extraordinary and dedicated individuals*. These included famous missionaries – Patrick in Ireland, Columba in Scotland, Columbanus in Gaul – and others whose names and stories are unknown. Often at great personal risk and with little or no official support, they carried the gospel beyond the frontiers and established

---

[17] Fletcher, *Barbarian*, 122.
[18] Fletcher, *Barbarian*, 118.

new Christian communities.[19] Others, like Ninian, Palladius and Ulfilas,[20] went as pastoral leaders to serve small Christian communities in otherwise pagan areas: they were not missionaries in the usual sense, but their role included preaching the gospel beyond their own communities. Also influential were spreading networks of monasteries, from which missionary monks dispersed to preach and teach.

Further work was also needed within the boundaries of Christendom, where many rural communities were relatively untouched by the faith of the cities, and in adjacent lands where Christian influences vied with paganism for the hearts and minds of tribal groups. Other missionaries, many trained in the monasteries, concentrated on this dual task, challenging paganism and encouraging deeper penetration of Christianity into these communities. Amandus from Gaul, three Englishmen, Wilfrid, Willibrord and Boniface, and the Frisian Liudger are those about whom we know most. Boniface was commissioned early in the eighth century to serve nominal Christians still steeped in paganism and those not yet Christian.[21] These missionaries extended the boundaries of Christendom into Frisia, Hesse, Thuringia, Franconia and Willibrord journeyed to Denmark.

In the eighth century, the expansionist ambitions of the Franks marked the end of the first phase of Christendom and the start of a more centralised and aggressive phase.

---

[19] This model of 'wandering mission' is popularly associated with 'Celtic' Christianity. Irish Christians were at the forefront of this, but it is doubtful that Celtic Christianity existed as a distinct entity.

[20] Ulfilas, a very effective missionary, was associated with semi-Arian theology and so has not been celebrated as his activities deserve.

[21] Fletcher, *Barbarian*, 206.

The Franks were becoming dominant in Western Europe and their championing of Christianity had significant implications for the continued progress of the Christian civilisation now flourishing among peoples who had not experienced Roman culture.

The expansion of Christendom between the fourth and eighth centuries can be more accurately described as the spread of 'adjacent but separate micro-Christendoms'.[22] Although Christian churches scattered across Europe knew they belonged together, the fragmentation and regionalisation that characterised this era precluded the monolithic organisation Christendom would become in the Middle Ages. A shared theology and story bound the churches together and conveyed a sense of unity stronger than other translocal influences, but this was not uniformity. 'In terms of custom and practice there were many churches in sixth- and seventh-century Europe, not One Church. Christendom was many-mansioned.'[23] But, as the Franks conquered more of Europe, these micro-Christendoms began to cohere into a Christian Empire.

From the eighth century, Christendom was enlarged by another mission strategy. Coercion in various forms had been used to complete the evangelisation of peoples whose rulers and upper classes had embraced Christianity, but now for the first time *coercive measures* were used by Christian rulers against those they were conquering. The partnership between soldiers and missionaries that characterised later European expeditions to the Americas was forged in this period: 'the combination of missionary zeal with a sense of cultural superiority, backed by the use of force, became a striking feature of early medieval Christian Europe.'[24]

---

[22] Brown, *Rise*, 364.
[23] Fletcher, *Barbarian, 92.*
[24] Brown, *Rise*, 41.

Charlemagne, the greatest Frankish king, pioneered this strategy in campaigns against the Saxons and Hungarian Avars. So brutal were his measures, including his personal supervision of the execution of over 4000 Saxon prisoners of war and the options of baptism or execution once conquest was complete, two historians comment: 'The fact that a Christian ruler could act with such savagery confronts us with fundamental questions about the degree of Christianization that had taken place among the Franks.'[25] But so effective was Charlemagne's conversion of the Saxons that in the tenth and eleventh centuries they were responsible for the enforced conversion of conquered Slavs! In each case, conquest involved forcible conversion and imposition of the death penalty for persisting with pagan practices and refusing to submit to baptism.

Charlemagne, who reigned for almost half a century from 768 and was crowned as emperor by the pope on Christmas Day 800, understood himself as standing in the line of Old Testament kings and was inspired by a vision of creating a Christian Empire. He interpreted Augustine's *City of God* to mean his Empire rather than the church. Hailed by church leaders as a 'new Constantine', he had a stronger sense of missionary responsibility than most previous Christian rulers for societies beyond Christendom; and he had no compunction about using force to persuade those he conquered to become Christians. His extensive but unwieldy Empire did not remain intact politically, but the kingdoms and principalities that emerged from it subscribed to the myth of a 'Holy Roman Empire' and operated within a shared Christendom culture that was more unified than anything in recent centuries.

The expansion of Christendom into Scandinavia, the one substantial area of Western Europe still predominantly

---

[25] Dale Irvin and Scott Sunquist, *History of the World Christian Movement* Volume I (Edinburgh: T. & T. Clark, 2002), 336.

pagan, occurred between the ninth and eleventh centuries. Reliable documentation is limited, but this was probably achieved initially through osmosis. Christian ideas infiltrated Viking communities in Ireland, Scotland, England and Normandy and were carried back to Denmark and Norway, and from there to new settlements in Iceland and Greenland. But for Christianity to become established, royal assent and patronage was needed. The Danish king, Harald Bluetooth, accepted Christianity in about 960 and encouraged his subjects to do likewise. Diplomatic links with England and Denmark influenced the spread of Christianity in Norway, before it was accepted in a public event in about 1022 (mentioned in a runic inscription noting 'twelve winters had Christendom been in Norway').[26] There is sporadic evidence for Christian influence in Sweden from the late tenth century, including the presence of the Polish wife of King Eric (Poland had recently accepted Christianity), but Sweden was finally incorporated into Christendom late in the eleventh century, after King Inge defeated a pagan usurper.

The establishment of Christendom in Scandinavia, therefore, was achieved through a combination of familiar methods. The spread of ideas paved the way for acceptance by national leaders and the conversion of the nation by coercion and inducement. The activities of individual missionaries are harder to detect from available evidence but these no doubt contributed. We lack detailed information about Bohemia, Poland and Hungary, but the story resembles the conversion of Scandinavia; by the beginning of the eleventh century, these kingdoms beyond the eastern frontier had also accepted Christianity.[27]

---

[26] Fletcher, *Barbarian*, 412.

[27] An additional factor in these areas, beyond the scope of this study, was the influence of Eastern Christendom.

During the twelfth century, the ideology of *crusade* became popular, directed towards both the re-conquest for Christendom of the Holy Land and the full evangelisation of Europe.[28] Among the first to suffer the consequences were Jewish communities in the Rhineland. The conversion of the Wends (a Slavic people north of the Danube) was accomplished by the application of this ideology. Bernard of Clairvaux clarified the stark alternatives they faced: 'We expressly forbid that for any reason whatsoever they should make a truce with [the Wends], whether for money or for tribute, until such time as, with God's help, either their religion or their nation be destroyed.'[29] This crusading approach, undergirded by the creation of new missionary orders, was responsible also for the conversion of Prussia, Finland and Livonia (roughly Estonia and Latvia) in the thirteen and fourteenth centuries.

Fletcher recounts the incident that formally completed the evangelisation of Western Europe and establishment of medieval Christendom:

> Jadwiga and Jogaila were to marry, their two countries were to be joined and the pagan Lithuanians were to accept Catholic Christianity ... On 15 February 1386 Jogaila was baptized at Cracow under the name Wladyslaw (Ladislas). Three days later he was married to Jadwiga. On 4 March he was crowned king of Poland. His leading men were baptized and in their turn undertook to bring about the baptism of their dependents. Medieval Latin Christendom was at last formally complete ... Something had been accomplished. Accomplished in a formal sense, at any rate. But Christianization was as slow in Lithuania as it was elsewhere.[30]

---

[28] See Jonathan Riley-Smith, *What were the Crusades?* (Basingstoke: Palgrave MacMillan, 2002).
[29] Quoted in Fletcher, *Barbarian*, 487.
[30] Fletcher, *Barbarian*, 507-508.

Over 1000 years had passed since Constantine accepted Christianity. To the south, North Africa had been lost to Islam and parts of Spain would be in Muslim hands for centuries, but to the north and west Christendom had made huge gains. In Lithuania, formal acceptance of Christianity was sealed by a royal marriage and the baptism of the aristocracy, a typical top-down arrangement. But Christianisation in Lithuania was just beginning. In Italy, Spain and elsewhere in southern Europe, Christianisation had been underway for centuries. The overwhelming majority throughout Europe was now officially Christian, baptised as infants into a society assumed to be Christian. Christendom had survived the demise of the culture in which it was born, rooted itself in the kingdoms that succeeded the Roman Empire, reinvented itself in the Frankish Empire and established itself as the uncontested spiritual heart of the medieval world. It transcended local cultures, dialects and political loyalties and formed 'an integrated social-religious construct that joined many little kingdoms and cultures into one more or less unified civilization.'[31] Something had been accomplished. But what?

How Christian was Christendom?

The fundamental question arising from this story is whether, and in what sense, Christendom was Christian. The next chapter will consider the Christendom *system* and assess whether the changes resulting from the Christendom shift were coherent with the original story and vision of the Christian faith. Was Christendom an authentic expression of Christianity? This chapter considers the *inhabitants* of Christendom. Did they perceive themselves to be Christians

---

[31] Irvin and Sunquist, *History*, 379.

and does the historical evidence support or challenge this perception?

A similar question about Constantine was examined with reference to the categories of 'believing', 'belonging' and 'behaving'. These categories are also helpful here. What did people believe in Christendom? To what extent did they belong to the church? How was their behaviour shaped by Christian values and the Christian story? Christendom developed over centuries and took different shapes in different contexts, so answers vary with time and place, but there are discernible patterns and tendencies.

Believing in Christendom

As Christendom matured there was increasing certainty about what Christians *ought* to believe. The theological controversies of the fourth and fifth centuries left a legacy of division and bitterness, which hindered the advance and unity of Christendom, but eventually one expression of Christianity triumphed, enshrined in definitive and obligatory creeds (though their theological niceties were unintelligible to almost all who repeated them).

But, because far less attention was given to instructing converts in the basics of the faith than to these theological definitions, the gulf between what Christians were meant to believe and what they actually believed was often wide. Providing proper instruction for huge numbers professing to be Christians, especially in the aftermath of military action, would have been demanding. But the absence of a process that effectively inducted converts into the Christian story and its implications meant the level of understanding was very low. Furthermore, conversions achieved through coercion and inducements were unlikely to result in comprehensive changes in belief, at least without the instruction that was generally lacking.

Unsurprisingly, there is widespread evidence of pagan beliefs persisting and co-existing alongside Christian beliefs. Missionaries noted the continuing attraction of tree worship, pagan festivals and consultations with soothsayers and diviners. Church councils repeatedly condemned magic and witchcraft, suggesting these remained popular. At grass-roots level there was friendly co-operation and mutual borrowing between Christian and pagan spiritual leaders; people turned to either or both for help. Christian rituals, symbols and liturgies (often in garbled form) were intertwined with pagan practices to produce local variations, especially where Christianity spread through osmosis rather than imposition. Sun worship was practised even in the heart of Christendom. Peter Brown reports:

> In 440, pope Leo was shocked to learn that, when they reached the top of the flight of steps that led up to the shrine of Saint Peter, many good Catholic Christians would turn their backs to the saint's basilica, to bow, with a reverential gesture, towards the rising sun.[32]

It is unclear how to evaluate this apparent confusion and syncretism, especially since church leaders adopted different perspectives. Some were deeply concerned about the persistence of pagan beliefs and practices, preached against these and attempted to wean their congregations off paganism. Others considered paganism a spent force and tolerated what they regarded as vestiges of a dying culture not worth worrying about. Others again recognised the importance of rooting Christianity in indigenous cultures and distinguished between beliefs and practices to be resisted and those that could be baptised into Christendom.

---

[32] Brown, *Rise*, 145.

We may query whether Christianity was rooted in local cultures through balanced applications of what Andrew Walls calls the 'indigenising' and 'pilgrim' principles.[33] Was this creative and sensitive contextualisation or irresponsible syncretism? Did some influential church customs and theological beliefs owe more to pagan influence than biblical teaching? Were pagan gods and goddesses subsumed into Christendom as saints to whom Christians could pray? Was Christianity paganised (rather than pagan beliefs christianised)? James Russell suggests Clovis' conversion, celebrated as the culmination of the Christianising of Europe, should be understood as symbolising the 'Germanisation' of Christianity.[34] An intriguing ninth-century example is *The Heliand*, which translates the story of Jesus into Germanic tribal culture and presents the disciples as warriors.

What is beyond dispute is that Christendom developed into a society that excluded or marginalised other religious options, where almost everyone regarded themselves as Christians and accepted without question a Christian worldview. The biblical story, the authority of the church and Christian terminology and concepts were imbibed through liturgy, art, sculpture, music, literature, architecture, legislation, customs and language. And people believed in Christendom itself as a Christian civilisation that provided a framework for political, economic, social, military and cultural life.

The depth of such beliefs is difficult to measure. There is extensive evidence of nominal Christianity throughout

---

[33] Andrew Walls, *The Missionary Movement in Christian History: Studies in the Transmission of Faith* (Edinburgh: T. & T. Clark, 1996), 7–9.

[34] James Russell, *The Germanization of Early Medieval Christianity: A Sociohistorical Approach to Religious Transformation* (New York: Oxford University Press, 1994).

Christendom, though some have suggested the overall feel of many communities gradually became more Christian than might be apparent from levels of personal belief.[35] Latourette writes: 'The experience of thoroughgoing moral and spiritual renewal was probably shared by only a minority of Christians. Enough of them had it, however, to give a tone to the Christian community.'[36] Church leaders knew only a small proportion of converts were serious about following Christ, though they rarely seemed unduly disturbed by this.[37] Many recognised Christendom had achieved breadth at the expense of depth and were willing to operate within this new context rather than wringing their hands over it. But this required a shift in the focus of belief:

> Before Constantine, one knew as a fact of everyday experience that there was a believing Christian community but one had to 'take it on faith' that God was governing history. After Constantine, one had to believe without seeing that there was a community of believers, within the larger nominally Christian mass, but one knew for a fact that God was in control of history.[38]

Belonging in Christendom

Whatever their actual beliefs, most people felt they belonged both in Christendom and to the church that was one of its main pillars. The baptism of infants, normative

---

[35] Robin Lane Fox, *Pagans and Christians* (Harmondsworth: Penguin, 1986), 21; Fletcher, *Barbarian*, 482, 512; MacMullen, *Christianizing*, 84.

[36] Latourette, *First*, 167.

[37] Kreider, *Change*, 64; MacMullen, *Christianizing*, 65–6.

[38] John Howard Yoder, *The Priestly Kingdom: Social Ethics as Gospel* (Notre Dame: University of Notre Dame Press, 1984), 137.

once first-generation converts were initiated into Christendom, expressed symbolically the automatic incorporation of everyone into the church and Christian society: as later chapters make clear, challenging this practice was profoundly disturbing, tantamount to questioning the whole Christendom framework.

Church leaders assumed everyone (except the Jews) belonged to the church. As was noted earlier, internal problems – heresy and schism – were more threatening than pagan vestiges. Christendom was a totalitarian culture: anyone challenging its beliefs or causing dissension was perceived as undermining society and dealt with severely. Those branded as heretics, including any who questioned infant baptism, were treated as political subversives rather than merely dissenters from theological beliefs asserted as orthodox by those in power. In a society where everyone belonged, everyone had to subscribe to the same beliefs, at least in public.

This shared belonging and believing was expressed and undergirded by participation in the rituals of the church. How many attended services, and how often, is difficult even to estimate, despite laws requiring regular attendance, and attendance often implied little interest in proceedings. Augustine complained about 'depraved persons who in mobs fill the churches in a bodily sense only',[39] and Martin of Braga referred to people playing dice and talking throughout church services.[40] Perhaps, however, this derived as much from liturgical changes as the spirituality of attenders. Services, especially in the cities, took place in huge buildings and consisted increasingly of complex liturgical performances that relegated attenders to the role of spectators.

---

[39] Augustine, *First Catechetical Instruction* 7.12.
[40] Herrin, *Formation*, 171.

The division of Christendom into parishes ensured almost everyone belonged to a parish church. This system evolved gradually during the medieval period as the basic unit of ecclesiastical administration and pastoral care. Boundaries were large enough for the parish to support a church and priest but small enough for all parishioners to gather in the church building. This system, which was also a secular administrative unit for many purposes, was more or less complete by the end of the twelfth century (with periodic adjustments for population shifts and anomalies, known as 'extra-parochial' places).[41] The transition by the eighth century from voluntary to mandatory tithing meant everyone was required to pay for this. In return, parishioners could expect from the church rites of passage, spiritual care, practical assistance in times of distress and other forms of pastoral ministry. Clergy and laity recognised their mutual obligations and knew they belonged in a Christian society and a culturally central church.

Behaving in Christendom

Evidence from as early as the fourth century suggests the behaviour of Christians was no longer distinctive as it had been in pre-Christendom. Markus concludes: 'Around 350 very little separated a Christian from his pagan counterpart in Roman society.'[42] A.H.M. Jones expands on this: 'Christianity thus became the official, and gradually also the normal, religion of the Roman Empire. The effect on the Church was mainly bad. As converts came in no longer by conviction, but for interested motives or merely by inertia,

---

[41] Norman Pounds, *A History of the English Parish* (Cambridge: Cambridge University Press, 2000).
[42] Markus, *End*, 27.

the spiritual and moral fervour of the Church inevitably waned.'[43]

The discipline and ethical lifestyle that had been so attractive began to lose coherence (even before Constantine adopted Christianity) as the church expanded and became respectable. But in the fourth century moral laxity increased markedly and Christians became harder to distinguish from pagans. Potential converts were now dissuaded by Christians' immorality and hypocrisy (the latter a new charge that would become common and persistent). A disturbing insight early in that century is provided by proceedings of the Council of Elvira, which was dealing with Christians involved in murder and pimping and church leaders involved in adultery and usury.[44]

One reason for this moral laxity was that the limited instruction provided for converts differed from the catechetical process of earlier centuries. The Old Testament rather than the New Testament was used, and doctrinal rather than ethical instruction predominated. Surveying this change, Everett Ferguson concludes: 'A more concentrated and thorough job was done of doctrinal and liturgical (sacramental) instruction than was done with biblical and moral teaching. The emphasis had shifted from the earlier days of the church ... Being a Christian was now defined primarily in terms of doctrine and not in terms of behaviour.'[45]

But loss of distinctiveness is most troubling among church leaders, who knew more about the ethical expecta-

---

[43] A.H.M. Jones, *Constantine and the Conversion of Europe* (Harmondsworth: Penguin, 1972), 238–9.
[44] Latourette, *First*, 286; Henry Chadwick, *The Early Church* (Harmondsworth: Penguin, 1967), 65.
[45] Everett Ferguson, 'Catechesis and Initiation', in Alan Kreider (ed.), *The Origins of Christendom in the West* (Edinburgh: T. & T. Clark, 2001), 267. See also Kreider, *Change*, passim.

tions of their faith but chose to ignore or reinterpret these. Although there were notable exceptions, the wealth, power and status they received in Christendom appear to have discouraged serious ethical living among church leaders. Many bishops were extraordinarily wealthy and often barely distinguishable from aristocrats and bureaucrats, participating unreservedly in the cultural pursuits of the privileged. Describing the lifestyle of a seventh-century bishop of York, Fletcher comments:

> Wilfrid's career shows us that the threshold between the world of the secular nobleman and that of the noble prelate was not one that was difficult or threatening to negotiate. The hurdle was not high; the leap not into the dark. Indeed, one may suspect that for some the threshold, hurdle or leap was to all intents and purposes invisible.[46]

What we know about Christian leaders between the fourth and fourteenth centuries suggests a colourful mixture of devout saints and thoroughly obnoxious characters led Christendom. Believing and behaving were not always well connected: some who struggled hardest to preserve what they regarded as orthodox doctrine were very unattractive personalities. Nor did strength of belonging safeguard behaviour: often the spiritual and moral qualities of church leaders fell well short of their parishioners. And methods used to strengthen the church's grip on society and extend Christendom leave much to be desired.

By the fourteenth century almost everyone shared, albeit to varying degrees and with varying enthusiasm, a common set of beliefs, a common sense of belonging and common norms of behaviour. They regarded themselves as Christians and called their culture Christendom: in many

---

[46] Fletcher, *Barbarian*, 180–1.

European languages Christendom equals Christianity.[47] But (recalling earlier questions) what was Christendom? Had Christianity triumphed over the Empire and created a Christian civilisation? Or had the Empire subverted Christianity?

More Questions

At the end of the last chapter various concerns emerged from the story of the coming of Christendom. Pursuing the story through the following centuries has underscored those concerns and raises further questions:

- Why was the definition of philosophical and linguistic points of doctrine more significant than instructing new converts?
- What kind of church results from the offer of inducements to convert?
- What justification is there for coercion in evangelism or persecuting those who hold other viewpoints?
- What have been the legacies of top-down mission strategies?
- Could hierarchical and militaristic tribes have been converted in any other way than top-down?
- Is the legal requirement of baptising infants significantly different from the forced baptising of conquered adults?
- What have been the implications of presenting Christ as a 'god of battles'?
- What ethical principles or ecclesiological practices were actually derived from paganism but through long usage have been accepted as Christian?

---

[47] Walls, *Cross-Cultural Process*, 36.

- What principles can guide those who attempt to contextualise the gospel and protect them from syncretism?
- How can the ideology of crusade be squared with the teaching of Jesus?
- Do the advantages of a clerical caste separate from the laity outweigh the disadvantages of this system?
- Was the transition from the depth of pre-Christendom Christian commitment to the breadth of Christian allegiance in Christendom worth making?

4

The Christendom Shift

Was Constantine's invitation to the church to receive not just toleration but imperial favour, status, wealth, power and social centrality a God-given opportunity, which it rightly seized to ensure the triumph of Christianity in Europe? Or did the acceptance of this invitation pervert the church, compromise its calling and hinder its mission, achieving by infiltration what 300 years of persecution had failed to achieve? Were the various changes that occurred as the church moved from the margins to the centre beneficial, regrettable but necessary, or illegitimate and corrupting?

This chapter will assess the claim that the Christendom shift radically re-engineered the church's DNA so that what developed became progressively alienated from the Christianity of the New Testament and pre-Christendom. It will begin with the 'nifty theological footwork' mentioned previously and the man most crucially involved in reshaping Christianity as an imperial religion: Augustine. Several fourth- and fifth-century theologians contributed. But responsibility for adapting Christianity to its new and unanticipated role fell primarily on the foremost theologian of the period, who undertook this with imagination and skill, and whose towering influence decisively shaped Western Christendom.

Augustine

If Constantine laid the foundations of Christendom, its main architect was Augustine. This brief study cannot survey the whole career and voluminous writings of this outstanding scholar, brilliant preacher and deeply pastoral bishop; its focus is on the innovations he introduced and his influence on the developing Christendom system.

Augustine was born in 354, in Numidia, to a pagan father and Christian mother. His mixed parentage reminds us Christendom was a recent development, but he was too young to remember Julian's attempt to revive paganism, so his whole life-experience was set against the background of the apparent triumph of Christianity and the search for new ways of understanding what it meant to be Christians at the centre instead of on the margins.

Augustine completed his education in Carthage and joined the Manichaeans, who were influential in the region and presented themselves as advanced Christians rather than members of another religion. He remained a Manichaean for nine years but became increasingly critical of their beliefs (though Manichaean influence is apparent in his writings). In 383 he moved to Italy, where he explored the philosophy of Neoplatonism, and in 385 became an orator in the employment of Valentinian II. During this period he was a catechumen and, attracted by the preaching of Ambrose, Bishop of Milan, he was baptised in 387. Four years after his baptism, during which time he struggled to integrate his philosophical ideas and Christian convictions, arguing and writing against Manichaeism, he was ordained a presbyter in his home province of Numidia. In 396 he became Bishop of Hippo and remained there until his death in 430.

We know more about the inner life and struggles of the young Augustine than about most of his contemporaries through the publication of his *Confessions*. This work, which inspired a tradition of spiritual autobiography, reflects on his family, education, philosophical influences, friends, mistress, career and finally his baptism and new career as a church leader. The central theme of this and many of his writings is God's grace upon which human beings depend.

Augustine wrote prolifically – sermons, exegetical works, theological and ethical treatises, letters and polemical material. His main opponents were the Manichaeans, Donatists and Pelagians, whom he perceived as threats to the Christian society that was developing, and against whom he campaigned vigorously. Apparent throughout his writings are theological principles, approaches to biblical interpretation, social and political commentary, pastoral and ethical teachings and convictions about the church and its mission. These are presented as orthodox but sometimes diverged markedly from what Christians had long accepted and practised.

Among these innovations (some of which contemporaries also taught) were:

- Introducing the principle of arbitrary predestination that consigned most of humanity to eternal punishment.[1]
- Theological justification of oppression and coercion of religious opponents.[2]
- Receiving as converts those who yielded to force or bribery rather than persuasion.[3]
- The first clear statement of the principle that 'error has no rights' upon which Christians have based the imposition of 'truth'.[4]

---

[1] Frend, *Early Church*, 198.
[2] Kreider, *Change*, 55, 72–3.
[3] MacMullen, *Christianizing*, 3, 62.
[4] Kreider, *Change*, 55. For a study of the outworking of this in Northern Ireland, see Joseph Liechty and Cecelia Clegg, *Moving Beyond Sectarianism: Conflict and Reconciliation in Northern Ireland* (Dublin: The Columba Press, 2001).

- Being 'the first Christian that we know of to think consistently and in a practical manner of making everyone a Christian'.[5]
- Acceptance that the visible church comprised a small proportion of serious Christians and very many nominal believers.[6]
- Initiating a 'baptismal revolution' so that baptising babies became normal.[7]
- Teaching that original sin was inherited from Adam through the lust involved in procreating children (which necessitated infant baptism).[8]
- The doctrine of 'indelibility of orders', whereby the ordained status of clergy was regarded as permanent.[9]
- Development of Christian catechetical teaching, for the first time in church history, on the basis of the Ten Commandments.[10]
- Application of the principle of tithing, detached from its biblical and cultural context, to Christians.[11]
- Adapting the classical 'just war' tradition to construct an alternative approach to war, replacing the pacifism of earlier centuries.[12]

---

[5] Brown, *Rise*, 91.

[6] Yoder, *Priestly*, 136; Kreider, *Change*, 57, 64.

[7] David Wright, 'Augustine and the Transformation of Baptism', in Kreider (ed.), *Origins*, 287–310.

[8] Frend, *Early Church*, 206.

[9] Everett Ferguson, 'The Congregationalism of the Early Church', in Daniel Williams, *The Free Church and the Early Church: Bridging the Historical and Theological Divide* (Grand Rapids: Eerdmans, 2002), 136.

[10] Kreider, *Change*, 62.

[11] Stuart Murray, *Beyond Tithing* (Carlisle: Paternoster Press, 2000), 117–20.

[12] A classic study of this subject and Augustine's influence is Roland Bainton, *Christian Attitudes Towards War and Peace: A*

These innovations would have profound and deeply disturbing consequences for the subsequent development of Christendom. Several things, however, should be said in defence of Augustine. First, he appears not to have appreciated how much he was innovating. The changed status of the church and the christianising society in which he lived hindered him from connecting with the beliefs and practices of the earlier church on the margins.

Second, although he welcomed the church's new status, Augustine was unsure about the place of the Empire in God's purposes. Richard Fletcher comments that Augustine 'was a discordant voice in the general chorus orchestrated by Eusebius in celebration of the Christian Empire'; for him the Empire was 'not part of a divine providential scheme; not the vehicle for the furtherance of God's purposes'.[13]

Third, though he advocated coercive measures against pagans and those he regarded as heretics and schismatics, his earlier writings indicate distaste for this approach. He changed his views reluctantly, and was frustrated that other measures were ineffective.[14] His writings contain both admonitions to desecrate pagan shrines and advice to leave this to secular authorities. He seems ambivalent about torture and consistently resisted the use of lethal measures against opponents.

Fourth, realising many of his congregation were nominal believers, he provided foundational teaching through ser-

---

[12] (*Continued*) *Historical Survey and Critical Re-evaluation* (Nashville: Abingdon Press, 1960).

[13] Fletcher, *Barbarian*, 28–30. See further R.A. Markus, *Saeculum: History and Society in the Theology of Saint Augustine* (Cambridge: Cambridge University Press, 1989).

[14] Augustine's views are described as 'a field of tensions' in Gerald Schlabach, 'The Correction of the Augustinians' in Williams (ed.), *Free Church*, 49.

mons and pre-baptismal catechesis. This was less thorough than in third-century churches but, by comparison with contemporary and later standards, relatively extensive.[15]

Finally, the way later church leaders used his writings to justify theological principles and ecclesiastical practices may misinterpret his intentions. His status throughout the medieval period and among both Catholics and Protestants after the Reformation meant they claimed his authority for many things based primarily on other arguments and justifications. Nevertheless, having made such allowances, Augustine

> had been innovating, presiding over a far-reaching alteration in the nature of the church and its relation to the 'world' ... For Augustine, a distinctively living Christian church had disappeared, as had the world. For him, a pioneer of Christendom, the church and the world were becoming so intermingled that they were indistinguishable.[16]

Whether or not he realised he was reinventing Christianity, Augustine, a 'pioneer of Christendom', believed his context required accommodation and reinterpretation. Many ideas and practices of Christians in previous generations were unrealistic in an Empire fast becoming Christian. What was needed was:

- Erosion of the old distinction between church and world.
- An understanding of church as a mixed company of wheat and weeds.
- An emphasis on God's grace rather than human discipleship.

---

[15] Kreider, *Change*, 61–5.
[16] Kreider, *Change*, 65.

- A united church across the Empire undisturbed by nonconformist movements.
- Ethical guidance for Christian politicians, aristocrats, economists, civil servants and military strategists with an Empire to run and defend.

Addressing these issues, Augustine developed an approach to biblical interpretation that enabled him to relate biblical teaching to the realities of Christendom.[17] He was committed to the supreme authority of Scripture and advocated careful textual study, drawing appreciatively (if surprisingly) on the exegetical rules of Tychonius, a Donatist. But his writings contain some extraordinary interpretations, often using allegorical interpretations to evade texts that challenged his convictions.

One aspect of his approach reflected a wider change in the fourth and fifth centuries that characterised biblical interpretation in Christendom: justifying from the Old Testament practices he could not easily justify from the New. Although, in his writings against Manichaeans and Pelagians, Augustine asserted either the consistent witness of both testaments or the primacy of the New Testament, the New Testament's teaching about economics and enemy loving disconcerted him. He resorted to a dualistic approach, urging Christian soldiers to love the enemies they killed. One extraordinary application of the story of Jesus clearing the Temple (Jn. 2) concludes: 'we do find Christ a persecutor.'[18] But the Old Testament rescued him. Augustine found there support for using force against the

---

[17] This section is indebted to David Nussbaum, 'Augustine, Scripture and Power: A Critical Appraisal of Scripture and Power in the Life and Thought of Augustine, and their Interrelation' (New College, Edinburgh: unpublished MTh dissertation, 1981).
[18] *Against Petilian* II.10.24.

Donatists, and he advocated tithing primarily from Old Testament texts.

Augustine also used the Old Testament to endorse the Christendom shift itself and the emerging culture (which he calls 'Christian times'), noting parallels between Israel and Christendom and interpreting Old Testament prophecies as foretelling a Christian Empire. And he found Old Testament support for the 'just war' theory that allowed, or even required, Christians to use force to defend this Empire and advance its interests.

But his interpretation of two Gospel texts did most to determine how the church and its role in society were understood in Christendom. The first was the parable of the 'wheat and weeds' (Mt. 13:24–30, 37–43). Jesus explicitly called this a parable of the kingdom and identified the field in which wheat and weeds grew as the world, but Augustine insisted it described the church (not mentioned in the parable) as a mixed community.[19] The collapse of boundaries between church and world in Christendom, and the identification of God's kingdom with the institutional church, required and were justified by such an interpretation.

The second text was a phrase from another parable: 'compel them to come in' (Lk. 14:23). Augustine used this to explain to a Donatist bishop, Vincentius, why he now advocated coercion.[20] In a sermon to his congregation he acknowledged this was a novel interpretation that demurred from the traditional non-coercive approach, but insisted that compelling people to choose well was legitimate.[21] Lacking other New Testament support for

---

[19] *The City of God* XX.9 and elsewhere, especially in anti-Donatist writings. He did not employ this text to argue against coercion despite the injunction against pulling up weeds ahead of time!

[20] Letter 93.5.17.

[21] Sermon 112 (62).

coercion, Augustine frequently used this text to undergird a position that depended on other considerations, but for which this offered apparent (though spurious) biblical support.[22] He insisted that unjust persecution *of* Christians was motivated by cruelty but 'just persecution' *by* Christians was motivated by love. This justification of coercion to enforce unity and theological convictions was original to Augustine and had terrible consequences throughout the centuries. Although he might not have endorsed later developments, many invoked his application of this text to justify inquisition, torture and execution.

Admirers of Augustine can argue legitimately that this critique does not adequately reflect his remarkable theological depth and breadth. Many studies applaud his achievements. Certainly books written towards the end of his life, including Augustine's study of the Trinity and *The City of God*, left a more positive legacy. He addressed issues earlier theologians had not adequately explored and his emphasis on grace corrects tendencies towards legalism and self-reliance. However, this section has been concerned with Augustine's influence on the development of Christendom and with identifying the roots of issues that need reassessing in post-Christendom.

Summarising the Christendom Shift[23]

Massive though Augustine's influence was, the Christendom shift did not depend on his activities or writings.[24] The

---

[22] See also Letters 173 and 185.
[23] This is a schematic overview, which does not explore nuances or chart gradual developments.
[24] Similar (though not identical) developments in Eastern Christendom, where Augustine's influence was minimal, suggest he should not be accorded undue credit or blame.

transformation in how the church understood itself and its role in society was not accomplished in one generation. Some developments had roots predating Constantine and would take centuries to develop fully. Over time, however, the Christendom shift involved:

- The adoption of Christianity as the official religion of city, state or Empire.
- Movement of the church from the margins to the centre of society.
- The creation and progressive development of a Christian culture or civilisation.
- The assumption that all citizens (except Jews) were Christian by birth.
- The development of a 'sacral society', *corpus Christianum*, where there was no freedom of religion and political power was divinely authenticated.
- The definition of 'orthodoxy' as the belief all shared, determined by powerful church leaders with state support.
- Imposition, by legislation and custom, of a supposedly Christian morality on the entire society (though normally Old Testament morality was applied).
- Infant baptism as the symbol of obligatory incorporation into Christian society.
- The defence of Christianity by legal sanctions to restrain heresy, immorality and schism.
- A hierarchical ecclesiastical system based on a diocesan and parish arrangement, analogous to the state hierarchy and buttressed by state support.
- A generic distinction between clergy and laity, and relegation of laity to a largely passive role.

- Two-tier ethics, with higher standards of discipleship ('evangelical counsels') expected of clergy and those in religious orders.
- Sunday as an official holiday and obligatory church attendance, with penalties for non-compliance.
- The requirement of oaths of allegiance and oaths in law courts to encourage truth telling.
- The construction of massive and ornate church buildings and the formation of huge congregations.
- Increased wealth for the church and obligatory tithes to fund the system.
- Division of the globe into 'Christendom' and 'heathendom' and wars waged in the name of Christ and the church.
- Use of political and military force to impose Christianity, regardless of personal conviction.
- Reliance on the Old Testament, rather than the New, to justify these changes.

The foundation of Christendom was a theocratic under-standing of society and a close, though sometimes fraught, partnership between church and state, the two main pillars of society. The nature of this partnership varied. Over the centuries, power struggles between popes and emperors resulted in one or other holding sway. Previous chapters have revealed one emperor presiding over a church council and another submitting to a bishop's authority. But the system assumed the church was associated with a status quo understood as Christian and had vested interests in its maintenance. The church provided religious legitimation for state activities; the state provided secular support for ecclesiastical decisions.

Christendom excluded or reinterpreted elements of New Testament teaching that had been important in pre-Christendom:

Faith and discipleship

- Faith in Christ was no longer understood as the exercise of choice in a pluralistic environment where other choices were possible without penalty.
- The term 'conversion' mainly described, not the start of the Christian life, but entrance into a monastic community.
- Discipleship was interpreted as loyal citizenship, rather than commitment to the counter-cultural values of God's kingdom.
- Preoccupation with individual eternal destiny replaced expectation of the coming of God's kingdom.

Church and society

- There was no longer any significant distinction between 'church' and 'world'.
- The state was no longer accorded a limited preservative function but had replaced the church as the bearer of the meaning of history.
- Church was defined territorially and membership was compulsory, with no room for believers' churches comprised only of voluntary members.
- Such voluntary communities, called 'churches' in the New Testament, were now called 'sects' and condemned as schismatic.
- The church largely abandoned its prophetic role for a chaplaincy role, providing spiritual support, sanctifying social occasions and state policies.
- The idea of God's kingdom was reduced to a historical entity, coterminous with the state church, or relegated to the future.

Church life

- Believers' baptism as the means of incorporation into the church was regarded as appropriate only for first-generation converts from paganism.
- Church services became performance-oriented as multi-voiced participation and the exercise of charismatic gifts declined.
- A sacramental and penitential system developed that enabled the church hierarchy to control and dispense 'salvation', often at a price.
- Clerical power and the disappearance of the 'world' meant church discipline was punitive, even lethal, rather than expressing pastoral care and mutual admonition.

Mission

- The church's orientation was now towards maintenance rather than mission, and mission was carried out by specialist agencies, not congregations.
- Pastors and teachers were honoured, while apostles, prophets and evangelists were marginalised or regarded as obsolete (cf. Eph. 4.11).
- Mission within and beyond Christendom was accomplished by top-down methods, including coercion and offering inducements.
- The vision of a new Christian nation, *corpus Christi*, scattered through the nations was replaced by a vision of an earthly Christian Empire.

Ethics

- The church became more concerned about maintaining social order than achieving social justice.

- Because the church exercised control, ethical choices were justified by anticipated outcomes or consequences rather than inherent morality.
- Pleas for religious liberty were forgotten and persecution was imposed by those claiming to be Christians rather than upon them.
- Enemy loving and peacemaking were replaced by the formation of a Christian army and the 'just war' theory or 'holy war' ideology.
- The cross was less a reminder of the laying down of life than a symbol carried into battle by those who would take the lives of others.

Illustrating the Christendom Shift

These were far-reaching changes in how Christians under-stood and practised their faith. A time-travelling first-century Christian would have found many aspects of fifth- or eighth-century Christianity unfamiliar and trou-bling. Other dimensions of the Christendom shift will be examined later, but two issues clearly illustrate its nature and consequences.

Baptism

The New Testament presents baptism as the initiation cere-mony whereby those who express faith in Christ are incorporated into the church. The symbolism of being washed clean and dying to the past is a powerful incentive to lives of whole-hearted discipleship. It is everywhere assumed that those who believed would be baptised, and the New Testament locates baptism close to the commit-ment to follow Jesus.

During the next 250 years the baptism of believers remained normal practice; but, as the church encountered people who understood little of God, Jesus' life and teaching and expectations of discipleship, an induction process was introduced to prepare them for baptism. Two further changes appeared: the baptism of young children and the belief that serious post-baptismal sin was well nigh unforgivable (to which Augustine's teaching was a helpful corrective). Baptising children lacks explicit New Testament mandate, although it is possible (some argue, likely) 'household baptisms'[25] included children. In the first three centuries those raised in Christian homes were normally baptised as young adults, but infant baptism developed as an exceptional pastoral measure, when children were not expected to survive to maturity.[26] Church leaders were ambivalent but willing to tolerate this if safeguards were in place.

The Christendom shift introduced new elements into baptismal thinking and practice. First, following the example of Constantine, baptised at the end of his life, perhaps to avoid committing unforgivable sins in his imperial role, *delayed baptism* became popular. No longer associated with the start of the Christian life but its end, 'clinical' baptism (after *kline*, bed) was understood not as commitment to a life of discipleship but as preparation for life after death, conferring immortality rather than forgiveness. Many Christians, even those who were serious about their faith, were catechumens throughout their lives.[27]

Second, *infant baptism* became, not exceptional, but first normal and then legally required (thereby discouraging delayed baptism). As late as the fifth-century, children from Christian homes were usually baptised after the age of

---

[25] Acts 16:15,33.
[26] Kreider, *Change*, 74.
[27] Jones, *Constantine*, 225.

twelve, but in most places by the sixth century infant baptism was normal. This also removed baptism from the start of the Christian life, linking it instead to the beginning of physical life; it meant entrance not into the church as a distinct community within society but into a sacral society in which the church was no longer a separate entity. Theological reasons were developed for this change of practice which, as so often, was justified on the basis of an Old Testament analogy – in this case, circumcision. Male infants were circumcised as a sign of membership in the sacral society of Israel; male and female infants were baptised as a sign of membership – by birth, not choice – in the sacral society of Christendom.

Third, there were many instances of *mass baptism*, where thousands were baptised together as Christendom expanded into new territory. Infant baptism would become normal in the next generation, but first-generation converts were baptised as adults. Following the conversion of the Frankish king, 'three thousand of Clovis' troops were baptised at the same time, presaging the collective tribal baptisms that occurred as Christianity conquered Western Europe'.[28] Cascading baptism occurred, illustrated by Lithuania's entrance into Christendom: first the king was baptised, then his nobles, who committed themselves to ensure the baptism of their followers.

Whether these baptisms had much in common with the baptism of 3000 at Pentecost seems unlikely; but in societies where identity is rooted in group solidarity, not personal choice, this approach may initially be inevitable. Missionaries have grappled with this issue in other societies through the centuries where operating according to the individualistic mindset of modern westerners seems inappropriate.[29] But this strategy requires careful

[28] Kreider, *Change*, 88.
[29] Walls, *Cross-Cultural Process*, 35.

instruction, before or after baptism, if conversion is to be more than nominal.

Fourth, some mass baptisms and the baptisms of some individuals must be designated *forced baptism*. As Christendom gathered pace, pagans within otherwise Christian territory were threatened with exile and confiscation of property if they refused to be baptised, and were also required to baptise their children. Jews were generally exempt from this requirement, but there are instances of some being forcibly baptised by zealous, if unauthorised, Christians. And in Spain, exasperation at the lack of progress of mission among Muslims resulted in some being coerced into baptism. Military campaigns that extended the boundaries of Christendom often required baptism as an indication of submission.[30] In these contexts, where refusal was a capital offence, not surprisingly the rush to baptism was considerable.

Finally, especially in contexts of rapid growth, *uninstructed baptism* was common. Deathbed baptisms often, as with Constantine, involved minimal instruction because of the urgency of the situation and the understandable reluctance of church leaders to withhold baptism from the dying. Where baptism was forced on adults or applied to infants, instruction might follow but was often regarded as unnecessary – the rite itself would suffice. Baptism functioned as a magical act.[31] In the case of mass baptisms, few were interested in receiving instruction. Where instruction was provided, this was often limited: in Christendom it was assumed people knew the story or would imbibe Christianity from the culture in which they lived.

---

[30] Fletcher, *Barbarian*, 210, 447.

[31] Adriaan Bredero, *Christendom and Christianity in the Middle Ages: The Relations Between Religion, Church, and Society* (Grand Rapids: Eerdmans, 1986), 357.

These significant changes shaped and were shaped by the sacral culture Christendom was becoming. Constantine publicly challenged traditional baptismal practices and Augustine provided a rationale for a new approach. Separating baptism from choice and counter-cultural discipleship was essential for Christendom as a unified society. David Wright writes of Augustine:

> Theologically he came to believe that infant baptism was the sole cure for the guilt of original sin; practically he came to advocate the universal baptism of infants soon after their birth. The result was a devaluation of baptism in the West which did much to determine the contours of Christendom.[32]

As Christendom fades, fewer infants are baptised – some because their parents are *not* Christians and see no reason to baptise their children; others because their parents *are* Christians and are not persuaded infant baptism is legitimate or helpful. Defenders of infant baptism offer theological justifications,[33] but in post-Christendom this practice will continue to decline. A major challenge will be developing an induction process to help converts learn the now unfamiliar Christian story and become counter-cultural followers of Jesus in an alien society. If baptism in Christendom symbolised entrance into normal society, in post-Christendom it means entrance into a deviant community.

---

[32] Wright, 'Augustine', 287.
[33] Few now adopt Augustine's argument that baptism rescues infants, infected by original sin, from eternal damnation. Most emphasise God's prevenient grace and covenant theology. Both arguments attempt to justify a practice that evolved for different reasons.

The Cross

The birth of Christendom can be traced, somewhat fanci-
fully, to Constantine's vision, in which he saw a cross and
received the instruction *in hoc signo vince* ('in this sign
conquer'). In obedience, Constantine apparently had the
sign of the cross painted on the military equipment his
soldiers were using and fought future battles under this
emblem. This use of the cross became standard in Christendom as Christian armies, who fasted and prayed before
battles, fought to defend or enlarge the Empire.

The sign of the cross was familiar in the early centuries
(as a hand movement when praying or seeking divine protection, rather than an artistic symbol). Its use as a military
logo was new and remarkable. The transformation of this
religious gesture and its public incorporation into Christendom was an impressive achievement. The cross, after all,
was an instrument of state execution – a potent reminder
Jesus Christ was crucified by the Roman state. Equivalents
from later centuries would be a noose, guillotine or electric
chair. To domesticate this subversive and scandalous symbol and invest it with entirely different significance in an
Empire now perceived as Christian rather than responsible
for killing Jesus was no mean feat!

From being a rough instrument of often summary justice
(or injustice) and appalling suffering, the cross became an
imperial symbol conveying the power and honour of Christendom. No longer a sign of self-sacrifice and love, it was
now a rallying point for armies shedding the blood of others, albeit in the name of the one who shed his own blood on
the original cross. No longer a private spiritual defensive
gesture, the cross was now a public military offensive symbol. 'Taking up the cross' now implied readiness not to die
but to kill. Crusades were 'expeditions of the cross' and crusaders were 'signed with the cross'. The New Testament

interprets the cross as the means by which Jesus disarmed the powers,[34] but in Christendom crosses adorned the weapons of the powers. Crosses were everywhere, Christian charms to protect travellers and homes, emblems of the church's dominance in society. 'As a victory-bringing sign, the Cross was known to warrior aristocracies throughout the Christian world.'[35] *The Heliand*, mentioned previously, though a creative attempt to contextualise the gospel, transmuted it into a story of warfare.[36] More than any other symbol, the ubiquity of the cross symbolised Christianity's triumph over the Empire – or its perversion and transformation into an imperial and violent religion.

The sign Constantine used as his military standard may not actually have been the cross, but a new symbol known as the *labarum*, that expressed his dual loyalty to the God of the Christians and the Unconquered Sun. Jones insists: 'It was not the Cross which Constantine used as the emblem of his new patron god, but a monogram ... it appears never to have been used before Constantine's day as a Christian symbol.'[37] Lactantius describes the sign Constantine devised: 'he marked on their shields the letter X, with a perpendicular line drawn through it and turned round thus at the top, being the cipher of Christ'.[38] This became known as the Chi/Rho monogram, using the first two letters of the word 'Christ', or Christogram. Alister Kee concludes: 'The symbol of Constantine's life is the labarum, through which

---

[34] Colossians 2:15.

[35] Brown, *Rise*, 378.

[36] For a positive appraisal, see Ronald Murphy, *The Saxon Savior: The Germanic Transformation of the Gospel in the Ninth-Century Heliand* (New York: Oxford University Press, 1989).

[37] Jones, *Constantine*, 100. See further Drake, *Constantine*, 201–4.

[38] Lactantius, *On the Deaths of the Persecutors* XLIV.

he brought terror to his enemies and freedom to his subjects. The symbol of Jesus, however, is the cross ... the victorious trophy of Constantine is covered in blood, but the blood of other people.'[39]

This was a massive, and largely uncontested, symbolic change that emptied the cross of its challenge, transformed it from a sign of shame and weakness into an insignia of honour, wealth and coercive power, and made possible the blessing of weapons in the name of Christ and the waging of war on behalf of the Christian Empire.

Objections to the Christendom Shift

But it was not completely uncontested. The symbolic, structural, theological, ethical and ecclesiastical changes resulting from the Christendom shift were questioned by some and opposed by others. From surviving sources, these dissenting voices appear to have been few and mostly restrained – the Christendom shift was achieved with amazingly little resistance given the changes it represented – but they are discernible.

Some objections came from those who remained within the system. Hilary of Poitiers and Eustathius of Sebaste were fourth-century bishops who publicly expressed doubts about changes flowing from the Christendom shift.[40] Martin of Tours protested about the execution of heretics, arguing this was a distortion of Christianity, and opposed the growing wealth of church leaders in Gaul. Basil of Caesarea continued to operate a demanding pre-Christendom-style baptismal policy and catechetical process. He also urged: 'one must not use human advantage

---

[39] Kee, *Constantine*, 125, 151–2.
[40] Kreider, *Change*, 42.

in preaching the gospel, lest the grace of God be obscured thereby.'[41] Christianity continued during the fourth century, at least in some places, to honour the traditions of earlier centuries.

Others responded in ways that took them outside the system but did not seriously threaten the system itself. The most influential and permanent, was *monasticism*, a reaction to several features of the Christendom shift. The assumption society was Christian muted the call to discipleship. Monasticism gave devout men and women an alternative way to respond: as noted above, 'conversion', largely redundant in a sacral society, connoted entry into religious orders. It offered discipline and a Christian community that was accountable instead of nominal Christendom congregations. The ending of persecution meant opportunities for martyrdom were restricted to frontier regions. Monasticism offered another form of heroism and self-denial: asceticism replaced martyrdom. Fletcher notes other factors:

> In part the call of the ascetic life could be interpreted as a movement of revulsion from what many saw as the increasing worldliness of the fourth-century church, the merging of its hierarchy with the 'establishment', its ever-accumulating wealth, the growing burdens of administrative responsibilities which encroached upon spiritual ministry.[42]

Monasticism played an ambiguous role in Christendom. Monasteries were centres of learning and spirituality, preservers of civilisation in chaotic times, dispensers of care and providers of hospitality. They gave women freedom

---

[41] Basil of Caesarea, *Maxims for those who Believe in the Lord*, 70:26.
[42] Fletcher, *Barbarian*, 27.

and opportunities unavailable elsewhere. They provided training centres and bases of operation for those engaged in mission within and beyond Christendom. Missionary monks, exempt from territorial restrictions of the diocesan system, travelled freely and made enormous contributions to the Christianising and educating of Christendom.

But monasteries could also be places of corruption and abuses of power; some were almost indistinct from the surrounding culture. James Campbell comments wryly, 'a late seventh- or eighth-century monastery often had many aspects of a special kind of nobleman's club'.[43] Despite the vow of poverty, many monasteries accrued incredible wealth and became occupied with administering their assets to the detriment of their spiritual ministry. Many were involved in selling supposed relics, regarded as having spiritual power, a lucrative trade in superstition that debased the monastic tradition. Among these were pieces of the 'true cross' – another perversion of the meaning of the cross. Attempts at reform, including the influential movement associated with the founding of Cluny in 910, had mixed results. Monastic corruption provoked derision and was one factor leading to the sixteenth-century Reformation.

The monastic tradition, at its best, represented determination to take seriously Jesus' teaching, acting as the conscience of a church finding this increasingly problematic. But this solution was itself problematic. Everett Ferguson writes: 'It was left for the monks to maintain the witness to a distinctive Christian lifestyle. Was all this the price of becoming the church of the Empire?'[44] Monasticism was a prophetic reminder of the discipleship of an earlier era,[45] but it excused the rest of the church from

---

[43] Quoted in Fletcher, *Barbarian*, 182.
[44] Ferguson, 'Catechesis', 267.
[45] Eoin de Bhaldraithe, 'Early Christian Features preserved in Western Monasticism', in Kreider (ed.), *Origins*, 153–78.

following New Testament teaching by legitimating two-tier Christianity.

More troubling objections came from individuals and movements who rejected the Christendom shift and were labelled heretical (unorthodox) or schismatic (orthodox but independent). Because 'history is written by the winners' and our knowledge of the losers comes mainly from their opponents' less than even-handed reports, we have limited information about what individuals actually said or how various movements really operated. Distorted and partial information is difficult to assess and attempts to compensate for bias can produce interpretations unbalanced in the opposite direction. Nevertheless, the challenges of some who objected to the Christendom shift and its implications should be registered.

As Christendom aged, such voices multiplied, forming a chorus from the margins that challenged the church at the centre. Two early voices challenged Augustine. The first was a movement labelled schismatic; the second was a man accused of heresy.

The Donatists

Donatism was an indigenous North African movement, orthodox but threatening to Christendom because it refused to accept the imperial religious system, now known as the catholic (universal) church.[46] Donatists re-baptised converts, opposed lax moral standards in the church, rejected monasticism as excusing others from discipleship and were more concerned about social justice than social order. Their opposition to Roman imperialism was motivated by nationalism and concern for the poor. M.P. Joseph comments: 'This is what the Donatists opposed. The God-image is not an ideological weapon for a hegemonic

---

[46] See Appendix 1.

emperor to extend his Empire; rather God is a refuge of the poor.'[47] W.H.C. Frend concludes that Donatism was 'the only force in the West who remained rootedly independent of the State. They retained to the last a theory of social justice grounded on a theology of the Holy Spirit'.[48]

Their leader, Donatus, on one occasion refused to co-operate with delegates of the emperor, Constans, asking a question that challenged a fundamental assumption of Christendom: *What has the emperor to do with the church?* Although Donatists had earlier appealed to the emperor and did so again when this seemed advantageous, this rhetorical question expressed their resistance to the state dictating church policies. Subsequent dissident movements would ask it again.

Donatism was not easily cowed by imperial pressure or persuaded by the arguments of catholic theologians. It was already a century old when Augustine confronted his opponents at the Council of Carthage in 411. He first applied the text 'compel them to come in' to the Donatists. Frustrated by the failure of years of persuasion, Augustine (whose influence probably ensured Donatism was classed as heresy after 405) now sanctioned coercion to crush opposition and impose unity. Although he advised against lethal force, the measures he encouraged were savage enough to provoke outraged protests from a pagan philosopher. Such internecine strife and use of violence was a wretched testimony to the good news of Jesus!

Coercion was effective in the short term, but ultimately it was disastrous. Donatism outlived Augustine and the damage this unhealed rupture caused and the suppression of

---

[47] M.P. Joseph, 'Heresy of the Majority: Donatist Critique of the Church-State Relationship', *Bangalore Theological Forum* 26.2 (1994), 70.
[48] Frend, *Early Church*, 237.

indigenous churches in North Africa paved the way for the triumph of Islam across the region (except in Egypt where the Coptic Church survived). Zablon Nthamburi concludes: 'When Saint Augustine co-operated with the civil authorities to suppress the Donatist Church he did not realize that he was sounding the death knell of his own church. He did not realize that by making Donatists weaker he was also weakening the Christian faith in North Africa.'[49]

Furthermore, his use of state power and justification of coercion provided a precedent for the treatment of many dissident movements throughout Christendom.

Pelagius

Pelagius was born in Britain but lived in Rome from about 384 to 409. A respected theologian, orator and spiritual counsellor with a reputation for moral integrity, asceticism and nobility of character, he was not ordained but was often regarded as a monk because of his simple lifestyle. In 409 he travelled to Sicily and was joined by Celestius, an aristocratic Roman converted through Pelagius' influence. Celestius became a fervent and unwise proponent of ideas Pelagius was exploring and for which he later became notorious. The two men sailed to North Africa hoping to meet Augustine, who was away. Pelagius went to Palestine, leaving Celestius propagating views that resulted in him being indicted for heresy and excommunicated.

The dispute followed Pelagius to the East with various bishops supporting or opposing him. Pelagius, Augustine and others wrote numerous books and tracts. Gradually issues were clarified and lines drawn, although Pelagius had

---

[49] Zablon Nthamburi, 'The Donatist Controversy as a Paradigm for Church and State', *Africa Theological Journal* 17.3 (1988), 204.

little interest in theological disputes and was concerned mainly with issues of discipleship. However, controversy was unavoidable and several synods considered the issues. Some condemned Pelagius, others acquitted him – all in his absence – until in 418 a council at Carthage excommunicated him. Dismayed, he protested his orthodoxy and longed to be reconciled to his main adversary, Augustine. But nothing came of this and shortly afterwards Pelagius disappears from history.

The issues at stake revolved around grace, sin and freewill. Pelagius protested that many Christians regarded sin as inevitable, rather than determining to live holy lives. He objected to Augustine's new and hitherto unorthodox views that original sin was passed genetically from parents to children, grace was irresistible and predestination meant freewill was illusory. Augustine became concerned at what he regarded as the undermining of God's grace and over-confidence in what redeemed human beings could accomplish. He insisted (with a novel interpretation of Romans 5:12) that in Adam all human beings were corrupted and that original sin was transmitted through sexual intercourse. God predestined some to be saved and to these his grace was irresistible. All human effort, before or after conversion, was worthless.

Careful examination of the arguments reveals strengths and weaknesses on both sides. Pelagius had an inadequate theology of atonement and gave little attention to the work of the Spirit. His teachings can be interpreted as undermining justification by faith and encouraging people to achieve salvation by moral living and self-reliance. Augustine was concerned lest biblical teaching was compromised and God's grace devalued. But Augustine so emphasised human depravity and divine predestination that the justice of God and moral responsibility of human beings were both in jeopardy.

Augustine's views were inconsistent with earlier Christian tradition. His explanation of original sin, insistence that human beings could not avoid sin and exposition of predestination were innovations. His antagonism towards Pelagius may indicate his opponent's teaching was touching a raw nerve with its call to discipleship and high moral standards. Pelagianism represented 'an onslaught on the languid, second-rate Christianity which blurred the line between a conventional Christian and the ordinary, pagan Roman'.[50] Pelagius envisaged the church as a disciplined and distinctive community; Augustine was laying theological and pastoral foundations for Christendom, where church and society were no longer separate.

Pelagius was excommunicated as a heretic; he should perhaps be remembered as a prophetic figure silenced by a church adjusting to an increasingly nominal form of Christianity. He advocated what was later called the 'priesthood of all believers' at a time when the clergy/laity divide was hardening and championed the right of women to learn to interpret Scripture. He advocated just redistribution of resources, concern for the poor, godly contentment and commitment to social justice, while Augustine concluded tithing was all he could expect from most Christians. Whereas many Christians used the Old Testament as the basis for ethics and marginalised the New, Pelagius encouraged his contemporaries to base their lives on Jesus' ethical teaching.

The similarities between Pelagius' teaching and the Donatists' views are significant. David Nussbaum writes: 'Pelagianism was, theologically, what Donatism was, ecclesiastically, in an important number of respects: both represented a desire for...purity, an attempt to hold on to the Christianity of earlier centuries, and to adopt a stand

---

[50] Markus, *End*, 43.

more independent from, and critical of, the institutional authorities.'[51]

Augustine's triumph ensured the smooth development of Christendom, but the issues Pelagius and Donatism raised would reappear on the margins of Christendom in the coming centuries.

Alternatives to the Christendom Shift

What did those who objected to the Christendom shift advocate instead? What other response might fourth-century Christians have made to the invitation to come in from the margins to the centre? How else than as a God-given opportunity could they have interpreted Constantine's adoption of Christianity?

Responses to these questions with the benefit of hindsight do not mean we should sit in judgment on fourth-century Christians suddenly confronted with an unimaginable opportunity or those who inherited a system seemingly destined to endure forever. But assessing their decisions and exploring alternatives is vital as we grapple with the challenges of post-Christendom.

Some have concluded that, despite the problems, there were no feasible alternatives to the Christendom shift. Lesslie Newbigin asks:

> How else, at that moment of history, could the Church have expressed its faithfulness to the gospel which is a message about the universal reign of God? It is hard to see what other possibility there was at that moment. The experiment of a Christian political order had to be made.[52]

---

[51] Nussbaum, 'Augustine', 36.
[52] Lesslie Newbigin, *The Other Side of 1984* (Geneva: WCC, 1983), 34. Cf. David Bosch, *Transforming Mission: Paradigm*

Newbigin implies that refusal to accept Constantine's invitation would have meant Christians abdicating responsibility for history and accepting a privatised gospel that did not engage with political and social realities. But is this so? Or is this judgement rooted in Christendom assumptions about the church's role and how God's reign operates in history?

There were other ways fourth-century Christians might have interpreted Constantine's adoption of Christianity and responded to his invitation.

- They might have recognised that all Roman emperors had used religion to impose order on the Empire: Constantine was acting in a typically Roman (not Christian) way.
- They might have questioned his continuing allegiance to the Unconquered Sun and the nature of his allegiance to Christ.
- They might have challenged him to become a catechumen earlier and to have prepared for baptism before he became terminally ill.
- They might have encouraged him to behave as a true Christian, rather than a normal emperor, accepting this might have resulted in his reign being brief.[53]
- They might have reflected on their survival and growth through 250 years of intermittent persecution and decided they did not need imperial protection or patronage.
- They might have differentiated between toleration and imperial endorsement, welcoming the former and courteously but firmly refusing the latter.

---

[52] (*Continued*) *Shifts in the Theology of Mission* (Maryknoll: Orbis, 1991), 222, 237.
[53] See Yoder, *Priestly*, 145–7.

- They might have explained to Constantine that massive basilicas and lavish bequests were inappropriate for followers of Jesus.
- They might have insisted the cross symbolised sacrificial suffering and was inappropriate as a military standard, explaining that Jesus' followers were a peaceful people, who would not fight to defend the Empire.
- They might have recalled their own experience of persecution and historic commitment to religious liberty[54] and refused to persecute or pressurise others.
- They might have listened to dissenting voices warning that the theological reinterpretations of Augustine and others were leading them away from their roots and core values.

The point of this discussion is not to blame those who accepted or presided over the Christendom shift, but to challenge the assertion that there was no alternative and to initiate discussion about appropriate post-Christendom strategies for Christians who want to see the church growing in numbers and influence but are wary of reinventing Christendom.

For the churches the Christendom shift was revolutionary; for the Empire it was minor, replacing one imperial religion with another. S.L. Greenslade comments:

> The toleration of Milan must not be misunderstood. It could not have implied the religious neutrality of a secular State, for at that time it was unthinkable that the State should not maintain official cults ... the real revolution would have come to

---

[54] Cyprian: *To Quirinius* 3.52; Irenaeus: *Against Heresies* 5.1.1.

pass if the emperor *had* renounced ultimate control over the
Church or any part of the life of his subjects. Constantine, of
course, had no such intention. As emperor he inherited the absolutist tradition.[55]

But what if fourth-century bishops had refused imperial
patronage and encouraged the emperor towards such a
revolution? Greenslade continues: 'had Constantine simply
tolerated Christianity, as in the Edict of Milan, some of the
troubles and temptations which were to beset the Church
would not have arisen.'[56]

Fourth-century Christians were evidently taken by surprise when Constantine decided to favour the church and
responded without thinking through the implications of
their grateful acceptance. There is no evidence any Christian before 312 had imagined this hypothetical situation or
considered its implications. The opportunity to turn the
tables on their persecutors appealed to some, who regarded
this as a legitimate expression of spiritual warfare, a form of
public exorcism. Undoubtedly, too, expansion in the third
century and changes in its internal life made the church
more amenable Constantine's proposals. Nigel Wright
concludes:

Modifications to its internal life, growing awareness of its
universality, pressures to move from its charismatic origins
towards hierarchy and institution, liturgical tendencies
towards a sacrificial dimension with its own priesthood and
ritual, growth through adhesion rather than conversion, and

---

[55] Greenslade, *Church*, 12–13. For the view that Constantine
promoted a religiously neutral state, see Drake, *Constantine*,
194.
[56] Greenslade, *Church*, 13.

the tension between remaining separate whilst reassuring
outsiders, were preparing the way for change.[57]

But the Christendom shift was massive, requiring huge
changes in theology, ethical principles, pastoral practice
and how Christians understood their role in society. They
might have responded differently. They might have spent
less time debating doctrinal formulations and more examining the ecclesiological implications of imperial support.
Even if they were caught off-guard at the beginning of the
fourth century, Christians might have protested against the
policy of Theodosius, when he decided not to pursue the
tolerant approach of Constantine and his successors but to
impose Christianity on all. This 'Theodosian shift' was
much more ominous than the 'Constantinian shift'. And
Christians in later centuries might have responded differently to developments catalogued in previous chapters,
many of which required them to abandon or radically revise
principles that inspired the early churches but now seemed
anachronistic.

Some have argued that, given the expansion of Christianity and the legacy of imperial religious patronage, if
Constantine had not made Christianity the imperial religion one of his successors would have. But this does not
take into account three factors: the inherent opposition to
imperial religion within early Christianity that
fourth-century Christians might have remembered; the
existence within the Empire of a movement like Donatism
that for over a century flourished without imperial endorsement (and with toleration might have thrived much longer);
and the contemporaneous experience of Christians in the

---

[57] Nigel Wright, *Disavowing Constantine: Mission, Church and
the Social Order in the Theologies of John Howard Yoder and
Jürgen Moltmann* (Carlisle: Paternoster Press, 2000), 15.

Persian Empire who flourished without being accorded official status.

Others have asked if Christianity could have spread across Europe and into the rest of the world without Christendom. We cannot know for sure. Obviously Christendom (rather than Christianity) could not have spread without the measures taken by the church and its imperial sponsor. But the continuing growth and influence of the kind of Christianity that flourished in earlier centuries could only have been accomplished *without* imperial patronage, coercive mission or the compromises the Christendom shift required.

However possible alternatives are assessed, most acknowledge there was a price to pay for the Christendom shift. If there were gains, there were also costs. Some were unintended and have often been ignored, such as the devastating impact on Christian communities in Persia. Constantine's adoption of Christianity abolished persecution for Christians within his Empire but unleashed persecution on Christians in Persia. In about 315 a letter from Constantine to Shapur II, intended to assist Persian Christians, resulted in an ominous change in official attitudes. Christians had been tolerated but were now regarded as representatives of a Roman Empire that had become Christian. Some 190,000 Christians may have died in the Great Persecution in Persia between 340 and 401 (far more than had died in the Roman Empire in previous centuries).[58]

Some costs were internal. The Christendom shift impacted the essence of the church and the gospel it proclaimed. Jürgen Moltmann concludes that, for its apparent victory over the Empire,

---

[58] Moffett, *Asia* Volume I, 137–45.

the church had to pay a high price: it had to take over the role of the political religion ... Now the church was there for everyone. Its mission reached everywhere. But as what? It reached everyone only as a component part of the political order – as the state religion of the political government.[59]

And Vinoth Ramachandra warns: 'A movement that proclaimed grace and practised justice, a faith that had at its centre a crucified man as the hope of human and cosmic transformation, could not have been converted to a religious civilization like any other without serious damage to its very essence.'[60]

This chapter has surveyed some areas in which this damage occurred; the next will examine further areas: biblical interpretation, mission and the nature of the church. It will also test the disturbing claim that the main price for the Christendom shift was the marginalisation of Jesus: for the church to come in from the margins to the centre, it had to push Jesus out from the centre to the margins of Christianity. It will follow the Christendom story to its zenith in the high Middle Ages. Seeds of a new way of being Christian were planted in the fourth and fifth centuries. What fruit would they bear in later centuries?

---

[59] Jürgen Moltmann, *The Power of the Powerless* (London: SCM 1983), 158.

[60] Vinoth Ramachandra, *Gods that Fail: Modern Idolatry and Christian Mission* (Carlisle: Paternoster Press, 1996), 214.

5

The Heart of Christendom

Pursuing the story through the centuries reveals how Christendom evolved once the triumph of Christianity seemed destined to be permanent. One chapter cannot begin to do justice to this complex period, passing in silence over fascinating individuals and movements. The focus is on how the Christendom ideology guided developments – especially in relation to biblical interpretation, mission and church. These topics take us to the heart of Christendom.

The Culture of Christendom

The high Middle Ages witnessed the flowering of Christendom, as Christianity inspired artists, sculptors, musicians, poets, architects and craftsmen. The biblical story and Christian theology provided the framework for literature, legislation and daily life. European history and culture is incomprehensible without this framework; even in post-Christendom those interested in their cultural roots must engage with Christendom. Plays, novels, art galleries and classical concerts become unintelligible without knowledge of this background. Christendom inspired the founding of schools, universities, hospitals and other institutions now incorporated into secular society. In this era

Christian philosophers and theologians produced classic treatises and liturgists developed resources that have nurtured generations of Christians.

But Christendom also became more oppressive, a totalitarian religious system, in which the church became phenomenally wealthy and seriously corrupt. Eleventh-century secular rulers exercised considerable control over the church and the choice of successive popes; but in the twelfth century the fluctuating struggle between church and state was resolved in favour of the church, which became dominant, exercising jurisdiction over the kingdoms and principalities of Western Europe. No secular ruler could rival papal wealth or authority, except in the late fourteenth and early fifteenth centuries when a papal schism threatened ecclesiastical domination. The church owned roughly one third of all arable land and developed an efficient administrative system to ensure its holdings were well ordered and funds flowed into its coffers.

An all-embracing diocesan and parochial structure provided pastoral care and social control. Church spires dominated the landscape; church bells pealed out across the countryside; church ceremonies punctuated the rhythm of the seasons and major life events. Churches 'hatched, matched and despatched' everyone in their parish. Bishops and abbots were not only spiritual leaders but involved in economic management and political activities. The feudal system and belief in the divine right of monarchs (both supported by the church) ensured the status quo was largely unchallenged; fear of inquisitors silenced all but the bravest dissenters. Despite periodic protests against injustice and grinding poverty, Christendom seemed impregnable.

Incorporation into the church of beliefs and practices with no biblical warrant and questionable coherence with Christianity, the ignorance and immorality of priests, the arrogance and abuses of power of popes and bishops, insensitivity to social injustice and persecution of dissidents can all be documented repeatedly. *Simony* (purchasing ecclesiastical appointments), *nicolaitism* (supposedly celibate clergy with concubines) and the sale of *indulgences* (granting release from punishment after death in exchange for service to the church) provoked protests but continued.

Less easy to discern are levels of belief and behaviour in society. Some detect regular and enthusiastic church attendance and suggest lay piety often exceeded clerical piety.[1] Others comment on how rarely most people received communion, note the proliferation of superstitious practices and doubt that Europe was ever effectively Christianised. Euan Cameron paints a graphic picture of debased and superstitious popular religion and warns us 'not to idealize the spiritual quality of late medieval piety'.[2] Jean Delumeau concludes Christianisation was superficial in many areas on the eve of the Reformation.[3] Richard Fletcher endorses a more generous interpretation but catalogues disturbing examples of the survival of pagan practices, ignorance of Christianity, monastic corruption and widespread disdain for the church.[4]

These issues concerned renewal movements that emerged during the medieval period; they also troubled dissenting movements on the fringes of Christendom. The church hierarchy reacted warily to such groups: some they tolerated or even honoured; others they persecuted fiercely. How an

---

[1] Eamon Duffy, *The Stripping of the Altars: Traditional Religion in England 1400–1580* (Yale: Yale University Press, 1992).
[2] Euan Cameron, *The European Reformation* (Oxford: Clarendon, 1991), 17.
[3] Jean Delumeau, *Catholicism between Luther and Voltaire: A New View of the Counter-Reformation* (London: Burns & Oates, 1977), 161.
[4] Fletcher, *Barbarian*, 508ff.

individual or group was treated depended as much on circumstances and personalities as substantive issues. The borderline between saint and heretic was thin: Francis of Assisi, founder of the Franciscans, was canonised, his near contemporary, Valdes, founder of the Waldensians, was persecuted. Franciscans, Cistercians and Dominicans were new religious orders. Lay renewal movements, like the Beguines and Beghards, introduced monastic lifestyles for women and men who continued to live in society. And popular preachers challenged ecclesiastical wealth and corruption and urged repentance, simple living and moral integrity.

The crucial issue in the authorities' response to these 'kingdom movements'[5] was neither *belief* nor *behaviour* (although they condemned both once they decided to oppose a movement) but *belonging*. What mattered was whether they threatened the Christendom system. Christendom could not tolerate dissent, whether expressed by unauthorised preaching, separate religious communities or criticism of the system. Conformity was essential. In 1229, facing the persistent challenge of Catharism,[6] a synod at Toulouse created the Inquisition, an investigative body responsible for discovering and prosecuting heretics. Torture was used to extract information about other heretics and encourage confession and reconciliation to the church. Unrepentant heretics were consigned to the state for execution. The logic of the Christendom shift led inexorably to totalitarian control and the Inquisition.

---

[5] Walls, *Cross-Cultural Process*, 15.

[6] A movement that flourished in southern France, held unorthodox beliefs and attracted considerable support. See Malcolm Lambert, *The Cathars* (Oxford: Blackwell, 1998).

Truth and Violence

During the Middle Ages many consequences of the Christendom shift reached maturity. Two hugely significant examples were oaths and war.

Oaths

Witnesses swore oaths to guarantee the truth of statements in court. Citizens swore to defend their state against attack. Clergy swore allegiance to lords on whose lands their churches stood. Kings swore to defend the faith (which included punishing those the church condemned). It was assumed those swearing oaths, which invoked divine judgement on lies or disloyalty, would not risk this but would speak and act faithfully. The political and legal framework of Christendom was built on oaths.

Oaths, invoking pagan gods to strike down those who were untrue, were common in pre-Christendom cultures. But early Christians refused to swear oaths. They resisted pressure to swear allegiance to Roman emperors regarded as divine but were also uneasy about oaths that called upon their own God as witness. Although there were biblical instances of oaths being sworn, many regarded Jesus' teaching ('Do not swear at all ... let your "Yes" be "Yes" and your "No", "No"'[7]) as definitive, prohibiting all oaths.[8]

But the Christendom shift necessitated reappraisal of this tradition. Primary allegiance was no longer to God's kingdom but to earthly rulers, so oaths of loyalty were vital. And in a nominally Christian Empire, truth telling in court could

[7] Matthew 5:34–37, echoed in James 5:12.
[8] See, for example, Justin: 1 *Apology* 14–16; 'Martyrdom of Apollonius' in Herbert Musurillo (ed.), *The Acts of the Christian Martyrs* (Oxford: Oxford University Press, 1971), 91–3.

not be guaranteed without threatening divine judgement, so Constantine required the use of oaths to encourage truthful testimony.[9] Augustine defended this contravention of the Sermon on the Mount as necessary rather than something he welcomed.[10] Once again, early church practice was abandoned and a familiar pagan practice was Christianised. Oaths were now sworn with the Christian God as guarantor of truth and loyalty, expected to act as the pagan gods, punishing oath-breakers.

To this aspect of the Christendom shift dissenting groups objected, but such protests were profoundly threatening. Abandoning oaths might undermine the whole sacral system. The oath's survival in post-Christendom, where it is still used in surprisingly diverse contexts, is remarkable testimony to how deeply this was embedded in the Christendom system.

War

We encountered the issue of war in the methods used to extend Christendom and the teaching of Augustine, who first formulated a coherent perspective on warfare that allowed Christians to take life. Christendom needed an approach to war that provided a convincing alternative to the pacifism of the early churches. With an Empire to run and defend, church leaders viewed pacifism as unrealistic (although monks and priests were excused participation in warfare as a concession to past principles – another example of two-tier Christianity). But principles were needed to decide when wars should be fought and when Christians should participate in them.

Until about 170, the churches were predominantly pacifist for several reasons: there was no universal conscription,

---

[9]   *Codex Theodosianus*, 11.39.3.
[10] Augustine, *On the Sermon on the Mount*, 1.17.51.

so Christians need not participate; Jesus' teaching seemed to preclude participation in war; love and killing appeared incompatible; military oaths of allegiance were pagan, conflicting with Christians' primary allegiance to Christ; few soldiers were converted, so the question of whether they could continue in the army arose infrequently; and the church's self-identity was a peaceful fellowship of those who followed the Prince of Peace. As a powerless and marginal community, whose views were not sought on political or military matters, they could not assess the justice of proposed campaigns. Their writings indicate they understood themselves as those who no longer used violence but were learning the disciplines of peacemaking.[11]

Between 170 and 313 changes can be detected. More soldiers were being converted and wondering whether to remain in the army; a distinction between serving in the army and killing was proposed; Christianity was becoming socially acceptable and converts from the higher echelons of society wanted to be both good Romans and good Christians; and there was susceptibility to the pagan critique that Christians benefited from imperial protection but refused to defend the Empire. But there was still robust resistance to diluting the traditional position and instances of martyrdom for throwing down weapons indicate antipathy to warfare remained strong.

In the fourth century, however, soldiers and army officers were among the crowds flooding into the churches. Christians gladly enlisted in an army now charged with defending and extending a Christian Empire. Theologians authorised killing in war and throwing down arms was no longer regarded as heroic. Christian citizens owed obedience now to both church and Empire, whose interests

---

[11] Jean-Michel Hornus, *It is not Lawful for Me to Fight: Early Christian Attitudes towards War, Violence and the State* (Scottdale: Herald Press, 1980).

generally coincided; if the emperor declared war, Christians were expected to support this decision. By 416, only Christians could join the army.

Clearly pacifism would not suit this Christian Empire, but memories of hesitations about fighting and killing were too strong to ignore: a more realistic approach was needed that nevertheless offered guidance on when war was justified. Augustine formulated this and several medieval thinkers, including Thomas Aquinas, refined it. The just war theory established criteria for wars to be considered justifiable. In its developed form this has six main components:

- War must be declared for a just cause.
- War must be fought with a good intention.
- There must be a reasonable expectation that more good than evil will result.
- War must be waged by proportionate means (avoiding civilian casualties).
- War must be the last resort after exhausting other options.
- War must be declared and fought by a legitimate authority.

This theory, accepted throughout Christendom and by most denominations (and incorporated into the Geneva Convention), has a curious history: 'It has never been promulgated as an official teaching by a council or a pope, never studied with great intensity, never formulated in a classical outline, and never applied with much consistency. It is dominant without being clear. It has taken over without being tested.'[12]

Advocates justified it from various Old Testament passages but drew heavily on the classical tradition of thinkers

---

[12] Yoder, *Priestly*, 75.

like Cicero. New Testament support is minimal and Jesus' teaching poses serious problems. How is warfare compatible with loving one's enemies? Augustine resolved this awkward issue by distinguishing attitudes and actions (killing can be loving) or personal and political spheres (loving personal enemies but killing state enemies). He seems uncomfortable, looking back wistfully to the church's traditional position but presenting this theory as a grim necessity.

The theory has significant merits. It does not glorify war. It regards war as unwelcome but sometimes, as the lesser of two evils, necessary to achieve justice. It establishes conditions necessary for Christians to participate. If applied properly, its stringent criteria make it almost impossible to justify any war. But it has rarely, if ever, been properly applied. Throughout Christendom, wars were designated 'just' with scant reference to the criteria; no official church statements ever condemned a war as unjust. Indeed, many wars involved one subdivision of Christendom fighting another, with bishops on both sides proclaiming 'just cause' and blessing opposing armies. The theory functioned as an ecclesiastical fig leaf.

There were two other approaches to war. The early church's pacifism continued to find advocates in marginal communities who opposed the Christendom shift. But 'holy war' or 'crusade', based on an interpretation of Old Testament wars that assumed the absolute evil of opponents and the holy duty of annihilation, offered a more frightening perspective. The 'just war' theory allowed Christians to approve wars waged by the state if certain criteria were met, but the church itself waged crusades as expressions of its mission. Popes summoned the faithful to crusades against Muslims and pagans, presenting these as penitential pilgrimages, wars of liberation and campaigns to extend Christendom or recapture ancient Christian territories.

Crusaders were promised material rewards and plenary indulgences. The blending of bloody violence and liturgical ceremonies reflected their sacred nature: many crusaders regarded participation as devotion to Christ.

Several twelfth-century crusades ultimately failed in their objectives but permanently soured Christian–Muslim relations[13] and left a damaging memory of the use of lethal force to advance the church's mission. During the thirteenth century, Pope Innocent IV insisted crusades needed 'just cause' (eroding the distinction between 'just' and 'holy' wars), but the assumption that Christ's interests were synonymous with Christendom meant justification was normally easy. The crusading mentality was not exhausted by failure to recapture the Holy Land but was turned inwards to galvanise fresh efforts to eradicate dissent within Christendom. 'Military orders' were founded to 'defend Christ's church with the material sword' against pagans, infidels, heretics and schismatics.[14]

Swearing oaths and justifying warfare are characteristic components of Christendom that further illustrate the nature of the Christendom shift. But the depth and scope of this shift is most apparent in relation to how three central features of Christianity were reinterpreted: the Bible, the church and mission. The fruits of this shift ripened in the Middle Ages, but the seeds were planted in the fourth century.

The Bible

Reading the Bible in Christendom differed in three interrelated ways from earlier approaches: it was used to support rather than challenge the dominant culture; the Old

---

[13] This probably resulted in the Muslim concept of *jihad* attaining a more militaristic meaning than it previously carried.
[14] Riley-Smith, *Crusades?*, 82.

Testament took precedence over the New; and Jesus' life and teaching was interpreted in ways that seemed feasible in a largely nominal Christian society.

Supporting the status quo

Having accepted political support, and understanding this as divinely providential, theologians naturally adjusted their interpretation of the Bible to reflect and undergird the new context. They used it to legitimise a social order that benefited both church and state, not to challenge the system. The traditional 'prophetic minority' critique was supplanted by a 'moral majority' stance.

Furthermore, the church's social centrality and involvement in the power structures significantly affected the presuppositions with which it approached Scripture. The view from the centre differs from the view from the margins. The story is the same, but it is read and applied differently. Texts like Romans 13, written to help marginal churches survive in a hostile environment, were now interpreted in ways that reflected Christendom requirements by inculcating loyal and uncritical citizenship.

Reflecting on the influence of Christendom on European biblical interpretation, liberation theologians identify a 'hermeneutic of order' as the controlling principle. According to José Miguez Bonino, Christendom interpreters asked 'what degree of justice ... is compatible with the existing order?' and found readings of Scripture that did not seriously challenge establishment values and interests. He proposes instead a 'hermeneutic of justice', insisting, 'the question of the Constantinian church has to be turned completely around. The true question is ... "what kind of order, which order, is compatible with the exercise of justice...?"'[15]

---

[15] José Miguez Bonino, *Towards a Christian Political Ethics* (Philadelphia: Fortress Press, 1983), 82ff.

Giving precedence to the Old Testament

New Testament teaching seemed designed for disciples in a non-Christian society, not a Christian Empire. Church leaders concluded it offered no guidelines for constructing and running the sacral society emerging in the fourth century. New Testament writers apparently did not envisage the triumph of Christianity, and provided no resources for developing a state religion. But there were helpful structures and perspectives in the Old Testament. Israel, at least during the period of the monarchy, seemed analogous to their Christianised Empire: both had borders to defend, armies to deploy, economic policies to determine, social institutions to maintain and a cultural heritage to transmit to future generations. Both recognised the ultimate government of God, mediated through chosen and anointed leaders. The roles of king and priest could be translated smoothly into the church/state partnership at the heart of Christendom.

The Old Testament provided insights on issues where the New Testament was silent or inapplicable in this changed situation. The extent to which Old Testament patterns and examples authenticated Christendom and adapted Christianity to this new context is remarkable. Theologians used the Old Testament to introduce tithing, defend oaths, develop the 'just war' and 'holy war' positions, justify compulsion in matters of faith, provide an analogy for infant baptism and greet emperors and kings as God's anointed rulers. Peter Brown records a classic instance, when bishops anointed Pippin king of the Franks because Israel's kings were anointed with oil: 'The ceremony took place in the most up-to-date manner possible for eighth-century Christians – that is, by a return to the Old Testament.'[16]

---

[16] Brown, *Rise*, 430.

Ecclesiastical and ethical issues were routinely decided by reference to the Old Testament. Theologians concluded it was impractical to require whole societies to accept New Testament ethics or to expect churches of largely nominal and passive members to operate as New Testament writers encouraged communities of committed disciples to behave, so they advocated Old Testament norms. And missionaries drew enthusiastically on Old Testament stories to encourage kings and warriors to trust the God of battles.

Consequently, the authority of the Old Testament (suitably interpreted) increased and much New Testament teaching was regarded as unreachable idealism – applicable still to clergy and the religious orders, but achievable by all only in the eschatological kingdom.

Marginalising Jesus

The increasing distance between Jesus' lifestyle and that of many church leaders necessitated marginalisation of Jesus' life and teaching. Seeing him as the example Christians should imitate, at least in their civic responsibilities, was unacceptable. Furthermore, some of his teachings were very difficult to apply in this new situation: how did Christian emperors love their enemies? How could Christian politicians 'take no thought for tomorrow'? The Sermon on the Mount especially presented problems: perhaps this was relevant only for inter-personal relationships rather than public life, or applied to attitudes rather than actions? Such ideas (contrary to consistent pre-Christendom interpretation) became 'counsels of perfection' rather than guidelines for everyday discipleship.

But the problem went deeper. For Christendom, Jesus of Nazareth, who taught radical discipleship rather than patriotic citizenship and was executed by the state, was hard to assimilate. It was fundamentally embarrassing that Jesus was crucified by order of the Roman Empire, acting through Pilate, its representative. The cross Constantine put on his soldiers' shields was not an ideal symbol for an imperial religion. Memories of Jesus challenging the authorities, championing the poor and criticising injustice were troublesome now bishops were establishment figures. Somehow, they had to loosen the connection between the radical Jesus and fourth-century Christianity.

Fourth-century theologians recast Jesus as a celestial figure, emphasised his divinity and allowed these dangerous memories to fade. Constantine honoured the God of the Christians, rather than Jesus. Eusebius accepted this and laid the foundations for the Christendom interpretation of an imperial and remote Jesus. Rosemary Radford Ruether writes:

> Christ becomes the Pantocrator, the cosmic governor of a new Christianized Empire. The Christian emperor, with the Christian bishop at his right hand, becomes the new Vicar of Christ on earth, governing the Christian state of the new redeemed order of history … The victory of Messiah as vindicator of the oppressed might have been seen as the radical levelling of all hierarchy and subjugation … Instead imperial christology wins in the fourth century as a sacralized vision of patriarchal, hierarchical and euro-centred imperial control.[17]

This radical change in how Jesus was understood impacted many aspects of fourth-century Christianity. It transformed artistic representations, which depicted Jesus in imperial rather than human images: stern portraits of an imperial judge, surrounded by a halo, superseded earlier rustic

---

[17] Rosemary Radford Ruether, 'Augustine and Christian Political Thought', *Interpretation* 29 (1975), 256. Cf Bosch, *Transforming Mission*, 202.

pictures of Jesus as good shepherd.[18] In the hymns, sermons, teaching of catechumens, creeds and theological treatises, Jesus' life and teaching received less and less attention. Compare, for instance, the catechetical instructions of late fourth-century Ambrose, based on Old Testament morality,[19] with the writings of second-century Justin[20] and the *Didache*,[21] which taught catechumens to apply Jesus' teachings to their lives. Fourth-century writers used the life of Christ devotionally rather than ethically.

This marginalising of Jesus is most striking in the creeds. These have had tremendous influence on generations of Christians. But they were written in the formative years of Christendom, when Jesus' life and teaching were being marginalised. They affirm his divinity and humanity but marginalise his life. The Nicene Creed, for instance, says Jesus 'was incarnate by the Holy Ghost of the Virgin Mary; and was made man. And was crucified also for us under Pontius Pilate'. It ignores his human life, moving straight from his birth to his death. Where are his miracles, relationships, teachings or subversive lifestyle? As in many fourth-century documents, where is Jesus? The other creeds contain this same startling omission.

Explanations can be offered – creeds cannot include everything and the human life of Jesus was not something fourth-century theologians were debating, so this was not included.[22] But this is precisely the point: Jesus' life and teaching were no longer the focus of attention. Christendom was comfortable with a divine Jesus – and with belief

---

[18] Drake, *Constantine*, 318–19.
[19] Ambrose, *De Mysteriis*, 1.1.
[20] Justin, *Apology*, 1:14–16.
[21] *Didache*, Ch. 1–6.
[22] Another explanation is that fear of Arianism precluded emphasis on Jesus' humanity.

that Jesus was also human – but struggled with the challenging reality of that human life. Although the creeds declare his humanity, this seems little more than an abstract philosophical principle. The Jesus in whom Christians expressed their faith as they repeated the creeds was an exalted figure, remote and powerful, a heavenly counterpart of the Christian emperor, no longer disturbing the status quo. Jesus was worshipped, but not followed. This has left a lasting legacy in European Christianity: the church was now at the centre, but Jesus was consigned to the margins.

The Church

Moving to the centre had consequences for how churches operated. Some things were already changing in the second half of the third century, as the church was growing and becoming respectable, but the Christendom shift was decisive in cementing these changes and for other innovations. The legacy of these changes is still evident, but the end of Christendom encourages us to assess their usefulness to churches no longer at the centre of society.

One obvious change in the fourth-century church was the *size* of congregations and buildings. The percentage of the population involved in the churches was expanding rapidly, so the church's self-identity was becoming centrist rather than marginal, and congregations grew large. Urban congregations gathered in massive basilicas. Gone were small communities meeting in homes, and even the public services in designated buildings that began in the third century were dwarfed by this development. Church leaders celebrated the advance of the gospel and began to believe Christ's millennial rule was imminent.

But size matters. As Christians have discovered through the centuries, large churches are different from small churches and develop structures and strategies to cope with their increased size. They are also prone to difficulties smaller churches avoid (though these face other challenges). What some greet as evidence of success and opportunity for enlarged ministry can jeopardise a church's internal health and impede its external mission. There are arguments for and against the development of large churches; but the size of fourth-century congregations required significant and lasting changes in church life. Jürgen Moltmann summarises these: 'Community with the church replaced community in the church. In this way what we nowadays call "the church from above" came into being, the church which takes care of the people, but in which the people themselves have no say.'[23]

The emergence of a *clerical caste* is detectable long before the fourth century, but this received an enormous boost following Constantine's adoption of Christianity. Their enhanced status, power and wealth resulted in clergy becoming, in effect, religious civil servants and forming a professional caste similar to that within other imperial organisations. In pre-Christendom, although church leaders had specialised roles and exercised considerable authority, they were chosen from within a congregation and generally stayed in it.[24] The main dividing line was still between church and world. In Christendom, this line disappeared, for there was no world outside the church; a sharp division between clergy and laity replaced it. The transfer of bishops from church to church and state interference in ecclesiastical appointments reinforced the separation of clergy from the churches. Incrementally, over the years, clergy gained privileges and alone performed functions once the task of all Christians. Soon they would adopt cleri-

---

[23] Moltmann, *Power*, 158.
[24] Ferguson, 'Congregationalism', 130–5.

cal dress, further separating them from others. Before long it could be said: 'The church consists in the clergy.'[25]

The clerical caste operated through a *territorial and hierarchical system* that fitted the Empire's structures and value-system, though this model – with its titles, perks and privileges – seemed distant from Jesus' teaching about leadership and authority. The Christendom church was settled, institutional and dependent on top-down authority. The gradual emergence of the Bishop of Rome as pope, whatever the theological arguments, was almost inevitable as the church mirrored the state. Like the state, the church needed a titular head; Rome was the obvious location. Diocesan and parish systems also mirrored imperial territorial arrangements and ensured that, eventually, churches would be within reach of every member of society. These were sensible arrangements, enabling churches to work efficiently and effectively within the Empire (although calling the pope *Pontifex Maximus* in the fifteenth century begs questions). As the Empire disintegrated, this church structure provided a framework on which to rebuild medieval Europe. But did this contradict fundamental gospel values?

In the enormous Christendom congregations clergy *performed services*, taking charge of more and more of the liturgy until the laity became almost entirely passive.[26] As liturgies became more complex, only trained professionals could perform them, in later centuries in Latin, a language most of the congregation did not understand. In the 360s the Council of Laodicea banned congregational singing and restricted singing to clergy and trained choirs. The architecture of church buildings suggested churchgoers were attending performances, not participating in communal

---

[25] Drake, *Constantine*, 357.
[26] Paul Bradshaw, 'The Effects of the Coming of Christendom on Early Christian Worship', in Kreider (ed.), *Origins*, 269–86.

events: congregations became audiences for awe-inspiring rituals, rhetorical sermons and front-led dramatic activities. Receiving bread and wine was one remaining form of participation, but even this was essentially passive, and before long most people refrained because they felt unworthy. Eventually, the laity received only bread; wine was restricted to clergy. The 'agape meals', once the communal context for breaking bread, fell into disrepute and the Council of Carthage in 397 forbade these.

One aspect of this move towards clerical performance was the increasing *dominance of monologue preaching.* New Testament and patristic texts suggest preaching was only one way early Christians learned together, alongside discussion and multi-voiced participation.[27] Why did this become dominant? It resulted from churches adopting from pagan culture assumptions about communication and a rhetorical model more concerned about demonstrating a preacher's knowledge and skill than the impact on listeners. Furthermore, thousands of nominal Christians were joining the churches. Monologue preaching by those with rhetorical skills (and loud voices) seemed the only realistic option in large basilicas and congregations with little understanding of even the basics of the faith. There were two additional reasons: now the church was part of the establishment, sermons by accredited preachers precluded unauthorised contributions that might rock the boat; and in this more institutional and hierarchical setting, clergy preached and laity listened.

Another dimension of church life profoundly affected by the Christendom shift was the practice of interactive pastoral care often called *church discipline.* That this term has for many a negative connotation indicates the distorting

---

[27] David Norrington, *To Preach or not to Preach: The Church's Urgent Question* (Carlisle: Paternoster Press, 1996).

influence of Christendom on a practice advocated in all
strands of the New Testament and comprising the only
explicit teaching on church life in the Gospels. 'Church'
appears in the Gospels only in Matthew 16 and 18: the former text conveys nothing about internal church dynamics,
but the latter envisages communities where conflict is handled sensitively and loving admonition is a mutual
responsibility of all. Just as churches could be communities
of interactive learning, so they should be characterised by
interactive pastoral care.

The Christendom shift transformed this into a punitive
and frightening practice. The text says nothing about
church leaders exercising church discipline, but in a cleri-
cally dominated church this became as inevitable as
monologue sermons. Church discipline became an exercise
of ecclesiastical control rather than an expression of communal discipleship. A process designed to restore
relationships mutated into a strategy for detecting and
quashing dissent. Furthermore, while clergy often winked
at immorality within the churches and in their own ranks,
they hounded godly dissenters as heretics and schismatics.
The collapse of the church/world boundary completes the
picture. In pre-Christendom, expelling disruptive members
(the final resort for any unwilling to receive communal pastoral admonition) meant consigning them to the world
beyond the church. But the world had disappeared in Christendom, so expulsion now meant 'extermination' (literally
'outside the boundaries') – either exile beyond Christendom
or execution. Church discipline had become lethal!

Mission

Another fundamental impact of the Christendom shift was
the church's preoccupation with maintaining its dominance

in a society now coterminous with the church itself. Christianising Western Europe took many centuries and involved both extension of the boundaries and deeper penetration of societies that had accepted Christianity. The persistence of paganism, the presence of the Jews and the rise of Islam prevented Christendom from becoming completely self-absorbed. But, over the centuries, the church became an *institution* rather than a *movement* and its energies were primarily directed towards *maintenance* rather than *mission*.

Constantine's invitation to the church to become the religious department of the Empire revolutionised its missiology. This is particularly evident in the *evangelistic* dimension of mission. From being a powerless and sometimes persecuted minority that nevertheless could not refrain from talking about Jesus and his impact on their lives, the church had become a powerful institution able to impose its beliefs and practices on society. Evangelism was no longer a winsome invitation to a deviant and dangerous way of living and into a puzzling and yet strangely attractive community. Mission now involved ensuring doctrinal conformity, enforcing church attendance, enshrining moral standards in the criminal law and eradicating choice in the area of religion. Methods used included education, persuasion, inducement and coercion.

Evangelism in its New Testament sense soon became irrelevant, except on the borders of Christendom. If the Empire was Christian, evangelism was obsolete. The church's role was providing pastoral care and teaching, ensuring church members became good citizens. This had consequences for the *nature and focus of church leadership*. The diverse ministry described in the New Testament[28] and evident in pre-Christendom – whether or not this should be

---

[28] Ephesians 4. Cf. Romans 12, 1 Corinthians 12.

understood in terms of designated roles – was deemed unnecessary in Christendom. Pastors and teachers remained vital, but evangelists were redundant, prophets were unwelcome in churches committed to supporting, not challenging, the status quo, and (though there were some itinerant preachers) apostles threatened the settled territorial system. Orientation towards maintenance rather than mission and a reduction in the diversity of ministry are Christendom legacies requiring scrutiny as we adjust to post-Christendom.

The churches did not abandon mission. Work was still needed beyond Christendom's boundaries and, for many centuries, within these boundaries among a population often barely Christianised. There were also irritating recurrences of heresy and schism that threatened to undermine the settled culture of Christendom – especially since some groups did not believe they lived in a Christian society and determined to evangelise their contemporaries, ignoring parish boundaries and ecclesiastical authorities. But mission was normally *delegated to specialist agencies* and disconnected from normal congregational life. Monastic mission orders led the way in educating nominal church members, combating dissent and taking the gospel into new regions. This divorce of church and mission, understandable in the Christendom context, has left churches ill equipped for post-Christendom.

A disturbing effect of the Christendom shift on mission was the *use of violence and coercion*. This was apparent in the story of Christendom's expansion, in Augustine's assertion that 'error has no rights' and his insistence on the necessity of compelling submission to the church. The Middle Ages witnessed the full horror of this mission strategy: crusades beyond Christendom, the treatment of Jews within Christendom and the use of torture by inquisitors to root out dissent. The persecution of Jews was a shameful aspect of Christendom. Jews fitted more easily into a pagan Empire than into Christendom! In a unitary culture they were different, non-conformist and threatening. Furthermore, as some theologians insisted, they were 'Christ-killers', responsible for the death of Jesus (whose own Jewishness was forgotten). The official church position (based on the doctrine of 'two swords') – that the state exercised coercive measures rather than the church, which handed offenders over to it – does not persuade those appalled by this story that the church was acting in accordance with gospel values.

The church's mission also involved offering *counsel to the state* on political, social, economic and ethical issues. Having been invited to participate in the reconstruction of the Empire, the church continued to partner the state in the diverse political systems that waxed and waned during the following centuries. This was difficult to manage with integrity: the church received so much from the state and benefited so greatly from partnership that legitimation and uncritical support was a persistent temptation. To their credit, bishops dared to challenge kings and emperors, urging policy changes in the direction of justice and humanity. Less creditable were attempts on both sides to buy the support of church or state. Given the opportunity to influence political decisions, it is hard to argue the church should have spurned this, but its identification with the wealthy and powerful, and other effects of the Christendom shift, meant it often offered counsel that had little connection with the gospel.

Christendom is sometimes presented as an alliance between church and state, but this discounts the integration of church and culture. Partnership with the state enabled the church to exercise influence throughout society and engage in *mission towards the whole culture*. The Middle Ages witnessed the most sustained attempt in history to shape a society through Christian theology. Just as we may endorse the church seizing the opportunity to influence the state, the desire to apply the Christian story and its values to all aspects of life was laudable. Those who defend Christendom rightly insist the transformation of culture is a noble aim; restricting mission to saving souls or planting churches is untenable given what we believe about God's redemptive purposes; but Christendom, which meant top-down rather than bottom-up transformation, distorted the vision of a Christian society that inspired this mission to culture. It was simply not Christian enough in its methods or expectations. It was compromised by confusion between the institutional church and God's kingdom, coercive methods, a moralising tone, unrealistic expectations of what was achievable in the present age and inability to distinguish Christendom ideology from the original Christian story.

Marginal Voices

These changes in biblical interpretation, church and mission were complex and far-reaching, but the system had internal consistency. The Christendom shift represented a recasting of the Christian story and different perspectives on the fundamental beliefs and practices of the churches. This inter-connectedness made it difficult to challenge a system widely regarded as permanent and simply 'the way things are'. Medieval Christendom was monolithic, totalitarian and seemingly impervious to critique.

But it had its critics – dissenting movements offering alternative perspectives and daring to suggest things could be different. As usual in totalitarian societies, reaction to these movements was vitriolic and vicious. Character assassination, suppression of their writings and sustained persecution means our knowledge of them is limited and some of what we think we know may be inaccurate. But enough has survived to show that these movements, springing up in different places at different times, had much in common. With little evidence of direct interaction, three factors may explain these similarities: rediscovery of the Bible (especially the Gospels); hostility towards the Christendom system; and subterranean piety sustaining radical ideas the authorities thought had been snuffed out.

A powerful image for this phenomenon is of a forest fire, which seems to have died down but is smouldering in the undergrowth, easily rekindled by another spark on a tinder-box of popular discontent and spiritual yearning. The spark might be different for each movement, but soon the broader dissident agenda is apparent again. These movements constitute an alternative Christian tradition on the edge of Christendom.[29] They offer those facing the challenges of post-Christendom different perspectives from the Christendom legacy. Opponents of the Christendom shift rejected oaths and participation in warfare and developed other approaches to the Bible, church and mission. As poor and uneducated groups, they had few interpretive tools and little sophistication, but their marginality enabled them to see things differently and in ways that were more congruent with the New Testament. Their knowledge of the early churches was limited but they sometimes unwittingly returned to pre-Christendom patterns of community and mission.

These were flawed and imperfect movements, but their story deserves to be told and their voices from the margins heard as we struggle to develop ways of being church on the margins today. Two movements must suffice here – one English and one French – that survived, battered and bloodied, into the Reformation period and were absorbed into

---

[29] See further Yoder, *Priestly*, 133.

the wider reform movement: the Lollards and the Waldensians.

Reading the Bible differently

Those who challenged the Christendom system usually began by interpreting the Bible in different and (to their opponents) socially dangerous ways. Dissident movements typically developed through several stages:

- Someone with access to the Bible and able to read was stirred by what they read to question the church's traditional interpretation of particular issues.
- Others listened and a group formed that explored alternative approaches to these issues and moved beyond discussion to action (including disseminating vernacular versions of the Bible).
- Reflecting on their activities – and the opposition these provoked – they asked whether the Christendom system itself was the problem, rather than particular issues.
- Continuing to read the Bible (or hear it, as many were illiterate), they noticed other issues where the church's beliefs and practices did not square with what they were reading.
- Once they decided the Christendom system was suspect, they became deeply suspicious that the Bible was being misinterpreted to legitimise it. They now looked at it through a different lens from the Christendom churches.
- This resulted in them thinking deeply about how to interpret the Bible and led to conclusions that further threatened the Christendom system.

Some movements began simply as attempts to take Jesus' teachings as directives for living and to practise what he taught. The Jesus they discovered as they read the Gospels challenged them personally, especially in relation to issues of lifestyle, and also suggested incongruities in the beliefs and practices of contemporary churches: the Sermon on the Mount, especially, inculcated values and attitudes not evident in the churches. It also appeared to forbid practices the churches endorsed: in particular, killing and swearing oaths. Many traditional beliefs and ceremonies had no basis in Jesus' teaching or the practice of his earliest followers.

The beginning of the Waldensian movement[30] in the conversion experience of Valdes is a classic example. In the several accounts of his conversion, reading the Gospels was a significant component. Valdes' reaction – by no means unique in the Middle Ages – was to take literally Jesus' words about giving to the poor and preaching the gospel. His starting point was not theology or criticism of the church, but rediscovery of Jesus' teaching, which challenged his priorities and transformed his life. Criticism of the church and the formation of a new movement followed, reluctantly on Valdes' part, as Waldensians contrasted the radical implications of Jesus' teachings with the status, priorities and activities of the churches.

If Waldensians began with a rediscovery of Jesus and renewed emphasis on following his teaching, other dissenting groups moved gradually towards this position as a result of reading the Bible for themselves and not allowing ecclesiastical traditions to dull its impact. This was true of the English Lollard movement[31] that popularised and developed the ideas of John Wyclif. Anne Hudson notes that among the Lollards 'the stress upon the Gospels amongst

---

[30] See Appendix 2.
[31] See Appendix 3.

the greater length of the Bible as a whole correctly reflects Wyclif's view that the core of the divine message was to be found within the four evangelists.'[32]

Other principles, apart from insistence on the centrality of Jesus, characterised the approach of dissident movements to the Bible:

- Their conviction that untrained lay Christians could understand Scripture challenged the clergy's interpretive monopoly.
- Their belief that the Bible was best understood in community challenged the individualism of scholarship.
- Their determination to apply it to their daily lives and communal practices challenged the prevailing emphasis on philosophical or mystical reflection rather than discipleship.
- Their suspicion that the Old Testament had been seriously misused to buttress a system built on wrong foundations challenged Christendom itself.

Being church differently

Rediscovering Jesus in the Gospels led to rediscovering the church in the rest of the New Testament. What dissidents found there they compared with the Christendom church; this further convinced them something was wrong. The churches were formal, full of superstitions, dominated by clergy, corrupt and subject to control by secular and ecclesiastical authorities. The New Testament, they believed, indicated the early churches were different. Some urged reformation and tried to introduce changes into existing

---

[32] Anne Hudson, *The Premature Reformation: Wycliffite Texts and Lollard History* (Oxford: Clarendon Press, 1988), 229.

churches; others developed alternative communities and structures. In time, separate networks of churches emerged, adopting what historians call the *believers' church* model.[33] This has several defining characteristics:

- The church is entered by choice rather than birth.
- Continued membership is voluntary rather than compulsory.
- Accountability is to other members in mutual submission rather than to ecclesiastical authorities.
- Church government is exercised from within rather than by external rulers.
- Congregations choose their own leaders.
- There is a high level of commitment, at least in the early years, and a low incidence of nominal believers.
- There is a sharp distinction between 'church' and 'world'.
- Although most do not claim all members are true disciples, or that no members of state churches are believers, they assume close correlation between true believers and members of the visible church.

Once they adopted this model, they subjected traditional components of church life to scrutiny. They questioned and often abandoned beliefs and practices for which they could not find New Testament warrant. Dissidents objected to (among other things) penance, priestly confession and absolution, the intermediary role of saints, growing reverence for Mary, purgatory, transubstantiation, pilgrimages, ascribing power to relics, veneration of crucifixes and

---

[33] Donald Durnbaugh, *The Believers' Church: The History and Character of Radical Protestantism* (Scottdale: Herald Press, 1985).

images, saints' days and indulgences. Different movements raised different issues but there was widespread criticism of wealth and complexity, and yearning for simpler forms of church life.

Infant baptism troubled most dissenting groups, for believers' baptism is a logical concomitant of the believers' church model, but this was costly to introduce. Since rebaptism of those baptised as infants was not just an affront to the Christendom church but had for centuries (since the Donatist controversy) been a capital crime, this was not a step to take lightly. Lollards queried whether infant baptism was necessary but did not baptise believers who joined them. Waldensians were unconvinced infant baptism was biblical and, though many still baptised their children, some groups did baptise those who joined the movement.

How did these movements assess other components of church life that had been distorted by the Christendom shift: clericalism, territorial and hierarchical structures, services as performances, the dominance of monologue preaching[34] and punitive church discipline? As marginal and persecuted groups, they were much smaller than the Christendom churches, but size was not the only factor. Continued engagement with the New Testament and the vision of church life they derived from this, together with deepening suspicion that mainstream churches were fundamentally flawed, encouraged them to abandon many traditional practices and explore alternatives.

Lollards were strongly anti-clerical, both because of corruption in the state churches and because of their commitment to the priesthood of all believers. They welcomed the participation of women, emphasised holiness

---

[34] Although in many church services in the medieval period there were no sermons.

rather than ordination and advocated simplicity rather than complexity and ritual. Although there were leaders, Lollards avoided hierarchical structures; their meetings were multi-voiced, involving all who attended in studying the Bible and discussing its application. Literature circulating around their 'reading circles' provided resources for study and dialogue rather than fixed dogmas.[35] They took discipleship seriously and practised mutual admonition.

Waldensians shared the Lollards' conviction that holiness rather than ordination was required for spiritual leadership: a common Waldensian saying was: 'As much as one has of holiness, just so much has one of power.'[36] They expressed their commitment to mutual accountability by rejecting the need for priests and hearing each other's confessions. They developed an alternative leadership structure, in which hierarchical patterns and the clergy/laity divide were reconfigured and relativised. As with the Lollards, women participated freely, and Waldensian groups were notorious among inquisitors for their biblical knowledge and passion for discussing the Bible together. The capacity of illiterate believers to learn huge chunks of Scripture amazed their opponents, but this was vital for participatory church life.

Although there is remarkable agreement on many issues within the dissenting tradition, it was not uniform. But believing the church had 'fallen' at the time of Constantine, criticisms of Christendom and persistent wrestling with the New Testament were common roots of a way of being church the authorities found very disturbing. These movements accepted the state's legitimate role in maintaining

---

[35] Hudson, *Premature*, 192.
[36] Euan Cameron, *The Reformation of the Heretics: The Waldenses of the Alps, 1480–1580* (Oxford: Clarendon Press 1984), 79.

order within society and did not participate in peasant revolts. But the model of church they advocated and practised represented subversion of the Christendom sacral state.

Disturbing also to both secular and ecclesiastical authorities were their deviant ethical perspectives. Although these were derived from the New Testament and resonated with the pre-Christendom churches, they dissented from views long endorsed within Christendom. This embarrassed inquisitors, who acknowledged the upright lives and exemplary behaviour of those they designated heretics, but ascribed this to demonic deception. Inquisitors were advised to arrest on suspicion of heresy any who seemed unusually godly; there were several instances when upright members of state churches were detained. Accusations of immorality were levelled against dissidents, but even their accusers seem unconvinced by these charges. What was troubling, however – and convincing evidence of unorthodoxy – was rejection of key elements in the sacral system: oath, tithe and just war.

Waldensians were committed to truth telling and most rejected oaths as contrary to Jesus' teaching. One of their mottos was 'curse not, lie not, swear allegiance to no man'. Lollards were uncertain: some opposed oaths as contrary to Jesus' teaching and a diabolical contravention of the ninth commandment; others taught oaths should be avoided if possible but were legitimate to save lives; still others insisted oaths sworn under duress (for example in heresy trials) were null and void.

On economic issues Lollards were the more radical. They challenged tithing as lacking New Testament foundations and suggested tithes should only be paid if church leaders deserved these. Some advocated abolition of private property and development of a communal system. Waldensians, too, challenged tithing and rejected greed and excess in

favour of living simply. Both movements criticised the
wealth and corruption of the churches and advocated
greater social justice.

Neither movement was entirely pacifist but both tended
in this direction. Some Lollards endorsed Wyclif's view that
war might be justified but other means were preferable; others opposed participation in war, making weapons, capital
punishment and self-defence when attacked; a few
defended 'righteous smiting' (an application of 'holy war'
ideology) and supported an attempt to overthrow the government. The collapse of this effort encouraged movement
away from violence towards pacifism. Waldensians occasionally resorted to violence under great duress but most
opposed violence of all kinds, rejecting crusades and warfare in general, the killing of Jews, execution of thieves
caught stealing food for their families in times of famine and
coercion in matters of faith. A common dissident claim was
that violent persecution of nonconformists proved the
Christendom church was not the true church, for such
behaviour was utterly contrary to the spirit of Jesus and the
New Testament.

Engaging in mission differently

If dissident perspectives on biblical interpretation, ethics
and church were threatening, different understandings of
mission were even more disturbing. Waldensians and
Lollards challenged the basic Christendom assumption that
they lived in a Christian society and reconnected church and
mission.

Wyclif taught, 'evangelization exceeds prayer and
administration of the sacraments to an infinite degree',[37]

---

[37] Margaret Aston, *Lollards and Reformers: Images and Literacy
in Late Medieval Religion* (London: The Hambledon Press,
1984), 15.

and advocated the formation of a new order of preachers. Lollard preachers were peripatetic, moving from place to place to spread their message and form new groups: this contrasted sharply with the maintenance-orientation of parish priests. Hudson calls them 'apostles' and 'prophets'.[38] Although she does not suggest Lollards used such terms themselves, Hudson is typical of historians describing dissident movements, choosing these terms to describe their leaders. Some Lollard preachers interrupted church services or persuaded local priests to surrender their pulpits. By the mid-fifteenth century, persecution had taken its toll and charismatic preachers had largely given way to less colourful figures travelling between communities, carrying books and greetings.

Mission, however, was not restricted to preachers but was the responsibility of all members. The spread of the movement relied on every-member evangelism. Converts were made through house-to-house visitation, evangelism in ale-houses, preaching in fairs and markets, conversations over meals in homes, distributing tracts and invitations to reading circles. Margaret Aston calls Lollardy 'the missionary church *par excellence*'.[39]

A similar commitment to mission is apparent among Waldensians. They have been described as proponents of 'the right and obligation of all Christians ... to preach the faith, guided by the Holy Spirit and without concern for ecclesiastical permissions and prohibitions, in response to Christ's unequivocal command'.[40] A remarkable feature of

[38] Hudson, *Premature*, 449.
[39] Aston, *Lollards*, 15.
[40] M. and R. Rouse:, 'The Schools and the Waldensians: a new work by Durand of Huesca', in Scott Waugh and Peter Diehl (eds.), *Christendom and its Discontents: Exclusion, Persecution, and Rebellion, 1000-1500* (Cambridge: Cambridge University Press, 1996), 87.

the movement was its determination to continue pressing ahead despite sustained pressure and opposition. Only in the darkest periods were their energies consumed with survival. At other times missionaries traversed Europe, risking their lives to spread their convictions and plant new congregations.

Much evangelism must have been cautious and through quiet conversations; public witness would have incurred severe penalties. There are accounts of evangelists as door-to-door salesmen, offering various goods and referring to 'more valuable treasures', which could be revealed if local clergy were not informed about the visit. Where there were positive responses, they shared the gospel and gave invitations to join study groups. The itinerant preachers, who exercised evangelistic and pastoral roles, were sometimes called 'apostles', although more often 'uncles' (*barbes*) – a deliberate and less hierarchical alternative to Catholic 'fathers.'

These movements, then, from their reading of the New Testament and convinced their society needed evangelising, restored the mission-orientation of the pre-Christendom churches. 'Poor preachers' were significant in both movements, but the involvement of all members in mission was distinctive, challenging the clericalism of Christendom and its separation of mission and church.

Dissident groups are frequently criticised for being sectarian and uninterested in the reformation and flourishing of society as a whole. The term 'sectarian' has a long and obnoxious history and, though sociologists employ it without the odium normally associated with its use by theologians, it often obscures rather than clarifies. The New Testament and pre-Christendom churches were sects, but this term is normally and dismissively applied to groups attempting to return to these models of church in the Christendom era. The Christendom shift has affected how we use language.

Whatever terminology is used, this criticism is rooted in Christendom assumptions. It is difficult for persecuted and marginalised groups to develop a positive agenda for a society from which they are excluded and which they cannot influence by normal means. Many critics are wedded to top-down strategies and Christendom-style social and political engagement. They fail to appreciate dissident groups were modelling alternative social, economic and political options. Certainly their persecutors found their activities extremely threatening, fearing their nonconformist behaviour and message could undermine the social and political system.

This chapter has taken us into the heart of Christendom, traced the origins of this culture back to the fourth-century Christendom shift and followed its development into the Middle Ages. It has made forays onto the margins and encountered dissidents raising serious questions about the entire Christendom edifice. We carry with us into the next chapter two different visions and expressions of Christianity.

6

The Disintegration of Christendom

In 1517, less than 150 years after Lithuania's acceptance of Christianity completed the formation of Christendom, an Augustinian monk, Martin Luther, nailed ninety-five theses to a church door in Wittenberg, urging wholesale reform. He and several others were troubled by doctrinal errors, abuses of power and moral corruption they perceived in the Catholic Church to which they belonged. The Protestant Reformers (as they were called) did not oppose Christendom or plan to establish rival churches, but their activities resulted in Christendom fragmenting into competing, then warring, mini-Christendoms. Lutheran Christendom appeared in Germany, Zwinglian Christendom in Zurich, Calvinist Christendom in Geneva and Anglican Christendom in England.

Eight years later, in January 1525, some friends in Zurich took the more radical, and illegal, step of baptising one another; this Anabaptist movement spread uncontrollably across central Europe, fiercely persecuted by Catholics and Reformers alike. Although Catholics and Reformers differed on many issues, they agreed Anabaptists[1] were subversive and dangerous. Like earlier dissident movements, Anabaptists rejected the Christendom system and

---

[1] See Appendix 4.

developed alternative perspectives on biblical interpretation, church and mission.

These developments represented sixteenth-century expressions of the two visions of Christianity evident in the medieval period. For all their laudable attempts to improve Christendom, the Reformers remained entrenched in the configuration of church and society that had survived the cultural and political turmoil of the past millennium. Through their alliances with political authorities, new forms of Christendom emerged. Anabaptists, heirs of the dissident tradition, paid the traditional price for opposing Christendom, but the availability of printing enabled them to disseminate their views widely, and the disintegration of Europe gave fleeing dissidents places of (usually temporary) refuge.

Christendom in Turmoil

Early sixteenth-century Europe was turbulent. Social, economic, political, cultural and religious questions were open to reappraisal. Developments and issues included:

- The final skirmishes in the centuries-long struggle for supremacy between pope and emperor.
- Gradual recovery from devastating plagues in the previous century, now less threatening but a dreaded memory.
- Severe economic problems and the complex ramifications of transition from feudalism to capitalism.
- A crisis of confidence in relation to cultural values and symbols once assumed to be permanent but now under threat.

- The cost of the church's unwieldy bureaucracy, its role as a major landowner, its moral corruption and its determination to defend its privileges.
- The possibility of reform movements being co-opted by national or regional authorities to assert their independence or advance political ambitions.

The Peasants' War (1524–1526), which disturbed central Europe, especially German-speaking regions, was a grass-roots protest against oppressive state and church practices. Assuming the Reformers would support them, the peasants' leaders were devastated by Luther's uncompromising advice to the German princes to crush this revolt.[2] Church and state remained partners. Luther, realising he needed the support of the political authorities, refused to embrace the peasants' socially disruptive agenda. Many disappointed peasants gravitated towards Anabaptism, hoping to pursue their dream of a just society through the alternative strategy of forming communities where they could introduce just practices.

Anabaptism was one option for those disillusioned with medieval Catholicism. After centuries of dominance, its monopoly had been broken. Individuals were beginning to exercise choice in matters of faith – just as medieval dissidents had advocated. There was still pressure to conform to the dominant religious tradition wherever they lived, but they could move to other Christendoms where their preferred form of Christianity was practised. There were even cities (Strasbourg, for instance) that hosted Christians representing various religious options and engaging in relatively friendly dialogue – unimaginable in earlier centuries.

---

[2]   The title of one of his tracts leaves his opposition in no doubt: *Against the Robbing and Murderous Hordes of Peasants*!

Catholicism remained the strongest form of Christendom. Despite the complaints of discontented theologians, philosophers, clergy and others, the thought of leaving the 'mother church' was abhorrent to most critics. They regarded as sacrosanct the unity of church and society and perceived schism as evil. If such convictions restrained the critics, inertia ensured most people continued to attend their parish church regardless of theological battles raging elsewhere. Furthermore, faced by the challenge of serious rivals for the first time in centuries, Catholicism embarked on its own internal reform process, the Counter-Reformation. Malcolm Lambert summarises its effects: 'The easygoing religion of the majority in the medieval age gave way to a more disciplined and often more aggressive Catholicism, organizing its membership more coherently, attempting to put down the remnants of pagan folk religion and bringing new religious orders to birth.'[3]

But in many places these changes were too late to prevent disaffection. Martin Luther, Ulrich Zwingli, John Calvin and others gained the support of monarchs and city councils for their reforming activities. Catholic Christendom became Lutheran or Reformed by decree. The Reformers were concerned to restore true doctrine, remove ecclesiastical corruption and provide effective preaching and pastoral care – to reform *believing* and some aspects of *behaving*. But they did not reform *belonging*: they maintained the state–church amalgam and endorsed Christendom ideology. Their strategy was to reform society gradually, relying on a combination of preaching and state-enforced changes of practice.

The result was the emergence of new political/religious entities where some version of Protestant Christianity

---

[3] Malcolm Lambert, *Medieval Heresy: Popular Movements from the Gregorian Reform to the Reformation* (Oxford: Blackwell, 1992), 361.

achieved recognition as the state religion. The Latin phrase *cuius regio eius religio* described this arrangement – the religion of the authorities determined the religion of their citizens.[4] This reformation process had similarities to the process by which the Roman Empire changed its religious allegiance during the fourth century. The Christendom mindset persisted and top-down methods were used. David Bosch concludes that the relationship between church and state in the sixteenth century 'was redefined in a more nuanced way, yet with little fundamental difference. The old, monolithic Christendom merely gave way to different fragments of Christendom.'[5] But there was one important difference. The relative independence of a transnational church from political control was lost: in the new mini-Christendoms church and state were more closely knit than ever.

Another difference was the availability of further options for those not persuaded any version of Christendom was legitimate. Spiritualists represented radical rejection of external forms of religion. They believed personal spirituality was the core of faith, relegating outward forms and ceremonies to non-essential status or regarding them as hindrances to spiritual growth and unity. The reform of the church was insignificant, if this meant concern with structural issues. This was an attractive option in an age of bitter disputes over such matters. Spiritualists might conform outwardly to whatever form of religion was required locally (since such conformity was irrelevant to spiritual life) and continue to practice their own beliefs.

---

[4] This phrase was used in the Peace of Westphalia (1648) that ended the Thirty Years' War, although the principle was operating earlier.

[5] David Bosch, *Witness to the World: The Christian Mission in Theological Perspective* (Basingstoke: Marshalls, 1980), 120.

The final option was Anabaptism. Anabaptists emphasised the centrality of Jesus, recovery of New Testament ecclesiology, separation of church and state, ethical renewal resulting in discipleship and mission in a society regarded as only nominally Christian. Although on many theological issues Anabaptists agreed with the Reformers, especially Zwingli and radical Lutherans, their reform programme was very different. Indeed, this is better described as restoration or restitution: Christendom was to be rejected, not transmuted. After initial attempts to gain political influence or attract support for an Anabaptist programme,[6] it soon became apparent this was not feasible. Anabaptists would not find territories where they could practise their faith without fear of persecution. Certain cities or regions tolerated them temporarily but they often faced choosing between conformity, migration or imprisonment and execution. But tens of thousands joined them. They were convinced the Spiritualists' denigration of the communal dimension of Christianity was as illegitimate as the competing state–church options; they also hoped that this grass-roots movement might achieve social justice and more radical reformation.

Reforming Christendom

Luther's response to the peasants' movement made clear social justice was not high on the Reformers' agenda. Reformation was not intended to threaten the alliance between church and state or the historic identification of church leaders with the wealthy and powerful in the social hierarchy. The Reformers' concerns required no such upheaval:

---

[6] For instance by Balthasar Hubmaier in Waldshut and later in Nicholsburg, and the disastrous attempt by extremists to turn Munster into an Anabaptist kingdom.

they could accomplish correct doctrine, moral reform and removal of ecclesiastical abuses by faithful preaching and pastoral leadership, backed up by state support to encourage compliance. Although they eventually conceded they could not achieve their aims without dividing Christendom and creating alternative churches, they were unwilling to abandon the Christendom system and its presuppositions.

Luther and some of his colleagues briefly considered a more radical approach but did not pursue this more costly strategy. They moved through three stages:

- Initially, they criticised blatant abuses, doctrinal errors and immorality without urging schism.
- Gradually, they accepted the inevitability of separation and toyed with radical ideas about the church and its relationship with the state and society (ideas not dissimilar to those of earlier dissidents).
- Finally, having secured political support, they rejected such radical ideas and established alternative expressions of Christendom, removing its objectionable features but maintaining its basic framework.

Although Reformers spoke warmly of the Waldensians and Lollards, claiming them as precursors, their reform programme was different from the medieval dissidents. This is apparent from their approach to biblical interpretation, church and mission and their attitudes towards characteristic Christendom practices such as infant baptism, oaths, participation in warfare and tithing.

The Bible

The Reformers advocated returning to Christianity's biblical roots and insisted the Bible, not church tradition, was

authoritative. How, then, did they approach biblical interpretation? During the past millennium, despite advances in
biblical understanding resulting from the labours of generations of biblical interpreters and theologians, the
Christendom mindset was dominant. Theologians consistently interpreted the Bible in ways that supported the
supposedly Christian status quo. The different application
of the Bible in the manifestos and tracts of the
sixteenth-century peasants' movement[7] indicates the unsettling readings of the dissidents had not been entirely snuffed
out. But these were marginal voices, which seemed to advocate unthinkable changes.

The Reformers introduced important changes but did
not challenge the Christendom mindset:

- They championed the plain sense of the text over
  allegorical interpretation and the Bible's supremacy
  over ecclesiastical traditions. Initially, they asserted
  the ability of all Christians to interpret, challenging
  the monopoly of popes, priests and councils. But
  they quickly withdrew this freedom when people
  advocated interpretations with which they disagreed.
- They rejected monasticism, removing the two-tier
  approach to discipleship, which excused people from
  applying the New Testament personally. But they
  persisted in using the Old Testament as their main
  source of ethical guidance.
- They emphasised the doctrine of justification by
  faith and focused attention on Jesus as saviour and
  his redeeming work on the cross. But this interest in
  Jesus did not mean his example and teaching were
  normative for discipleship.

---

[7] Tom Scott and Bob Scribner (eds.), *The German Peasants'
War: A History in Documents* (Atlantic Highlands: Humanities
Press, 1991).

- They insisted on the freedom of biblical interpretation from the scrutiny of ecclesiastical or political authorities, but in practice frequently deferred to these. Operating with a 'hermeneutic of order' rather than a 'hermeneutic of justice' they were wary of interpretations that threatened political, economic, social and ecclesiastical norms.

Consequently, their return to the biblical roots did not mean subjecting ethical and ecclesiastical issues to the same scrutiny they applied to doctrine. They rejected the peasants' calls for reform of the oppressive tithing system and vilified those who advocated communitarian models of economic sharing. And they refused to address the peasants' concerns about church structures and local accountability.

Reformers affirmed traditional views on the necessity of oaths for the ordering of society. Heinrich Bullinger peered over the abyss into the chaos that would ensue if oaths were abolished: 'The oath is the button, which holds together the authorities and covenants, relationships of obedience, etc ... So if you now take away the oath, this is all dissolved, counts for nothing, and altogether becomes nothing, resulting in such complete confusion and disorder that it is impossible to describe.'[8] This illustrates the concern to uphold the status quo that hindered Reformers from challenging traditional biblical interpretation.

Reformers also endorsed 'just war' thinking and urged Christians to take up arms against those the state designated their enemies – even if this meant slaughtering

---

[8] Cited in Edmund Pries, 'Anabaptist Oath Refusal: Basel, Bern and Strasbourg, 1525–1538' (PhD thesis: University of Waterloo, 1995), 266. For statements on the oath by other Reformers, see Martin Luther, *On Worldly Authority* and Philip Melanchthon, *On Christian Doctrine*.

other Christians. Luther advocated a violent response to the peasants' movement. Zwingli died on the battlefield. Calvin defended the right and duty of governments to engage in just wars:

> kings and people must sometimes take up arms to execute such a public vengeance. On this basis we may judge wars lawful ... princes must be armed not only to restrain the misdeeds of private individuals by judicial punishment, but also to defend by war the dominions entrusted to their safekeeping, if at any time they are under enemy attack.[9]

Knowing Anabaptists based objections to this viewpoint on the Sermon on the Mount, Reformers employed traditional strategies to counter their challenge: applying its teaching to intention rather than action; claiming it described life in the eschatological kingdom; regarding it as unattainable idealism to encourage dependence on God's mercy; and distinguishing the private and public spheres in which Christians lived. Luther's 'two kingdoms' approach (Christians were to behave differently in the public and private realms) was similar to Augustine's efforts a millennium earlier to evade the implications of this demanding passage. It just as effectively marginalised Jesus.

Given their acceptance of support from the political authorities and their continued endorsement of the Christendom framework (if not its Catholic expression), the Reformers could hardly have interpreted the Bible on these issues in any other way. They consistently advocated interpretations of the New Testament that legitimised the social order and opposed alternative readings that might threaten the interests of those in authority. When opponents challenged them with awkward New Testament texts, they retreated to the Old Testament: if establishing a New

---

[9]   Calvin, *Institutes*, 4.20, 10–11.

Testament basis for infant baptism was difficult, the Old Testament practice of circumcision provided a helpful analogy; and if the New Testament seemed to advocate pacifism, many examples of Old Testament warfare were available to refute this.

The church

Reformers rarely planted new churches. Their strategy was to achieve political and popular support to convert Catholic churches into Protestant churches. Reformation would be achieved through biblical preaching, purging the churches of superstitious practices and improving the religious life of people and clergy alike. They abolished or reformed practices earlier dissidents had challenged – the mass, veneration of relics and images, pilgrimages, prayers to the saints and for the dead and fast days. Scrutiny of traditional teaching also resulted in changes dissidents would have welcomed: reliance on grace rather than works for salvation; assurance of direct access to God without the necessary mediation of Mary or a priest; and rejection of the concept of purgatory.

But reforming existing churches generally leads to less radical changes than planting new churches. The Reformers inherited an ecclesiastical system and assumptions about church life they generally chose not to question. They knew others were critical of the limited reforms in the state churches and were planting churches that operated differently. Occasionally they dreamed of more radical possibilities. Luther, in 1526, described the kind of church he longed for but concluded: 'I neither can nor may as yet set up such a congregation; for I do not as yet have the people for it.'[10] But they would not jeopardise political or

---

[10] Leonard Verduin, *The Reformers and their Stepchildren* (Grand Rapids: Eerdmans, 1964), 127.

popular support by introducing changes they thought unnecessary. Dependence on the Old Testament and reluctance to subject church life to the same biblical scrutiny as other areas of doctrine did not encourage radical reform.

Consequently, many aspects of church life remained unreformed. Although the pope was dethroned as head of the church, the hierarchical and clerical structure that had governed the church throughout Christendom survived intact. They adjusted terminology and organisational arrangements, but the clergy/laity divide persisted – despite talk of the 'priesthood of all believers' – and they replaced the monopoly of the priest with the monopoly of the preacher.[11] Reformers restored preaching to church services (medieval services often lacked any preaching component due to the ignorance of local clerics), but clerical performances and monologue sermons still dominated services, with congregations participating little more than when their churches were Catholic. As Anabaptist evangelist Hans Hut complained, 'our new evangelicals, the tender scribes, have thrown the pope, the monks, and the parsons from their thrones and they establish – God have mercy on us – a worse popery than before over the poor man.'[12]

Nor, sadly, did they abandon punitive church discipline. As before, doctrinal errors and moral failings were normally excusable provided culprits remained in the church. Indeed, now the penitential system had been abolished as another tradition without biblical warrant, lack of discipline in Protestant churches provoked derision from their

---

[11] R. Paul Stevens, *The Abolition of the Laity: Vocation, Work and Ministry in a Biblical Perspective* (Carlisle: Paternoster Press, 1999), 45–7.

[12] Hans Hut, 'On the Mystery of Baptism', in Michael Baylor (ed.), *The Radical Reformation* (Cambridge: Cambridge University Press, 1991), 54.

opponents. But they pursued as vigorously as ever heresy and schism that threatened the unity of church and society, using familiar coercive and violent methods. There were places of refuge in fragmented sixteenth-century Christendom, but the mutual persecution of those claiming to be Christians was as great a blight as the persecution of dissidents in earlier centuries. Catholics imprisoned, interrogated, tortured and burned Protestants; Protestants similarly abused Catholics, though they generally beheaded them. Both state churches persecuted Anabaptists (at least 3000 of whom were executed, with many more imprisoned or exiled). Such treatment convinced Anabaptists Christendom could not be truly Christian. Dirk Philips wrote: 'True Christians must here be persecuted for the sake of truth and righteousness, but they persecute no one on account of his faith ... Those who persecute others on account of their faith can nevermore be counted as a church of the Lord.'[13]

Mission

One aspect of Anabaptism that outraged Reformers and Catholics was its refusal to respect territorial boundaries that defined spiritual responsibility within Christendom. Ignoring the parochial structure and sensibility of parish priests, Anabaptists followed the tradition of the unauthorised and unlicensed preachers of the dissident movements. They evangelised, baptised and formed new congregations without regard for whose ecclesiastical toes they trod on.

But far more threatening than this ecclesiastical discourtesy was their conviction Christendom needed evangelising. Reformers acknowledged problems with both belief and behaviour but continued to operate on the basis that

---

[13] Walter Klaassen, *Anabaptism in Outline: Selected Primary Sources* (Scottdale: Herald Press, 1981), 298.

Europe was Christian and everyone belonged to the church. The church needed reformation, but pastors and teachers were required, not evangelists (or apostles and prophets). They endorsed the orthodox position for the past millennium – a position challenged only by dissident movements and now by Anabaptists – that the Great Commission was accomplished centuries earlier and Europe was a Christian society. Evangelists were obsolete, their task completed long ago. Reformers did not recognise the legitimacy of evangelism in an officially Christian society, and they regarded mission beyond Christendom as God's responsibility, not theirs.[14]

Unsurprisingly, Reformers defined the church in relation to the preaching of true doctrine and proper administration of the sacraments. Pastors exercised what became known as 'ministry of Word and sacrament' and operated essentially in maintenance mode. As in past centuries, everyone living in the parish was baptised into the church shortly after birth and remained within it by default. The idea that the church might be a missionary community and evangelism a component in the work of ministers was unthinkable while the Christendom framework remained intact. Bosch writes: 'The Reformation definitions of the Church were silent on its missionary dimensions. Ecclesiological definitions were almost exclusively preoccupied with matters concerning the purity of doctrine, the sacraments and church discipline. Mission had to content itself with a position on the church's periphery.'[15]

It was not that Reformers lacked a sense of mission, but they understood mission in the Christendom sense of imposing beliefs, legislating morality, controlling culture,

---

[14]   There were just two Protestant missionary enterprises beyond Christendom in the Reformation era, both initiated by political authorities. See Bosch, *Transforming Mission*, 246.
[15]   Bosch, *Witness*, 169.

monitoring behaviour, enforcing church attendance, encouraging loyalty to the state and pursuing dissenters. Mission was top-down and essentially coercive. Church leaders continued to legitimise and sanctify state occasions and policies and offer the authorities advice on diverse issues. They also continued to expect the state to uphold their privileges and punish dissidents – who now included members of churches previously regarded as orthodox.

Reformation applied not only to internal church matters but also to the whole of society; the church's mission embraced all aspects of culture. Daily life and work were newly sanctified as spheres of service and vocation, although different standards applied in business than in church. Social engagement was essentially conservative and resistant to radical demands for social justice. Reformers made strenuous efforts to purge society of cultural practices once regarded favourably but now deemed unchristian, superstitious or even idolatrous. Abolishing the cult of the saints and suppression of similar traditional forms of spirituality were intended to lead to religious reformation and renewal. However, hearts and minds had generally not been won and the cerebral and less visual forms of Christianity that Reformers advocated were unsatisfying. In some communities, attempts at reformation resulted in unexpected upsurges in traditional pagan practices to compensate for the loss of Christianised versions of these.

The Reformation caused enormous upheaval and produced lasting divisions in the church and European society. But actually *nothing much really changed*, at least in relation to Christendom. All the defining structures, attitudes, methods, reflexes and processes were still in place. Those who regard the Reformation as a turning point in European history, restoring true doctrine and order to the church, will find this assessment surprising. But Reformers, despite initially considering more radical changes, rejected this option, validated Christendom and continued to operate within this system. They refined it, fractured it and shifted the balance of power within it towards the secular authorities. But they were not prepared to dismantle it. And they strenuously and violently opposed Anabaptists for their temerity in disagreeing with them.

Rejecting Christendom

Anabaptist writings were not destroyed like those of earlier dissidents, but antipathy towards any movement regarded as sectarian precluded serious consideration of those who challenged Christendom. Until the second half of the twentieth century, students of the Reformation encountered Anabaptists only as brief and dismissive footnotes to the main story of the rivalry between Catholics and Reformers. But in the past sixty years the disintegration of Christendom has encouraged historians to investigate this movement, read its own writings as well as its opponents' polemics and suggest their approach to biblical interpretation, church and mission might be helpful.

Anabaptists, like medieval dissidents, were mainly uneducated and poor, although early leaders included ex-monks, scholars and ex-priests. Anabaptism flourished in areas where earlier movements had left at least a subversive memory. And within this movement dissident beliefs and practices re-emerged and lay piety found renewed popular expression. In their approach to biblical interpretation, church and mission, Anabaptists inherited and developed the dissident tradition. They hoped to galvanise radical reform, but the Reformers and their sponsors would not embrace changes that might unsettle society and threaten the gradual reforms they wanted to introduce. Disappointed Anabaptists realised reforming the state–church system was inadequate and began to form believers' churches. They concluded the fourth-century 'fall' of the church was fundamental, with infant baptism its primary symbol. Identifying the Christendom shift as the root problem, they examined Christendom beliefs, structures, symbols and practices and reached similar conclusions to earlier dissidents.

Whenever movements identify the Christendom shift as the central issue and remove the Christendom blinkers, they rediscover the centrality of Jesus and find traditional approaches to issues such as baptism, church life, evangelism, warfare, economics, the oath and the role of the state need to be revised.

The Bible

A grass-roots approach to biblical interpretation energised Anabaptism. Although literacy was still limited, the increasing availability of vernacular translations enabled Christians across central Europe to gather in small groups to listen to the Bible, learn it by heart and discuss its meaning and implications. Anabaptists under interrogation frequently amazed and irritated their inquisitors with their biblical knowledge, which was far in advance of those who attended the state churches. Like earlier movements, Anabaptists were struck by the dissonance between what they read and what they saw in Catholic and Protestant churches. And, as before, this resulted in them developing different approaches to biblical interpretation:[16]

- They too rejected two-tier discipleship with different standards for different classes of Christians but,

---

[16] Stuart Murray, *Biblical Interpretation in the Anabaptist Tradition* (Kitchener: Pandora Press, 2000).

unlike the Reformers, they applied New Testament standards to all. Jesus' life and teaching was normative, so ecclesiastical and ethical issues were not decided solely by reference to the Old Testament.

- They insisted New Testament teaching should be obeyed whatever its social implications. They rejected readings of Romans 13 that required excessive deference to political authorities and operated not with a 'hermeneutic of order' but a 'hermeneutic of obedience'.
- They welcomed Reformers' early confidence that all could interpret but did not share their growing unease about this. They were convinced uneducated Christians could, with the help of the Holy Spirit, understand and obey the Bible.
- They perceived their marginal and persecuted status as advantageous, seeing this as analogous to the early Christians, giving them insights into the Bible's meaning that were inaccessible to their persecutors, who were in thrall to political and economic power structures.
- They insisted the Bible should be interpreted in the congregation because all members of this community had insights; this had significant implications for their understanding of church life.

The central Anabaptist insight was *Christocentrism*. They rejected the marginalising of Jesus that was necessary for the Christendom shift but had disturbed the medieval dissidents. They were determined to listen to Jesus and follow him. The Sermon on the Mount was not a wonderful collection of unattainable ideals but a guide for daily living. They reconnected spirituality and discipleship: in the words of

Hans Denck, 'No one can know Christ unless he follows after him in life.'[17]

This motif of *following Jesus* characterised the Anabaptist movement. From early in the Christendom era there had been reticence about using Jesus' life as a model for Christian living. Worshipping an exalted and imperial Christ was less demanding than following the radical Jesus. Inevitably, many reacted against this remote imagery. The cults of the saints and especially the Virgin Mary can be interpreted as compensatory: these intermediaries were less austere and more accessible than the remote Christ of Christendom. Mystical and monastic writers painted a more intimate picture of Jesus. In the medieval period the theme of 'imitating Christ' was very popular. But, though this resulted in spiritual benefits and renewed interest in Jesus' human life, it did not generally lead to behaviour that threatened Christendom. However, the dissidents' conviction that following Jesus meant applying his teaching in ways that challenged political, economic and social norms provoked persecution.

This caused problems for Anabaptists too. Neither Catholics nor Reformers welcomed the reappearance of this disturbing perspective. Reformers also feared the Anabaptist emphasis on discipleship undermined their principle of justification by faith and meant a return to the 'works-righteousness' they detected in Catholicism. Anabaptists countered that Reformers replaced 'works without faith' with 'faith without works', failing to recognise Jesus as teacher and example as well as saviour. Michael Sattler pronounced a blessing on those who remained 'on the middle path', turning aside neither to the 'works-righteous' nor to those who 'teach in the name of the gospel a faith without works'.[18]

---

[17] Klaassen, *Anabaptism*, 87.
[18] Klaassen, *Anabaptism*, 57.

Among the 'works' Anabaptists advocated were deviant approaches to traditional Christendom perspectives on warfare, oaths and economics. Although in a diverse movement there were different views on these issues, a developing consensus rejected oaths and participation in warfare. Most Anabaptists believed Jesus' example and teaching precluded both practices and encouraged the development of habits of truth-telling and peaceful living. They identified the fourth century as the time when the church compromised ethically.

For 500 years the Anabaptist tradition has insisted Christians, as followers of the Prince of Peace, are called to non-violence and peacemaking. In Menno Simons' writings a description of the church common in pre-Christendom but unfamiliar in Christendom reappears: 'They are the children of peace who have beaten their swords into ploughshares and their spears into pruning hooks, and know war no more.'[19] Together with the Quakers, Anabaptists constitute a 'peace church' tradition that recovers this early church perspective and advocates alternatives to the dominant 'just war' tradition and occasional lapses into crusading.

As for oaths, Anabaptists believed Jesus' teaching precluded these and insisted they were irrelevant for those committed to consistent truth telling. Promising truthfulness under oath implied lower standards on other occasions. Oaths guaranteeing future behaviour (for instance, refraining from further illicit Anabaptist activities) were presumptuous, indicating they were unwilling to obey the call of God. Nor, of course, would they swear

---

[19] Menno Simons, *Complete Works 1496–1561* (Scottdale: Herald Press, 1956), 93. Examples from pre-Christendom writers include Origen's *Letter to Julius Africanus*, 15 and Justin's *Dialogue with Trypho*, 110.2–3.

oaths of political allegiance that might require them to bear arms.[20]

Anabaptists' refusal to bear arms and swear oaths caused others in central Europe to label them subversives, but their radical approach to economics worried English authorities. There were hardly any Anabaptists in England (refugees seeking asylum from persecution were imprisoned, interrogated and either executed or deported); but fear of the movement resulted in Anabaptists being named in the Church of England's foundational document. The thirty-eighth of the *Thirty-Nine Articles of Religion* (1571) states: 'The riches and goods of Christians are not common, as touching the right, title, and possession of the same, as certain Anabaptists do falsely boast; notwithstanding every man ought of such things as he possesseth liberally to give alms to the poor, according to his ability.'

Some Anabaptists (the Hutterians) had formed common-purse communities that were profoundly threatening to a hierarchical society deeply committed to private property and pursuit of wealth. Most, however, practised 'mutual aid' and emphasised simple living and generosity towards those in need. They opposed tithing, because it lacked New Testament support and undergirded a system they regarded as corrupt.

Their opponents' response to these challenges involved relying on the Old Testament. The use of Old Testament texts to countermand Jesus' teaching had been familiar for centuries and was essential for maintaining the Christendom system, but Anabaptists agreed with medieval dissidents this was illegitimate. According to Leonard Verduin, Anabaptists 'complained loudly that the weapons which the reformers used ... were weapons taken from the Old Testament arsenal. They looked upon the policy of

---

[20] Klaassen, *Anabaptism*, 283–9.

sliding from the Old Testament to the New as a master evil, one from which all sorts of evils come.'[21]

The church

Anabaptists expressed similar concerns about the use of the Old Testament to justify church structures and practices. The model of church operating within Christendom seemed to them an Old Testament model; persistent calls to restore New Testament models of church and discipleship characterised their debates with Reformers.

The issue of baptism assumed central importance. By baptising one another Anabaptists decisively broke with the Christendom system. As they had been christened as infants, legally this amounted to rebaptism, which carried the death penalty – so seriously did both church and state regard this flagrant challenge to social unity. They themselves rejected the term 'anabaptist' (re-baptiser), claiming their earlier baptism was invalid, but the charge and the label stuck. Further trouble ensued when they refused to allow their own children to be christened. So worried were the authorities, an imperial edict in 1529 authorised execution without trial for anyone publicly criticising infant baptism. Medieval dissidents expressed doubts about infant baptism, but Anabaptists replaced this distinctive Christendom ceremony with the baptism of believers. They did so for four interrelated reasons:

- They understood baptism as an expression of faith and commitment to a life of discipleship within the Christian community.
- They believed in voluntary church membership rather than involuntary incorporation shortly after

---

[21] Verduin, *Reformers*, 210.

birth, regarding infant baptism as a violation of religious liberty.

- They could find no New Testament basis for baptising infants and were not persuaded by arguments about the inclusion of infants in household baptisms.
- They regarded the analogy with circumcision and Reformers' reliance on the Old Testament to justify infant baptism as illegitimate.

The debate about baptism reflected deeper questions about the nature of the church and its relationship to state and society. Anabaptists rejected the Catholic state–church model, which the Reformers adopted, with its assumption the church comprised all members of society. They pioneered a 'free church' model. Here churches, comprised of those who chose to belong and accepted the discipline of the community, governed themselves without reference to the state. This profoundly challenged Christendom.

Across central Europe Anabaptists planted hundreds of new churches, free from state control but liable to persecution as unauthorised and subversive. Although there were larger congregations, most were small and met in homes, woods and anywhere they might escape notice. Inevitably, they developed structures and practices that fitted this different way of being church. Simplicity, domesticity, egalitarian values and biblical precedent guided them. Although they knew little about earlier dissidents, similarities soon appeared.

Church membership was not territorial but relational. Anabaptists insisted they no longer belonged to the state churches but to their own Christian communities. This claim was difficult for secular and ecclesiastical authorities to understand, let alone accept. In 1575, some Anabaptists seeking refuge in England from persecution in the Netherlands were arrested and imprisoned. The Bishop of London, after failing to convince them of their errors, threatened to expel them from his church. The prisoners responded: 'How can you expel us from your church, when we have never yet been one with you?' The bishop's reply was uncomprehending and uncompromising: 'In England there is no one that is not a member of God's church. I condemn you all to death.'[22]

The leadership model Anabaptists developed, though it became more conventional over time, was initially very different from the clerical and hierarchical Christendom pattern. They chose leaders from the congregation on the basis of spiritual maturity and holiness of life, rather than educational qualifications or official authentication. They followed through the Reformers' idea of the priesthood of all believers more radically than in the Reformers' churches, empowering all to participate in many aspects of church life. Women had more scope for participation and leadership and all members were expected to contribute to multi-voiced gatherings. Anabaptists held three convictions about how God spoke to people: first, listening to the Holy Spirit was more important in understanding Scripture than education or ordination; second, the Spirit might speak through any Christian as they meditated on the Bible; and third, discerning the meaning of God's word was a community practice, so dialogue and interaction were vital.

Although Anabaptists did not abandon sermons, they were wary of monologues and criticised the lack of participation in Catholic and Protestant churches, arguing from Scripture that this was wrong. An Anabaptist tract, quoting Paul's instruction in 1 Corinthians 14 that when the church gathered all should contribute, complained: 'When some

---

[22] Thieleman van Braght, *Martyrs' Mirror* (Scottdale: Herald Press, 1950), 1009.

one comes to church and hears only one person speaking, and all the listeners are silent ... who can or will regard or confess the same to be a spiritual congregation?'[23] Many congregations moved away from monologue towards a more interactive style. Under interrogation in 1527, Ambrosius Spitelmaier, an Anabaptist leader in Nicholsburg, explained: 'When they have come together, they teach one another the divine Word and one asks the other: how do you understand this saying? Thus there is among them a diligent living according to the divine Word.'[24] A drift back towards more passive forms of church life is apparent as the movement aged, but there are glimpses later in the sixteenth century of multi-voiced community.

One further difference concerned Anabaptists' approach to church discipline. They rejected as erroneous and unchristian coercive and often lethal application of church and state power against them. They also criticised the lack of true church discipline in the state churches and consequent low moral standards. To the Reformers' 'word and sacrament' definition of the true church Anabaptists added a third element: the true church exercised church discipline ('fraternal admonition'). They linked this with the baptism of believers, who submitted in baptism to mutual accountability. Matthew 18 was their biblical basis for church discipline within the movement.[25]

Anabaptists did not always handle well its practical outworking. Vindictive attitudes, harsh application of principles, insensitivity towards human failings, disruption

---

[23] Paul Peachey, 'Answer of Some who are called (Ana)baptists why they do not attend the Churches: A Swiss Brethren Tract', *Mennonite Quarterly Review* (1971), 7.

[24] Klaassen, *Anabaptism*, 124.

[25] Klaassen, *Anabaptism*, 213–31.

of family life, mutual excommunication of congregations who disagreed on issues of interpretation, psychological pressure and perfectionism blighted the application of a pastoral process intended to nurture discipleship and prevent breaches of relationship. At least, unlike the church discipline Catholics and Reformers practised, it was non-lethal: there was a world outside the church into which rebellious members could be consigned. And some Anabaptists exercised discipline graciously and creatively. But the tradition represented by movements like Anabaptism, as it attempted to restore practices obscured or distorted by the Christendom shift, was flawed. If we would draw inspiration from this tradition in reconfiguring church life for post-Christendom, we must engage critically with the models and examples it offers.

Mission

The way Anabaptists practised church discipline may have been flawed, but they were distinctive in refusing to condone coercion in matters of religion. They criticised Reformers not only for failing to exercise proper pastoral church discipline but also for applying coercive discipline. They were early advocates of *religious liberty*.

For persecuted movements to advocate religious liberty may seem unsurprising, since they will be beneficiaries of this policy. But we can too easily, in an era where such liberty is almost universally championed in Western culture, take for granted the idea that religious convictions should not be coerced. This was not obvious in Christendom where the dictum 'error has no rights' and the need to preserve society from dissent combined to override sensitivity to individual conscience. The Reformers appeared to challenge this, but within territories under their control they operated in the traditional coercive manner.

Anabaptists argued for religious liberty – not just for themselves but for all, including Jews and Muslims. Hans Denck insisted: 'No one shall deprive another – whether heathen or Jew or Christian – but rather allow everyone to move in all territories in the name of his God.'[26] Kilian Aurbacher declared: 'It is never right to compel one in matters of faith, whatever he may believe, be he Jew or Turk ... Christ's people are a free, unforced and uncompelled people.'[27] Such statements are important antecedents of later declarations of religious liberty.

Contemporary arguments for religious liberty are often based on the assumption that truth claims are illegitimate and accompanied by resistance to the idea of evangelism. A later chapter will examine this anaemic form of toleration, but the Anabaptist vision was different. Convinced faith could not be coerced, they also believed *evangelism* was crucial in a society they did not perceive as Christian. While pressure to believe should not be exerted, every effort should be made to persuade people to become disciples of Christ. Through unauthorised preaching, interrupting church services, itinerant evangelism, conversations at work and in homes, Anabaptists evangelised their communities, baptising any who received their message and incorporating them into their churches.

Anabaptism (like the medieval movements) has been designated a classic example of a *missionary movement*, in which community and mission were integrated rather than separated.[28] Reformers accepted the Christendom claim that the Great Commission had been fulfilled centuries

---

[26] Klaassen, *Anabaptism*, 292.
[27] Klaassen, *Anabaptism*, 293.
[28] C. Peter Wagner, *Leading Your Church to Growth: The secret of pastor/people partnership in dynamic church growth* (London: MARC/BCGA, 1984), 154.

ago,[29] whereas few biblical passages appear as frequently in Anabaptist writings as Matthew 28:18–20. This text underscored their conviction about believers' baptism and called them into mission to make disciples and teach them to follow Jesus. Hans Schlaffer wrote: 'Our faith stands on nothing other than the command of Christ in Matthew 28 and Mark 16. For Christ did not say to his disciples: Go forth and celebrate Mass, but go forth and preach the Gospel.'[30] Sixteenth-century court records testify that this inspired the rank and file of the movement, not just designated evangelists; grass-roots evangelism was the primary means of growth.

This missionary perspective also impacted the movement's leadership. Once again the *marginalised ministries* of evangelists, prophets and apostles reappeared alongside pastors and teachers. Itinerant bookseller and evangelist Hans Hut baptised thousands in a brief but dynamic ministry, and Hutterite communities in Moravia commissioned hundreds of men and women to traverse Europe evangelising those they met (many of these, like Hut, were arrested and executed). Peter Rideman explained how Hutterites viewed apostolic leadership (differentiating this from pastoral leadership): 'Paul saith that God set first apostles in the Church. These are they who are sent out by God and his Church in accordance with the command of the gospel to go through the country and establish through the word and baptism the obedience of faith in his name.'[31]

Anabaptists, like others dismissively labelled 'sectarian' by those still operating with Christendom assumptions,

---

[29]   Matthew 28:18–20 was used in the medieval period almost exclusively as a proof-text for the Trinity.
[30]   Cited in Wilbert Shenk, *Anabaptism and Mission* (Scottdale: Herald Press, 1984), 19.
[31]   Peter Rideman, *Confession of Faith 1545* (Rifton: Plough, 1970), 82.

have often been charged with lacking vision or strategy for *engaging with wider culture*. In Richard Niebuhr's classic categories,[32] they have been assigned the 'Christ against culture' position and accused of withdrawing into separatist enclaves and refusing responsibility for governing or developing society. Undoubtedly a separatist tendency is apparent in the early years of the movement,[33] which has recurred over the past five centuries, but this is not the full story. Niebuhr provides no evidence to justify locating Anabaptism in the 'Christ against culture' category, and the record of Anabaptists in areas of social engagement, such as disaster relief, restorative justice, agricultural and economic development, conflict mediation, campaigns against war and capital punishment, provision of mental health services and education, compares well with most other traditions.

Why have critics not acknowledged this dimension of mission? Perhaps Christendom categories have again been definitive: because Anabaptists regarded involvement in the army or magistracy as inappropriate, and because critics regarded their stance on issues of truth telling, violence and economics as idealistic, they have been dismissed as separatist and unwilling to engage with wider social concerns. But Anabaptists did not deny the legitimate role of government, even if they were less convinced than the Reformers that governmental action tended to advance the cause of the gospel.

Government, according to most Anabaptists, was appointed by God and performed a divine function,

---

[32] H. Richard Niebuhr, *Christ and Culture* (New York: Harper Row, 1951), especially 56. This categorisation has rightly been criticised as flawed and simplistic but continues to exercise considerable influence.

[33] The Schleitheim Confession (1527), around which Swiss Anabaptists rallied, was strongly separatist in ethos.

whether it was benevolent or tyrannous. This function was to reward the good and punish the evil. It kept order by force in a world in which Christ's spirit had not yet captured all hearts and made them obedient. Anabaptists never disputed this use of force. Because governments were instituted by God and acted in God's stead, they should be obeyed. Taxes should be paid without resistance (although Hutterites refused to pay taxes to support war or capital punishment). On all this, Reformers and Anabaptists agreed. Where they parted company was on a Christian's relation to government. Luther argued Christians must participate in government out of love for their neighbours and be ready to coerce and kill to protect them, which they could do with good conscience because they were carrying out a divine mandate. Anabaptists were unconvinced those in government needed to be Christians and were sure Christians should *not* participate in lethal aspects of government out of love for their neighbours. Servants of Christ must not coerce or kill because this was contrary to Christ's commands. Some Anabaptists rejected all participation in government for these reasons – and also because any sixteenth-century Anabaptists participating in government would soon find themselves prosecuting members of their own church.[34]

Anabaptists, therefore, excluded themselves from certain forms of engagement with wider culture, both because of their understanding of biblical principles and because of their socio-political context. Some opted for separatism but many were concerned about society: they just did not engage with social issues in the ways normally associated with state churches:

---

[34] Klaassen, *Anabaptism*, 246–63.

- As a marginal and persecuted movement, active and public promulgation of their principles was dangerous and likely to be ineffective.
- As a movement committed to non-violence and opposed to oaths, it is difficult to see how they could participate in public service or governmental roles (even if they had been tolerated).
- As a refuge for many involved in the peasants' war, commitment to social justice permeated the movement, together with recognition political action had been ineffective.
- As a community largely comprised of poor and powerless people, their instinct was towards grass-roots action rather than top-down strategies.
- As a tradition guided by a 'hermeneutic of justice', not a 'hermeneutic of order', they tended towards radical criticism of society rather than advocating reformation and improvement.

The pertinent issue is not *whether* Anabaptism had a vision for engaging with culture but *how* such a vision might be expressed without subscribing to coercive methods and centralist perspectives. Sixteenth-century Anabaptists engaged with economic and political issues in two ways: by modelling within their own communities distinctive practices based on principles derived from the New Testament; and by commending these principles and practices through their writings and testimonies. In a different social context, where other forms of government are operative and other perspectives than the dominant one can be expressed without fear of persecution, a more overtly political strategy is possible. But for marginal communities this approach – modelling alternatives and speaking as a prophetic minority – may be the most effective strategy.

Reflecting on Christendom

The two different expressions of Christianity evident in the medieval period are also apparent in the changed and chaotic sixteenth-century context. The Reformers hoped to transform society from the centre, but challenged none of the essential components of Christendom. Anabaptists rejected Christendom, embodying alternatives in marginal communities and commending these to any who would listen.

There are resources in both traditions for faithful discipleship and witness in post-Christendom, but there are also choices to make between the approach to biblical interpretation, church and mission that resulted from the Christendom shift and the alternative approach of those who rejected this shift. As in some earlier chapters, it may be helpful to carry forward a number of questions:

- What are the advantages and disadvantages in post-Christendom of the 'grass-roots community' and 'strong institution' models of church?
- Are there good reasons for persisting with the practice of infant baptism in post-Christendom?
- What principles might guide post-Christendom churches in interpreting the Bible – and especially the Old Testament?
- Does the use of coercion and killing have any place in the life and witness of churches in post-Christendom, or can we become 'peace churches'?
- What relevance, if any, does the long-running dispute over swearing oaths have today?
- If the Christendom model of state–church relationships was flawed, what can we suggest as an alternative in post-Christendom?

- What modes of engagement with wider culture are appropriate for churches in post-Christendom, and what expectations are realistic?
- If we draw on the dissident tradition, does this mean accepting church life in post-Christendom will be marginal and our influence small?
- Can we find resources, inspiration and perspectives from the mainstream and the margins, and can the pre-Christendom churches help us discern what may be helpful in both traditions?

7

The Christendom Legacy

Christendom survived the sixteenth-century upheaval, but seeds of destruction had been sown. This chapter will examine the causes of its gradual but inexorable demise over the next four centuries and its headlong collapse in the late twentieth century. But, though this collapse is surely terminal and irreversible, Christendom has left a powerful legacy. Vestiges of Christendom are scattered throughout our culture. The Christendom mindset and Christendom reflexes will continue to shape our reactions and expectations. Furthermore, new forms of Christendom have appeared elsewhere. So we must consider our responses to the Christendom legacy.

The Demise of Christendom

The history of the past four centuries is complex but major factors in Christendom's demise can be identified. These are interconnected and it is difficult to distinguish causes and effects:

- Disillusionment with religion resulting from incessant warfare between supposedly Christian nations.

- The reliance of philosophers and scientists on reason and experimentation rather than revelation.
- The impact of industrialisation and urbanisation on traditional beliefs and structures.
- Postmodernism, pluralisation and fragmentation.
- The persistence of dissent and emergence of the 'free church' tradition.
- The globalisation of the church and its mission.

The sixteenth-century disintegration of Christendom resulted in the emergence of religious nationalism. Medieval Christendom was an all-embracing civilisation, engaging in crusades against other cultures but not internecine religious warfare. Wars between European states were not perceived as conflicts between variant forms of Christianity. But during the sixteenth and seventeenth centuries bitter and prolonged wars between the mini-Christendoms that emerged from the Reformation caused sensitive people to question the legitimacy of religion if it inspired such antagonism.[1] Christians killing other Christians in the name of Christ and bishops legitimising these wars and blessing weapons on both sides undermined the authority of the church and its message. Was Christianity a source of conflict rather than a resource for peace?

During the eighteenth century many sought a more secure foundation for society. This period, known as the Enlightenment and the birth of the modern era, witnessed an explosion of philosophical and scientific enquiry challenging long-held convictions and priorities. Scientific explanation replaced sacral interpretation. Attention was

---

[1] Although it may be more accurate to see these 'wars of religion' as inspired by rising nationalism than by religious convictions. See Vinoth Ramachandra, *Faiths in Conflict?: Christian Integrity in a Multicultural World* (Downers Grove: InterVarsity Press, 1999),149 –51.

on this world rather than the next, on the body or mind rather than the spirit. Reliance on reason was preferred to dependence on revelation; experimentation and logic seemed to offer better prospects for certainty and harmony.

Many of those involved remained within the church and subscribed to belief in God (although often deism rather than theism[2]); the Enlightenment was not explicitly anti-Christian. Nor was it without precedent. The Renaissance that flourished between the fourteenth and sixteenth centuries asked similar questions and recovered the literature and philosophies of classical paganism and early Christianity. Christendom absorbed its challenge and coerced into submission those whose discoveries threatened it, but this was not feasible in the eighteenth century. The Enlightenment worldview – 'scientific materialism', 'secular humanism', 'rationalism' or simply 'modernism' – brought great benefits and a culture that became increasingly intolerant of religious ideas and institutions. Although many Christians understandably regard it with hostility, perhaps we should celebrate its achievements. The Enlightenment can be interpreted as God-given liberation from a corrupt Christendom.

A consequence of the technological revolution the Enlightenment sparked was rapid transition from agriculture to industry. Accompanying this was urbanisation – expanding cities and the dissemination of urban values. These trends impacted home and family, working practices, transportation systems, political structures, legislation, economics and cultural issues. They also hastened the disintegration of Christendom: moving to the city disrupted family life and the inter-generational process of handing on the faith; individuals, uprooted from traditional community structures, felt less

---

[2] Deism, which rejects revealed religion and bases belief in a supreme being on nature and reason, was presented as a rational, non-divisive system encouraging self-reliance and critical engagement with the world.

obligation to remain churchgoers; work in mechanised factories detached people from the land, the rhythm of the seasons and traditional religious practices; and church structures, designed for a different context, adapted slowly and ineffectually.

But industrialisation and urbanisation accelerated rather than caused the demise of Christendom. The alienation of the poor from the churches is evident long before these trends removed remaining social constraints that ensured many still attended church. While employers required employees to attend church, they did; but once this requirement was lifted they left in droves. And the strength of rural religion can be exaggerated and romanticised. Christendom was already fading. Nevertheless, post-Christendom arrived first in the cities.

Neither of the nineteenth-century theological responses to the Enlightenment helped the cause of Christianity. Conservatives, rejecting scientific explanations and trying to maintain a stranglehold on debate, weakened its appeal by associating Christianity with obscurantism and blinkered traditionalism. Liberals, attempting to reconfigure Christianity to fit comfortably into the culture of scientific rationalism, produced an anaemic religion that attracted little commitment and decreasing numbers. As in the fourth century, church leaders faced profound challenges; apportioning blame is less helpful than reflecting on consequences. Christendom, with its legacy of antagonism towards new ideas and accommodation to culture, offered inadequate resources to chart a more creative course through this turbulent period.

The outcome was the increasing alienation of those who welcomed the Enlightenment and were unimpressed by the church's response. The influence of the Christian story and the church's embedded social position ensured Christendom would not collapse immediately: church attendance remained high throughout this period. But inexorable decline in institutional Christianity and the influence of Christian ideas had begun. 'Revivals' and 'awakenings' in the eighteenth, nineteenth and twentieth centuries promised briefly to recapture lost ground and reverse decline, but could not prevent the gradual erosion of Christendom.

Another major influence during the twentieth century was the experience of two world wars and multiple regional conflicts. Churches on both sides again endorsed as 'just' wars declared on each other by 'Christian' nations, and a 'Christian' nation perpetrated the most horrific of many Christendom outrages against the Jews – the Holocaust. While some found faith in Christ through their wartime experience, many others abandoned faith and never returned to the churches. The post-war revival in Britain associated with Billy Graham's campaigns stemmed the flow and even briefly reversed it (church attendance rose in this period), but, like previous revivals, was short-lived.

In the 1960s, another factor emerged, though its roots can be traced back to the 1930s. Postmodernism, whatever else this elusive concept means, exhibits deep suspicion towards truth claims, whether based on religious, scientific, rational or experiential foundations. The interpretation of the universe Christians offered and the alternative explanations of modernist scientists and philosophers are equally untenable, according to postmodernists. Both make claims that fail to acknowledge the distorting effects of their cultural context, assumptions and vested interests. From this perspective, the Enlightenment is a secularised form of Christendom! Walter Brueggemann writes: 'The unquestioned claims of Christendom were decisively challenged in the rise of Enlightenment rationality ... And yet it seems fair to insist that even the Enlightenment was a European affair that operated within the confines of Christendom and continued to make absolutist, universal claims.'[3]

---

[3] Walter Brueggemann, *Cadences of Home: Preaching Among Exiles* (Louisville: Westminster John Knox Press, 1997), 39.

Postmodernism represents a more thoroughgoing deconstruction of Christianity than modernism. Modernism challenged Christian truth claims and relegated religion to the private domain; postmodernism relativises all truth claims. Modernism had alternative explanations of reality; postmodernism suspects all explanations of being partial and oppressive. To the 'hermeneutics of order' and 'hermeneutics of justice' options from the Christendom era, it adds a 'hermeneutics of scepticism'. Postmodernism not only challenges Christianity but presents a powerful critique of Christendom: its unwitting captivity to dominant social values, authoritarian and institutional ethos, oppressive attitudes, domination by a male professional caste and marginalising of dissent are all glaringly visible in the searchlight of postmodernist scrutiny.

Christianity is remarkably adaptable, having been translated into numerous cultures and eras. Postmodernism offers both challenges and opportunities. Christians will dissent from some aspects of postmodernism; others we will affirm – including its critique of the pretensions of modernism – as offering fresh possibilities for telling the Christian story. But Christendom is inflexible; its values, structures and models are even less appropriate in postmodernity than in modernity. Postmodernism sounds its death-knell. For Christianity to thrive in postmodernity, Christendom assumptions and attitudes must go.

Explaining Christendom's demise in this way provokes questions. First, why did its collapse occur so precipitately from the 1960s? Various explanations are offered for accelerating decline during the past half-century. Most persuasive is the suggestion Christendom's foundations had been undermined by the cumulative impact of the above factors, but institutional and cultural scaffolding prevented implosion. Cultural shifts in the 1960s merely triggered the collapse of the Christendom house of cards.

Second, are we witnessing the demise of Christendom or the decline of Christianity? We may celebrate the former, but surely we should mourn the latter. The problem is that Christianity and Christendom were inseparable in this period. Christendom values hindered effective responses to philosophical challenges and cultural changes eroding the church's influence. The demise of Christendom and decline of Christianity were mutually reinforcing. We face the challenge of rediscovering Christianity without the Christendom framework.

Third, where was God in all this? The explanations sound deterministic – social and philosophical developments causing Christendom's demise and Christianity's decline. But if Christendom was illegitimate, perhaps its demise was God's doing, using these developments to destroy an oppressive system in order to liberate church and society. The frustration of the Babel building-project and scattering of the workers[4] can be interpreted as acts of judgement or grace; the demise of Christendom initially spells similar dismay and confusion, but this might be the launching pad for a new phase of Christian engagement with Western culture.

Two final factors in Christendom's demise were internal: forms of church growth that undermined its foundations.[5] The first was the proliferation of free churches in the mini-Christendoms created in the sixteenth century. The dissident tradition grew and dissipated – Separatists, Congregationalists, Puritans, Baptists, Quakers, Moravians and Methodists.[6] Many distinguished real from nominal

---

[4] Genesis 11:1–9.
[5] These will be explored further in Chapter 8.
[6] Meic Pearse, *The Great Restoration: The Religious Radicals of the 16th and 17th Centuries* (Carlisle: Paternoster Press, 1998); Christopher Hill, *The World Turned Upside Down*

Christianity, undermining the foundations of Christendom by emphasising individual rather than public religion. In the nineteenth and twentieth centuries denominations proliferated. Instead of a parish church for each community, multiple options existed even within parish boundaries, with many more within reach of a more mobile society.

The second development was the modern missionary movement. The expansion of Christianity into a global faith had dramatic consequences for Christendom. Although missionaries, imbued with Christendom assumptions, transported its structures and values into other societies, the old wineskins could not contain this new wine. In Asia and Africa, non-coercive strategies, non-established churches and indigenous forms of Christianity not identified with particular territories drove unaccustomed wedges between Christendom and Christianity. Andrew Walls calls the missionary movement both 'the last flourish of Christendom' and 'a departure from Christendom'.[7] Wilbert Shenk comments: 'The dark shadow of Christendom considerably complicated the missionary's task by making it difficult to see the situation fully; but in the long run, Christendom itself could not survive in the crucible of mission.'[8]

Massive church growth in Africa, Asia, Oceania and Latin America and a shrinking European church have all resulted in the end of Christendom as a territory or civilisation. 'Christian Europe' is nonsense when numerous missionaries from other continents are evangelising pagan

---

[6] (*Continued*) (Harmondsworth: Penguin, 1972) and Andrew Bradstock and Christopher Rowland (eds.), *Radical Christian Writings: A Reader* (Oxford: Blackwell, 2002).

[7] Walls, *Cross-Cultural Process*, 42–3.

[8] Wilbert Shenk, *The Transfiguration of Mission* (Scottdale: Herald Press, 1993), 21.

Europe! Boundaries between Christendom and 'heathendom' have collapsed, and non-Christendom Christianity
has subverted the Christendom mindset.

Whether we regard Christendom's demise as tragic or
hopeful, the evidence indicates a new era is beginning. This
includes declining trends in most indicators of Christian
believing, behaving and belonging.[9] There are anomalies,
including the increasing popularity of church schools. But
church attendance and membership have decreased
steadily, and more now belong to other churches than the
established church. Many Anglicans are urging disestablishment and reform of the parish system and infant
baptism. Missiologists no longer label historic Christendom as 'sending nations' and other societies as 'receiving
nations': mission is 'from everywhere to everywhere' and
there is a reverse flow of missionaries. Christendom categories are collapsing.

The demise of Christendom is not proceeding uniformly
across Europe or even within nations. Inner-city communities are a generation ahead of suburbia. Ways of thinking
and levels of churchgoing in Belfast are different from those
in Birmingham. Post-Reformation mini-Christendoms
took different forms (established church, national church
or *Volkskirche*); they have also lost coherence in different
ways. Grace Davie notes the dissimilar experience of Catholic and Protestant nations:

> In the Protestant North ... a model emerged in which the state
> Church remained prominent, indeed influential, amidst a
> largely secular population ... In Latin Europe, in contrast, the
> confrontation between the Catholic Church and the advocates
> of the enlightenment became heavily politicised ... one result

[9] See Chapter 1, and Peter Brierley, *The Tide is Running Out:
What the English Church Attendance Survey Reveals* (London:
Christian Research, 2000).

in this part of Europe was the emergence of a parallel 'church' in the form of the apparatus of a secular state.[10]

Furthermore, the demise of Christendom in Western Europe may not mean the end of Christendom. Walls anticipates, 'Christianity without Christendom ... determined by the southern continents'.[11] But the missionary movement exported Christendom and may spawn Christendoms in Africa, Asia and Latin America.[12] In post-communist Eastern Europe, a new Christendom is emerging, with demands for national churches with monopoly positions. And in America, though constitutional separation of church and state officially precludes Christendom, the Christendom mindset is pervasive and resilient. The honoured place of the flag in church buildings, conflating 'the American dream' with hopes for God's kingdom and identifying American values and interests as 'Christian' demonstrate Christendom's ability to flourish where officially it should not exist. Christendom is persistent! Its assumptions infuse movements as disparate as Christian Reconstructionism and Liberation Theology. John Howard Yoder identifies this phenomenon as 'neo-Constantinianism' – transmuted Christendoms that share assumptions about the church's role in society.[13]

Nevertheless, for Western culture:

The fourth and twentieth centuries form bookends marking transition points in the history of the church. Just as the fourth century adoption of Christianity by Constantine forced the church to struggle with its self-understanding as the new center

---

[10] Davie, *Europe*, 142.
[11] Walls, *Cross-Cultural Process*, 45.
[12] See Chapter 1.
[13] Yoder, *Priestly*, 142–3.

of the culture, twentieth century Christians must now struggle to understand the meaning of their social location in a decentered world.[14]

But Nigel Wright insists we must not simply acknowledge the church is in a 'post-Constantinian' situation, but evaluate this. He continues: 'To concede the dissolution of Christendom in the face of pluralism is less than appropriating it theologically.'[15] We must interpret and respond to this new situation. Hopefully, lessons learned in this transitional period will help churches elsewhere as they grapple with the Christendom system we have exported.

Vestiges of Christendom

Christendom as a political arrangement, Christian civilisation or sacral culture may be defunct; but vestiges of Christendom survive in our supposedly post-Christendom society. This is understandable after so many centuries. Some may be as harmless as pagan vestiges early missionaries chose to ignore, assuming these would eventually wither and die. Others are inappropriate for a marginal church in a plural culture but are defended on grounds other than those that originally undergirded them (arguments for infant baptism based on prevenient divine grace and covenant theology are classic examples). Some vestiges may be wholesome, representing the church's maturation during Christendom, rather than its deviation from earlier and healthier traditions. Others may compromise our witness and jeopardise our ability to engage sensitively in mission in post-Christendom.

---

[14] Alan Roxburgh, *The Missionary Congregation, Leadership, and Liminality* (Harrisburg: Trinity Press, 1997), 218.
[15] Wright, *Disavowing Constantine*, 4.

We should identify these vestiges and assess their significance. We need not indulge in mindless iconoclasm or adopt a postmodern 'hermeneutic of scepticism' that interprets everything in the worst possible light. But we will be suspicious of vested interests and historic privileges, sensitive to others in a plural society and guided by a 'hermeneutic of justice', not a 'hermeneutic of order'. In post-Christendom, which vestiges are unjust or inappropriate, and how do we deal with these? What follows is not exhaustive but indicates the scope and diversity of vestiges in Britain.[16]

Ecclesiastical vestiges

- The Church of England is the established church, acknowledging the monarch as supreme governor and claiming official status by its very name, which by implication excludes other denominations.
- The self-identity of the non-established Church of Scotland is of a national church.[17]
- The monarch appoints Anglican bishops, on the recommendation of the prime minister, from a shortlist of candidates the church prepares. The state can veto episcopal appointments.
- Church leaders participate in state ceremonies, during which they engage in acts of worship (although increasingly representatives of other faiths also participate).

---

[16] Some have parallels in other nations, but examining these would make this section too complex.

[17] In 2001 The 'Church without Walls' report offered a trenchant critique of Christendom assumptions undergirding the church, and proposals for transformation. See www.churchwithoutwalls.org.uk

- Some decisions of the Church of England's General Synod require state endorsement (the requisite majority of the 'three houses' approved the decision to ordain women, but this needed ratification by both Houses of Parliament).
- The parish system symbolises and implements the ubiquity of the established church, regardless of the presence of other congregations.
- The Church of England is legally obliged to provide marriage and funeral services. Clergy of many denominations act as state registrars.
- The Church of England is a major landowner and, despite falling income and rising costs, a very wealthy institution.
- The Chi-Rho symbol, Constantine's labarum, adorns many churches and chapels instead of the cross.
- The cross is associated in many communities with conquest and coercion, not suffering and self-giving love.
- Many church buildings contain military paraphernalia, including regimental flags, plaques commemorating war casualties and soldiers' graves.
- Most denominations endorse the 'just war' theory.
- Although many denominations have more members elsewhere than in Europe, representatives of historic Christendom nations dominate their structures and culture.
- Many denominations and agencies maintain structures that perpetuate outdated 'sending nations' and 'mission fields' concepts.
- Infant baptism is still widely practised (not only in the state church), but there are concerns about indiscriminate christening.

- Leadership structures in many newer denominations mirror Christendom arrangements (albeit with different titles).
- The dominance of monologue sermons is evident in all denominations (with longer sermons in newer churches).
- The popularity of tithing in newer churches is encouraging Anglicans and Catholics to return to an abandoned Christendom practice.
- Church discipline is not taught in theological colleges, congregations are not equipped to practise this and attempts to exercise discipline are frequently ineffective or authoritarian.
- Inherited or chosen architectural styles of church buildings maintain aspects of Christendom ecclesiology. Many resemble lecture halls or theatres, disabling multi-voiced worship.
- Special clothes continue to designate a clerical caste with special powers and privileges.

Social vestiges

- The monarch's coronation takes place in Westminster Abbey and involves senior church leaders, who present a Bible as a 'rule for the whole life and government of Christian Princes', anoint the monarch with oil with reference to Old Testament kings, present a sword for the monarch to 'protect the holy Church of God' and bestow a ring with a ruby cross, urging the monarch to be the 'defender of Christ's religion'.
- The monarch swears to 'maintain the Laws of God and the true profession of the gospel'; 'maintain in the United Kingdom the Protestant Reformed Religion established by law'; 'maintain and preserve

inviolably the settlement of the Church of England, and the doctrine, worship, discipline, and government thereof, as by law established in England'; and 'preserve unto the Bishops and Clergy of England, and to the Churches there committed to their charge, all such rights and privileges, as by law do or shall appertain to them or any of them.'

- The National Anthem combines unquestioning support for the monarch with prayer for military success.[18]
- Coins carry inscriptions committing the monarch to defend the (Anglican) faith (D.G.REG.F.D[19]).
- The Union Flag comprises crosses of St George, St Andrew and St Patrick, the 'patron saints' of England, Scotland and Ireland.
- Remembrance Day ceremonies offer prayers of thanksgiving for military success.
- State-funded chaplains serve in the armed forces and accompany them to war, implicitly supporting their actions.
- Christian prayers take place daily in both Houses of Parliament.
- Two archbishops and twenty-four diocesan bishops are 'Lords Spiritual' sitting in the House of Lords.
- The English legal system includes 'canon law', which governs church affairs, and ecclesiastical courts.
- Anyone on the parish electoral role (whatever their religious views) may vote to elect churchwardens.

---

[18] Another verse continues: 'O Lord our God arise, scatter our enemies and make them fall; confound their politics, frustrate their knavish tricks; on Thee our hopes we fix; God save us all.'

[19] *Dei Gratia Regina [Rex] Fidei Defensor* – 'by the grace of God Queen [King], defender of the faith.'

- The launching of ships involves a 'christening' ceremony, invoking God's blessing on the vessel.
- Blasphemy laws (though rarely invoked) protect only the Church of England, not other denominations or religions.
- Churches enjoy the presumption their activities are charitable and so receive significant tax benefits.
- Schools must provide daily acts of collective worship 'wholly or mainly of a broadly Christian character'.[20]
- School, college and bank holidays are planned around or associated primarily with the Christmas and Easter festivals.
- Despite continuing erosion, there are still restrictions on economic and social activities on Sundays.
- Use of oaths in the courts and legal processes (although affirmation is now available) remains normal.
- People in various institutions swear oaths of allegiance. Members of the police force, for instance, swear oaths in an annual service.

How should we assess these leftovers? Are they worth bothering about? Should we simply accept them as aspects of our cultural heritage? Do any have continuing value and legitimacy in post-Christendom? Should we divest our churches of such vestiges? Should we cling to residual privileges, acquiesce without resistance to their eventual removal or campaign for their abolition in cases where

---

[20] The 1996 Education Act, Section 386(2). The following subsection states acts of worship should reflect 'the broad traditions of Christian belief without being distinctive of any particular Christian denomination.'

legislation is required? What theological principles under-gird our strategy? We might ask the following questions:

- Is the vestige merely anachronistic or is an issue of justice involved?
- Are there explicit biblical challenges (albeit requiring interpretation) to this practice?
- Does a vestige offend others, and how does this affect the church's work and witness?
- How would we feel as a minority community if another established religion insisted on this practice?
- How much time and energy is required to effect change, and will the outcome justify this?
- What alternative practice might replace a vestige, and how helpful would this be for church or society?
- What of value would be lost if a vestige were eradicated?
- Would the removal of a vestige result merely in a more secular culture or a culture where Christian witness is less compromised and more effective?
- How might the reputation of the church (and the gospel) be enhanced by firm adherence to traditional practices?
- How might its reputation be sullied by futile attempts to retain privileges being prised from us?
- What does resistance to tackling certain vestiges indicate about the mindset of those who resist?

We may respond differently to different vestiges. Some are ancient practices adopted from paganism through indiscriminate syncretism or attempts to contextualise the gospel; others were derived from the Bible (primarily the Old Testament) and adapted for Christendom. Some flowed from the alliance of church and state and the privileges entailed; others reflect the permeation of Christianity into European culture. We can eradicate some through internal church decisions; others need legislation to remove or change. Some will involve minor adjustments; others might have serious economic, political and social consequences.

There has already been progress towards ameliorating the effects of some vestiges, as with the requirement of oaths in the courts. It seems perverse to require witnesses to swear by a God they may not believe in to speak truthfully lest this God strikes them down, which nobody in the court believes will happen – and to do this holding a book whose authority they may not accept and in which some detect prohibitions of oaths! The introduction of a right to 'affirm' is welcome (although those choosing this are often made to feel awkward), but maybe we should encourage further reform to abolish oaths entirely.

On some issues there have been attempts to strike a balance between introducing change and maintaining traditions. The 1996 Education Act, while requiring schools to ensure acts of worship are 'broadly Christian', does not require Anglican liturgy and, like previous legislation, permits withdrawal of pupils from acts of worship. The section on religious instruction reads: 'Every agreed syllabus shall reflect the fact that the religious traditions in Great Britain are in the main Christian whilst taking account of the teaching and practices of the other principal religions represented in Great Britain.'[21] Although some criticise this for conceding too much to other faiths and others for conceding too little, it seems reasonable in this transitional period. Given Christianity's pervasive influence on British culture, prioritising this helps children understand their cultural heritage. But prescribing 'broadly Christian' worship indefinitely in post-Christendom is neither feasible nor desirable.

---

[21] The 1996 Education Act, Section 375(3).

On other issues there is increasing momentum for change. Archaic blasphemy laws will surely be superseded by measures protecting all faith communities from those inciting religious hatred, removing the injustice in a plural society of favouring one community. The offence of blasphemy originated in Luther's use of this term (rather than 'heresy') to persecute Catholics, Jews, Anabaptists and peasants.[22] Those who resist changing blasphemy provisions may feel a beleaguered minority today but should feel some discomfort knowing such laws were used to persecute minorities in the past. Ignorance of history may mean Christians supporting policies and practices that injured their forebears.

Removing some vestiges will require enormous persistence, as the long campaign to abolish tithing demonstrates.[23] There is growing support for disestablishment among Anglicans, although many still vehemently oppose this. The House of Lords debated this for the first time in 2002, and several senior church leaders favour severing links with the state.[24] This would remove many vestiges, but so entwined are church and state, a decade of parliamentary work could be required for full disestablishment. As this is not high on the political agenda, whittling away at links may be more effective than full-scale assault. One possibility under discussion is detaching the church

---

[22] Richard Webster, *A Brief History of Blasphemy: Liberalism, Censorship and 'The Satanic Verses'* (Southwold: The Orwell Press, 1990).

[23] Murray, *Beyond Tithing*, passim.

[24] See Colin Buchanan, *Cut the Connection: Disestablishment and the Church of England* (London: Darton, Longman & Todd, 1994); Kenneth Leech, *Setting the Church of England Free: The Case for Disestablishment* (Croydon: Jubilee Group, 2001); and < www.disestablish.co.uk >.

from the monarchy but retaining its established status. Other creative ideas are needed. But disestablishment of a state church can be achieved, as the uncoupling of the Lutheran Church from the Swedish state in 2000 demonstrates. And there are many precedents for non-established Anglicanism (including Wales, Scotland and Ireland): the Church of England is the only established church in the worldwide Anglican Communion.

But eradicating Christendom vestiges is threatening to Christians desperate to retain remaining privileges. Recent campaigns have tried to persuade a post-Christendom society that Christians should continue to dictate how it operates. The 'Keep Sunday Special' campaign achieved temporary success before its inevitable defeat.[25] There were positive aspects of this campaign, which publicised probable consequences of liberalised Sunday trading and licensing regulations – pressure on family life, loss of rest, exploitation of workers and growing consumerism. But it was marred by its reliance on a Christendom-oriented interpretation of the Old Testament, its blatant appeal to Christians' self-interest ('your Sunday is under threat') and its susceptibility to derision for presenting an utterly predictable reaction to the threat of forfeiting a Christendom vestige.[26]

Such campaigns demonstrate resistance to change is not restricted to members of the established church. Indeed, many Anglicans are troubled by the church–state link and are more sensitive to issues of justice in a plural society than

---

[25] The 1994 Sunday Trading Act ended any possibility of retaining the traditional Sunday ethos, although the campaign continues. See < www.jubilee-centre.org/kss >.

[26] Stuart Murray, 'Make Wednesday Special', *Third Way* (October 1991), 26–7. This attempt to raise these issues produced incomprehension from a representative of the campaign.

members of other churches. Senior Anglicans have been more critical of government policies than colleagues in other denominations. Within most denominations some want to preserve privileges (or regain lost ground), while others welcome the removal of Christendom vestiges. Nor does theological or political liberalism necessarily locate someone on the side of reform: some liberals support establishment as ensuring religion and politics are not disconnected.

Despite their historic opposition to establishment, many Free Church Christians are 'vicarious establishmentarians': although they do not belong to the established church, they regard it as a bulwark against the incursions of secularism and other religions. In September 2002, a letter to the *Baptist Times* argued: 'The Christian church faces many challenges. On the one hand there is the growing secularism which may lead to the disestablishment of the Anglican Church and a consequent weakening of Christianity as the dominant faith, and on the other hand, the rise of other faith communities.' Oblivious of his Baptist heritage, he represents many Free Church Christians dismayed by proposals for disestablishment. He identifies three threats: the philosophy of secularism, the weakening of Christianity as the dominant faith and the growth of other faith communities. His argument is clear: an established church guarantees Christian dominance and benefits all Christians.

This letter suggests that if the Church of England is eventually disestablished, many Christians in other denominations will face a serious identity crisis. Not only is their Free Church identity not rooted in theological convictions; it appears parasitic on establishment. The disintegration of Christendom has produced a society much closer to what the dissidents demanded, but unless the dissident tradition is reclaimed more wholeheartedly than in most denominations, disestablishment may be liberating for Anglicans but disorientating for Free Church Christians. Rediscovering an identity that is more than 'not established' is crucial for Free Churches in post-Christendom.

Resistance to dismantling Christendom vestiges pervades the churches, but there may also be unexpected disquiet elsewhere, though this may diminish as post-Christendom develops. Many today are deeply critical of Christendom, which encourages us to dismantle its relics; but residual affection for the trappings of Christendom may hinder their removal. Church buildings are more attractive for weddings than registry offices and impart something 'spiritual' to the occasion. The solemn and colourful participation of archbishops enhances state pageantry. Closure of, or alterations to, church buildings can provoke hostility from local residents, who never attend services but feel the building symbolises something in the community. Many still turn to churches in times of local or national distress, reminding us we are in transition from Christendom to post-Christendom.

How do we interpret this? Should we retain some vestiges and encourage those who approach churches occasionally for rites of passage or public ceremonies to move beyond 'folk Christianity' into discipleship? Or should we draw sharper lines between 'church' and 'world', discouraging civic and sentimental Christianity? There are strategic and theological issues. What will we gain or lose by providing services for the diminishing, but still substantial, number who do not participate regularly but expect churches to be there in emergencies?

We may also be intrigued – or disturbed – by evidence of support for establishment from some Jewish and Muslim community leaders in Britain! Why do they urge continuation of preferential treatment for Christianity? The main reason is fear that the only alternative is a secular state that might become less tolerant than this vestigial Christendom arrangement. We must consider this if we propose disestablishment and avoid naïve assumptions about the tolerance or neutrality achievable in a society based on secularism. But it is unlikely the anaemic form of Christianity embodied in the Christendom vestiges will offer lasting protection against secularism, intolerance or social fragmentation.

The Christendom Mindset

Christendom lasted a long time. For centuries its assumptions, spirit, values, priorities and expectations permeated church and society, shaping the institutions and processes that sustained the system and the mindset of all who lived within Christendom. This mindset – a way of thinking, judging issues and responding to situations that are both conscious and reflexive – comprises Christendom's most significant legacy. Even if the church/state partnership is dissolved and the vestiges are removed, Christendom thinking will persist. And if the vestiges were not restricted to the established church, the mindset is stronger in younger denominations and churches, blissfully unaware of Christendom values and assumptions (dressed up in radical phraseology) permeating their theology, ethics, structures and expectations. The Christendom mindset includes:

- Orientation towards maintaining (but perhaps tweaking) the status quo rather than advocating radical and disturbing change.
- Wanting to control history and bring in God's kingdom (even coercively) rather than trusting the future to God.
- Assuming Christians would govern nations more justly and effectively than others or that having more

Christians in influential positions (especially in politics) would be beneficial.[27]

- Over-emphasising church and internal ecclesial issues at the expense of God's mission and kingdom.
- A 'moral majority' stance on ethical issues, assuming the right of churches to instruct the behaviour of those beyond the church.
- A punitive rather than restorative approach to issues of justice and support for capital punishment as 'biblical'.
- Disgruntlement that Christian festivals (particularly Christmas and Easter) are no longer accorded the spiritual significance they once enjoyed.
- When reading the Bible, identifying naturally with the perspective of the rich and powerful.
- Readily finding analogies between Old Testament Israel and Britain (or America) as a 'Christian nation', reapplying biblical prophecies.
- Confusion about the relationship between patriotism and ultimate loyalty to God's kingdom and the transnational Christian community.
- A 'mainstream' interpretation of church history that marginalises the laity, dissident movements, women and the poor.
- Euro-centric theology that marginalises other perspectives on mission, church and biblical interpretation.
- Inattentiveness to the criticisms of those outraged by the historic association of Christianity with patriarchy, warfare, injustice and patronage.

---

[27] See further Jonathan Bartley, *The Subversive Manifesto: Lifting the Lid on God's Political Agenda* (Oxford: Bible Reading Fellowship, 2003).

- Using 'spiritual warfare' language without reflecting on issues of violence and insensitivity to its effect on users and observers.
- A latent persecution mentality that lacks theological or ethical objections to imposing beliefs or behaviour on others.
- Partiality for respectability, top-down mission and hierarchical church government.
- Predilection for large congregations that support a 'professional' standard of ministry and exercise influence on local power structures.
- Approaches to evangelism that rely excessively on 'come' rather than 'go' initiatives.
- Thinking the Christian story is still known, understood and widely believed within society.
- Reluctance to conclude Christendom vestiges inoculate rather than evangelise.
- Celebrating survey evidence that seventy per cent of the population claim to be Christian, as if such notional Christianity is significant.
- Assuming churchgoing is a normal social activity and that most people feel comfortable in church buildings and services.
- Attitudes towards church buildings that imply these are focal points of God's presence.
- Orientation towards maintenance rather than mission in ministerial training, congregational focus and financial priorities.
- Proliferation of church activities that are inappropriate and exhausting for marginal communities in a mission context.
- Preferring authoritative pronouncements, preaching and monologue over dialogue, conversation and consensus.

- Pontificating and lecturing, often in a sanctimonious tone that understandably irritates others.
- Discomfort among church leaders if members ask questions or express doubts or disagreement.
- Performance-oriented services and the tendency of short-lived multi-voiced developments to revert to the default mono-voiced position.
- Solemnity, formality and even morbidity when breaking bread and sharing wine in contrast to the joyful and domestic informality of the early churches.
- Despite decades of decline and marginalisation, triumphalist theology and language (especially in our hymnody).
- Consequentialist and utilitarian approaches to ethics, more concerned with outcomes than right motives and means.[28]
- Attitudes to other faith communities that vary from opposition to tolerance but assume Christianity should be accorded centrality and privileges.
- Expectations that imminent revival will restore the fortunes and influence of the churches in society.

These attitudes, priorities and reflexes are not all equally apparent in all churches! Today, most Christians vigorously reject some of these aspects of the Christendom mindset; other aspects find ready defenders. But many appear in books, articles, sermons, conferences, songs, programmes and conversations. Some are rarely expressed openly and are instinctive, not conscious; but challenging them uncovers strong feelings and indicates the continuing influence of Christendom thought patterns. Stanley Hauerwas concludes: 'Constantinianism is a hard habit to

---

[28] Yoder, *Priestly*, 135–47.

break.'[29] The Christendom mindset is the 'default' position, which we must subject to persistent scrutiny. As with the vestiges, we need discernment about which reflexes should be valued and retained and which jettisoned or revised in post-Christendom.

The Christendom mindset is also found beyond the churches. This is understandable, for our roots are in Christendom even though our society has largely rejected this heritage. Thus, New Testament phrases intrude occasionally into conversations, though often interpreted in ways that reflect Christendom filtering rather than their biblical meaning. Especially poignant are 'turn the other cheek' and 'go the second mile' – examples of Jesus' counter-cultural teaching now diluted to imply passivity in difficult situations.[30] Discussions of ethical issues refer, often unconsciously, to Christendom categories and terminology; for example, the language of 'just war' (or 'crusade').

Surveys consistently indicate a large majority in Britain believe in God and identify themselves as Christians. 'Default Anglicanism' is the preferred option of any without active church connections; many still equate 'Christian' with 'British' or use this term to differentiate themselves from other faith communities. Some 'social churchgoing' persists and large suburban churches may still have a (declining and ageing) fringe of occasional attenders. Furthermore, some regard the churches not with hostility but with a combination of indifference and gratitude; they are there when needed. Grace Davie refers to 'vicarious religion' and a 'latent sense of belonging': 'Europeans, by and large, regard their churches as public utilities ... this is the

---

[29] Hauerwas, *After Christendom?*, 18.
[30] For alternative readings, see Walter Wink, *Engaging the Powers: Discernment and Resistance in a World of Domination* (Minneapolis: Fortress Press, 1992), 175–93.

real legacy of a state church history and inextricably linked to the concept of vicariousness.'[31]

Post-Christendom is not pre-Christendom revisited. Centuries of tradition undergird this perception of the church's role in society. Nor is it entirely obvious whether this latent sense of belonging should be discouraged or nurtured. Whether this tenuous link between the churches and post-Christendom society will survive as memories of the Christian story fade is doubtful, but some argue it should not be severed.[32]

But we should not ignore those whose hostility towards Christianity results from their knowledge of Christendom and the church's reluctance to admit and repudiate dark aspects of its heritage. Nor should we discount the resistance of those who know little of this history but have inherited perceptions of the church, often expressed in familiar phrases, reflecting Christendom practices, such as 'the church is only after your money' (an echo of the tithing system).[33]

More problematic is the assertion Britain is a Christian nation. This is used by church members to justify preferential treatment, by other faith communities to criticise the standard of Christianity practised by British people and by fascist groups to advocate excluding 'non-Christians' from Britain! This component of the Christendom mindset should be challenged vigorously and persistently.

---

[31] Davie, *Europe*, 43–4. See further Grace Davie, *Religion in Britain since 1945: Believing Without Belonging* (Oxford: Blackwell, 1994).
[32] Hugh Montefiore, *Credible Christianity: The Gospel in Contemporary Society* (London: Mowbray, 1993), 175.
[33] Recent research reveals considerable hostility. See Nick Spencer, *Beyond Belief: Barriers and Bridges to Faith Today* (London: LICC, 2003).

Reflecting on these Christendom thought patterns, we can ask similar questions to those used to assess responses to the vestiges. There are strategic issues to consider as we ponder whether they repulse or attract more people, but there are also theological and ethical issues. Are these assumptions, priorities and reflexes truly Christian?

Responding to the Christendom Legacy

There is also the larger issue of how we evaluate the end of Christendom and from what perspective we engage with its legacy. There are several options:

Denying

Despite accumulating evidence, many Christians are in denial regarding the demise of Christendom. They perceive this as a temporary phenomenon that might yet be reversed (and celebrate scattered instances of renewed support for traditional patterns). Church leaders preach, pastor congregations and organise conferences as though nothing had changed, but many are working harder with less impact. Some long ago abandoned efforts to engage with a changing society, taking refuge in churches offering stability and the comfort of familiarity. Others urge whole-hearted revisiting of once-effective forms of mission and church, confident 'gospel rallies' can turn the tide. Some pursue strategies to recover ground they refuse to concede is irretrievably lost: Rodney Clapp calls this 'retrenchment' and presents conservative and liberal examples.[34] Others are still strategising as if European churches were definitive and the

---

[34] Clapp, *Peculiar People*, 20–1.

old model of world mission made sense.[35] Many hope and pray for revival (a backward-looking concept steeped in Christendom thinking), assuming the divine strategy includes resuscitating a dying era.

Defending

Not all believe the Christendom shift resulted in disastrous distortions of Christianity or that Christendom should be cheerfully abandoned.[36] They accuse its critics of capitulating to secularism and colluding with assaults on Christianity: attacking the historical roots of Christianity (and Western culture) undermines church and society. Denouncing Christendom, they argue, is easy but misguided: not a daring critique of a corrupt system still enjoying wide support, but tame submission to liberal orthodoxy, abandoning attempts to present Christianity as public truth, and retreat into whatever private space secular and postmodern society allows. The Christendom shift was a legitimate and inevitable development from pre-Christendom. Although its historical expression was marred, its achievements outweigh its deficiencies, and the best hope for the future is a reconstituted Christendom. Those arguing thus rightly note that the decline of Christian faith has had negative consequences in European society. They imply the alternative to Christendom is conniving

---

[35] David Smith, *Mission After Christendom* (London: Darton, Longman & Todd, 2003), 6–7.

[36] See Aidan Nichols, *Christendom Awake: On Re-energising the Church in Culture* (Edinburgh: T. & T. Clark, 1999); Oliver O'Donovan, *Desire of the Nations: Rediscovering the Roots of Political Theology* (Cambridge: Cambridge University Press, 1999); Paul Avis, *Church, State and Establishment* (London: SPCK, 2000).

with the privatisation and decline of Christian faith in Western culture. They regard denunciations of Christendom as sterile and defeatist, offering no alternative vision of church and mission.

This critique demonstrates how locked into Christendom thinking we are, unable to imagine different ways of engaging with culture. But objections to Christendom were not pioneered by liberals and secularists but by medieval dissidents, for very different reasons. These and the Anabaptist movement explored other ways of engaging with society. The dissident tradition must be reconfigured for post-Christendom, but its objections and alternative strategies are more pertinent than Christendom's defenders recognise.

Dismissing

Some accept the transition to post-Christendom and realise adjustments are needed, but respond pragmatically rather than theologically. This may help reconfigure the church and its mission. But failing to acknowledge the dark side of its history or investigate the deeper legacy of the Christendom mindset evades moral and spiritual issues, leaving us ill prepared for challenges ahead. Accepting Christendom's demise without questioning the legitimacy of a system many perceive as oppressive and corrupt surely dismisses the past too lightly.[37] The end of Christendom means, in the long run, *imposing Christianity does not work*; only if we celebrate this and move beyond dismissing Christendom to a more repentant response will we be truly free to develop a different strategy.

Dismissing Christendom also risks dismissing how individuals and communities feel about the passing of an era.

---

[37] A serious deficiency in the otherwise helpful writings of Mead, *Once and Future* and Jackson, *Hope*.

Regarding the Christendom shift as illegitimate does not mean writing off everything that happened in the mainstream during the next fifteen centuries! Nor does it preclude grief. Brueggemann insists: 'congregations must be, in intentional ways, *communities of honest sadness*, naming the losses'.[38] And Nigel Wright concludes: 'Christendom's vision of society has its own coherence ... It was not all bad and, when compared with its alternatives or replacements, there is much that could be said in favour of it. But the fact is that it has been lost and will never be recovered.'[39]

David Smith offers a similar analysis but invites us to move beyond grief to hopeful anticipation: 'The long era of Western Christendom is over ... Yet even as we despair at what has been lost and grieve over the fragmented and weakened condition of the churches, can we begin to catch the indications that God is inviting us to participate in something quite new?'[40] Merely dismissing Christendom will not enable us to make this transition.

Dissociating

Christians in new churches sometimes suggest these issues are relevant only in older denominations. Explicitly or implicitly they dissociate themselves from Christendom, assuming they are not influenced by its legacy. Especially in movements energised by 'restoring New Testament Christianity', interest in church history over the past 2000 years is limited. The impression given is that little of significance

---

[38] Brueggemann, *Cadences*, 4 (italics his).
[39] Nigel Wright, *New Baptists, New Agenda* (Carlisle: Paternoster Press, 2002), 96–7.
[40] David Smith, *Crying in the Wilderness: Evangelism and Mission in Today's Culture* (Carlisle: Paternoster Press, 2000), 78.

occurred between the end of Acts and 1970, and none of it is relevant today. Consequently, many are oblivious to how their attitudes, structures, expectations, songs and sermons exhibit the Christendom mindset. Most are less prepared for post-Christendom than older churches whose leaders understand the issues.

In some newer churches there is growing interest in church history, although this is often selective and superficial. Uncritical and eclectic pillaging of liturgical resources, forms of spirituality and approaches to mission may be enriching and offer welcome alternatives to repetitive and unreflective church life; but this can mean Christendom perspectives are unwittingly imbibed. There are rich (Catholic, Orthodox, Reformed, Celtic, monastic and other) resources from Christendom, but a 'pick-and-mix' approach, though quintessentially postmodern and initially attractive, is not the best way to proceed. Some have discovered the dissidents (usually via Anabaptism) and claim them as spiritual and ecclesial forebears; but this identification is often too easy and demonstrates little understanding of the issues at stake.

We may choose to listen to Donatus and Pelagius rather than Augustine and Ambrose, to Valdes and Wyclif rather than popes and inquisitors, to Marpeck and Menno rather than Luther and Calvin. We may sense greater kinship with those on the margins than those at the centre (although we will probably find individuals in various locations to whom we are drawn). Some groups may inspire us more than others. But we cannot dissociate ourselves from family members we dislike. The whole story is our heritage. There will be incidents that grieve and appal us and individuals or institutions we wish had played no part in the story. We may want to disown these elements and question whether they were in any sense Christian. But unless they were disowned at the time as unchristian (which mainly applied to dissidents we may want to retain!), this is hard to sustain. Certainly critics of the church will not let us off so lightly.

Demonising

Our analysis of Christendom's history and legacy could tempt us to demonise those involved. In the darker recesses of the story undoubtedly lurk dreadful acts of cruelty, barbarism, violence, oppression and inhumanity: 'demonic' may be the only adequate description of such behaviour. But Christendom also nurtured remarkable expressions of creativity, beauty, compassion, intellectual prowess and spirituality. Within its institutions were wonderful saints and dedicated disciples, rogues and charlatans, murderers and sadists. Demonising Christendom and all involved in it is unhelpful: however we, with the benefit of hindsight, evaluate the Christendom shift, many of our forebears believed they were serving Christ and seeking God's kingdom as much when they tortured heretics, fought in crusades and imposed morality as when they translated the Bible into the vernacular, wrote inspiring liturgies and ministered to the poor. Demonising obscures much that was good (in motive and action); it also hinders us from recognising our own darkness, mixed motives and complicity in structures of injustice.

We must also resist the temptation to idealise dissident movements. Earlier chapters offer an affirming interpretation of these and of some individuals traditionally labelled heretics. But communities under pressure tend towards legalism and extremism, both for community survival and because they lack time to explore nuances. Judgemental attitudes and perfectionist traits are unattractive features of dissident groups. Many consisted mainly of poor and uneducated people, with neither ability nor leisure to produce theological works. Their contribution was to protest and explore alternative possibilities rather than develop comprehensive approaches to ethics or ecclesiology. Nor did they always live up to their own ideals. We need to be as discriminating in our assessment of this tradition as of the Christendom mainstream.

Disavowing

Nigel Wright suggests 'disavowing' the history and legacy of Christendom.[41] This is the most appropriate response. Disavowing differs from demonising or dissociating ourselves from Christendom. It is more nuanced, charitable towards those who endorsed the Christendom shift and finding treasures in Christendom, but assessing the shift and the system it created as fundamentally flawed and choosing no longer to defend, justify or maintain this. Disavowal requires repentance and humility. Christendom reveals the church as sign and counter-sign of the kingdom – faithful and corrupt, entrenched but capable of renewal. Summarising the church's horrendous record through the centuries and regretting official statements that ignore its sinfulness, Hugh Montefiore writes: 'The church has often betrayed its title deeds ... Those who have a high doctrine of the church must reckon with the grim reality of its actual history.'[42] Disavowal means telling the truth about our history.

However we evaluate the benefits and drawbacks of Christendom, disavowal means repudiating this way of thinking. It means facing forward into a new era, not looking wistfully backwards, celebrating rather than mourning Christendom's demise. It means endorsing the judgement of Herbert Butterfield:

---

[41] Wright, *Disavowing Constantine*, in his discussion of John Howard Yoder.
[42] Montefiore, *Credible*, 172–3.

After a period of fifteen hundred years or so we can just about begin to say that at last no man is now a Christian because of government compulsion, or because it is the way to procure favor at court, or because it is necessary to qualify for public office, or because public opinion demands conformity, or because he would lose customers if he did not go to church, or even because habit and intellectual indolence keep the mind in the appointed groove. This fact makes the present day the most important and the most exhilarating period in the history of Christianity for fifteen hundred years.[43]

Disentangling

With disavowal as our basic approach, we can reflect further on the vestiges and reflexes. The connections between church and state, church and nation, church and society, church and culture are deep-rooted and complex. The task of unravelling and disentangling will not be completed quickly. We must assess priorities, asking which connections raise critical theological and ethical problems, which seriously impede the church's mission in post-Christendom and which require most re-education in the churches. Some vestiges are freestanding and can be removed easily. Pulling at other threads will reveal complications. And we will not want to cause unnecessary damage or pain, or confuse what must be excised with what we can retain.

Action is needed in many places – denominational headquarters, training institutions, local congregations, publishing houses, home groups and conversations. Hearts and minds must be won, re-reflexing us, weaning us off Christendom thought processes, helping us move forward

---

[43] Herbert Butterfield, *Christianity and History* (New York: Charles Scribner's Sons, 1949), 135.

in an uncertain period without props we have relied on, and enabling us to find a path between despair and unrealistic expectations. We are still in the twilight years of Christendom and cannot yet see clearly what lies ahead; many decisions will be provisional. And we cannot do this in a detached forum: in a period of decline we cannot disengage from other mission tasks to disentangle the effects of Christendom.

Deconstructing

Does this mean our primary response to the Christendom legacy is deconstruction? Yes and no.

Deconstruction cannot be the ultimate goal. A criticism of dissident movements is that they were better deconstructors than constructors. They 'knew' what was wrong with the system, but had less to say about alternatives. This criticism is unfair historically. These groups were marginalised and persecuted; they had no incentive for developing alternative policies or any way to test recommendations they might have made. But it applies in our situation, where Christendom is collapsing, opening up opportunities to explore different approaches. We will for the foreseeable future be a minority church in a plural society, but we will have as much freedom as others to advocate economic, social, political, ethical and cultural policies.

What will we advocate? How might we want to guide the reconstruction of post-Christendom culture? If Christendom is not how to incarnate gospel values in society, what is? If partnership between church and state is not how we should participate in politics and work for the transformation of society in light of our vision of God's kingdom of justice, peace and joy, what is? And if there is renewed interest in the story of Jesus in the years ahead and opportunities for greater influence, how will we respond? Some pose this challenge: if Christians again comprised a majority, what responsibility should we assume for society? This, after all, was the situation in which fifth-century Christians found themselves and is becoming the case elsewhere in the world. If we are not to consign the church to perpetual social insignificance, what alternative is there to reinventing Christendom and taking control again?

These are legitimate and probing questions, which point us beyond deconstruction to developing an alternative strategy for the church in post-Christendom. Some of them will be explored in the following chapters.

But while deconstruction cannot be our complete response to the Christendom legacy, it may be our primary response in this transitional period, for three reasons. First, trying to rebuild is unwise until we have dismantled the old structures. Superficial disavowal of the Christendom legacy and half-hearted repentance for the compromise, suffering and marred witness of that era will undermine efforts to form an authentic post-Christendom strategy. Thorough deconstruction may need to be followed by a pause for reflection before attempting reconstruction. Second, building new structures in a period of cultural turbulence may be unhelpful, especially if we accord them more than provisional significance. Tentative and experimental ways of proceeding may be more appropriate than grand schemes. Third, suspicion of our motives and expectations will linger until memories of Christendom fade. It should eventually be possible to make truth claims about Jesus Christ without implying these should be received uncritically or that other faith communities should not make their own truth claims. But memories of imposition and cultural imperialism mean that for some time yet many will be deeply suspicious of such claims.

Disembarking

Post-Christendom is our future. We may not yet be able to describe what this means for our witness to Jesus, community life or engagement with culture, let alone build structures to facilitate these things. But we must be clear that we cannot simply continue as before. The imagery of the sinking of the Titanic is overused, but it is as if we are being urged to leave the apparent security of a still-impressive but doomed liner and entrust ourselves to a tiny lifeboat bobbing up and down on the waves in the darkness. Disembarking from Christendom will require courage, and some may choose instead to rearrange the deckchairs once more, but hope for the future lies in the vulnerability of the lifeboat, wherever it may carry us.

8

Post-Christendom: Mission

We know of few 'missionaries' in pre-Christendom. Mission depended primarily on the witness of unknown Christians – countless acts of kindness, family and friendship connections, provocative discipleship and significant conversations. Evangelism was a lifestyle, not a specialist activity. The Christendom shift fractured this integration of church and mission. Mission became the task of civil and ecclesiastical authorities, specialist organisations and monastic orders. Churches became maintenance-oriented. In post-Christendom we will need to recover the pre-Christendom paradigm.

This chapter examines the implications of the demise of Christendom for mission in Western culture.[1] What approach to evangelism is appropriate in post-Christendom? How can churches pursue social transformation without exercising control? What type of political engagement is feasible for marginal churches?

Mission in Late Christendom

Although Christendom churches were maintenance-oriented, mission persisted and found fresh expression in

---

[1] On the implications for global mission, see Smith, *Mission*.

the past four centuries. Christianity spread into new areas and penetrated further into societies already officially Christian. It expanded beyond historic Christendom and became global; and there have been mission initiatives, evangelistic and cultural, within Christendom. What is the legacy of mission in late Christendom?

Mission beyond Christendom

Catholics, Reformers and Anabaptists adopted different perspectives on mission and followed divergent trajectories. Maintenance-oriented Reformers, assuming Europe was Christian, opposed mission-oriented Anabaptists, who believed Europe needed evangelising. Catholics, meanwhile, amidst the fragmentation of Christendom, were embarking on a new mission strategy: explorers were discovering a 'new world' and Catholic monarchs quickly recognised the potential for conquest and mission.

Soldiers and priests accompanied these explorers, instructed by their royal sponsors to extend European authority over these new realms and convert the inhabitants. Nobody doubted these were virgin territories, ripe for incorporation into Christendom, needing to be civilised by adopting European culture. For European Christendom was the most powerful civilisation on earth – economically, politically, technologically, militarily – and its divinely favoured Christian culture was self-evidently superior to native cultures. Europeans were responsible for evangelising and civilising other cultures, by force if necessary. Mission beyond Christendom meant exporting Christendom.

The story of the conquest and conversion of the Americas is complex – high adventure, bravery and nobility jostle with brutality, cruelty and inhumanity. Versions from the perspective of the vanquished require revision of popular accounts of Christopher Columbus and his successors.[2] Typically, history from the underside and the margins looks different: the Americas were invaded, pillaged and raped, not discovered. Even the conquistadors' records furnish abundant evidence of Christendom-style mission in a new context – which they report sure of divine approval. The smashing of idols and temples, inducements to convert, sword-point baptisms, top-down pressure and other accoutrements of crusade and inquisition all reappear. Richard Fletcher comments: 'The techniques and experiments of the thirteenth and fourteenth centuries furnished models and precedents and warnings (not much heeded) for the missionaries of the fifteenth and sixteenth centuries. The spiritual conquest of Prussia and Livonia points ahead to that of Mexico and Peru.'[3]

This 'spiritual conquest' was impressive if measured in Christendom categories: mass baptisms, sometimes thousands a day, as millions of Indians across Central and South America were incorporated into churches built to European designs. As in medieval Europe, some deplored the use of violence to spread the gospel: well-known examples are Bartolome de las Casas and Fray Antonio de Montesinos. Despite such protests and other more positive aspects, the conversion of the Americas added significantly to the Christendom legacy of coercive mission and cultural imposition.

These exploits were celebrated in Catholic Europe and used in the propaganda war against Protestants, who seemed uninterested in mission. David Smith reports their defensive response:

---

[2] George Tinker, *Missionary Conquest: The Gospel and Native American Cultural Genocide* (Minneapolis: Augsburg Fortress, 1993); Tzvetan Todorov, *The Conquest of America: The Question of the Other* (New York: HarperPerennial, 1982).

[3] Fletcher, *Barbarian*, 491.

> Roman Catholics had often pointed out the failure of the Re-
> formers and their successors to engage in mission ... Some
> Protestants reacted to this Catholic polemic with the argument
> that Christ had never intended mission to be an abiding mark
> of the church. Johann Gerard, for example, taught that the
> Great Commission had been given exclusively to the apostles.[4]

To this argument they added others: evidence from distant
lands indicated they had been evangelised long ago, proving
the Great Commission had already been fulfilled; heathen
nations were barbarous and did not deserve the gospel; and
the conversion of the heathen depended on God's initiative
and required no human intervention.[5]

However, some Protestants thought differently, especially those influenced by the dissident tradition.
Anabaptists themselves, despite embracing the Great Commission, had not engaged in mission beyond Christendom
and gradually abandoned mission within Europe. Persecution resulted in them exchanging mission for quiet survival
or migration in search of refuge. In the twentieth century,
Anabaptists recovered their initial mission dynamic and
embarked on new and distinctive global initiatives. But,
meanwhile, two other movements with links to the dissident tradition emulated their commitment to mission.

The Moravians originated in the fifteenth-century
Hussite movement and particularly those associated with
Peter Chelčhický who became the *Unitas Fratrum* ('unity of
brethren').[6] They had connections with Waldensians and
influenced early Anabaptists but were almost destroyed by

---

[4] Smith, *Crying*, 4.
[5] Durnbaugh, *Believers' Church*, 230.
[6] Peter Chelčhický's best-known work, *Net of Faith*, presents a
passionate call to mission and urges recovery of New Testament
practices.

sustained persecution. The movement was reborn in 1722 when Count Zinzendorf, a German Lutheran and Pietist, provided asylum at Herrnhut for Moravian refugees. In 1727 this community introduced round-the-clock prayer, with a man and woman assigned to every hour. 'The longest prayer meeting in history' continued for over a century. In 1732, they commissioned missionaries to St Thomas in the West Indies.[7] Hundreds more followed and this example inspired others.

William Carey, citing Moravian missionaries, encouraged Baptists to follow their example. In his *Enquiry into the Obligations of Christians to Use Means for the Conversion of the Heathens* (1792), he denied the Great Commission had been fulfilled and urged action. English Baptists emerged in the early seventeenth century from Puritan and separatist roots. Their relationship with Anabaptism is debatable: there are common beliefs and practices, but also differences; there were human links, including John Smyth's involvement with Dutch Mennonites; but most historians resist construing decisive influence.[8] Nevertheless, Carey's departure to India and formation of what would become the Baptist Missionary Society[9] owed much to mission perspectives nurtured in earlier dissident movements.

Eventually, other Protestants joined Moravian and Baptist pioneers and the Great Commission became the cornerstone of

[7] Joe Cooper, *The Moravian Church* (London: Moravian Book Room, 2000).
[8] H. Leon McBeth, *The Baptist Heritage* (Nashville: Broadman, 1987), 49–63 and Pearse, *Great Restoration*. Cf. Ernest Payne, 'Who were the Baptists?', *The Baptist Quarterly* XVI (October 1956), 339–42.
[9] Brian Stanley, *The History of the Baptist Missionary Society 1792–1992* (Edinburgh: T. & T. Clark, 1992).

the modern missionary movement. Hundreds of missionary societies and thousands of missionaries transformed Christianity into a global faith, making Christendom boundaries obsolete. But their methods, though less coercive than the conquistadors, reflected the Christendom mindset. Blatant bribery accompanied dubious forms of inducement (the phenomenon of 'rice Christians') where converts knew colonial authorities would reward them with material help or favourable treatment. Some argued this was simply extending the benefits of Christian civilisation, but not all agreed – especially those who rejected these inducements or experienced exploitation by those who represented the gospel. The partnership of missionary and merchant is as disturbing as that of missionary and mercenary.

Furthermore, wherever European missionaries went, they imported their cultural assumptions and preferences. They expected converts to adopt European forms of dress, styles of architecture, musical instruments, modes of church government and other 'Christian' cultural norms. Christendom had eradicated tensions between gospel and culture, leaving missionaries ill equipped to differentiate these or contextualise the gospel in other cultures. Consequently, converts were detached from their own people and became dependent on missionaries. Christianity appeared as a European religion legitimating colonial oppression – with devastating long-term consequences.

But some missionaries refused to employ such methods, recognised the gospel must be expressed in culturally appropriate ways and acted as catalysts, encouraging the development of indigenous churches. Their experiences undermined the Christendom mindset they brought with them, which in turn eventually undermined colonialism.[10]

---

[10] Lamin Sanneh, *Translating the Message: The Missionary Impact on Culture* (Maryknoll: Orbis, 1990). See further Ramachandra, *Faiths in conflict?*, 127–8, 168.

Gradually this perspective became normative in mission agencies (but not before the Christendom legacy was exported, storing up problems). Nevertheless, so successful was this missionary movement that sixty per cent of Christians now live in Africa, Asia and Latin America, and a reverse missionary movement is underway.[11]

Mission within Christendom

This reverse missionary movement is responding to accelerating decline in European churches, despite belated acceptance by Catholics and Protestants of the maligned Anabaptist conviction that mission was needed in Europe.

Catholic efforts to nurture a well-instructed and more disciplined membership were noted previously.[12] In Protestant nations, movements advocating religious experience and discipleship rather than cognitive assent and churchgoing challenged nominality. Pietism, a Lutheran renewal movement, was inspired by Philip Jakob Spener's *Pia Desideria* (1675), which urged cultivation of 'heart religion', not 'head religion'. This spread across northern Europe, revitalising churches and galvanising mission within and beyond Europe. Via Zinzendorf and the Moravians it impacted Wesley and the Methodist movement in England, spreading from there to New England Puritans.[13]

Similar emphases characterised 'awakenings' and 'revivals' that stirred Europe and North America in the eighteenth and nineteenth centuries. Itinerant evangelists

---

[11] Walls, *Cross-Cultural Process*, 31 and passim.

[12] See Chapter 6.

[13] Ted Campbell, *The Religion of the Heart: A Study of European Religious Life in the Seventeenth and Eighteenth Centuries* (Columbia: University of South Carolina Press, 1991).

and revivalists organised 'campaigns', 'crusades' and 'missions' to preach experiential Christianity and moral uprightness. Organisations and denominational departments of 'home mission' sprang up as counterparts to those servicing 'foreign mission'. Most mission work, however, depended on individual enthusiasm or voluntary societies: congregations remained firmly maintenance-oriented. The language and methods of twentieth-century evangelism hail from this period – modes of preaching, models of conversion, mass meetings, Jesus as 'personal saviour' and evangelism as invitation to events. Although the impact on individuals was profound and sometimes resulted in recognisable social changes, such evangelising has bequeathed to us an ambivalent legacy and has imparted to our society a justifiable suspicion of evangelism.

For, although the assumption that society did not need evangelising was abandoned, undermining Christendom by insisting on personal conversion rather than cultural conformity, evangelism operated within a Christendom framework. Although the term 'conversion' was ubiquitous, this was 'insider-conversion', not 'outsider-conversion'. Since the Christian story was familiar, evangelism primarily involved attempts to re-energise faith and challenge lukewarm discipleship. Evangelists encouraged renewed commitment to the gospel through Bible reading, attending church regularly, living respectably and caring for others.

Because church and state were partners, and church leaders were respected members of society, top-down evangelism was implemented by the educated, articulate, wealthy and powerful. This impacted the message preached, which was generally moralistic and inculcated conformity to middle-class culture. Sin was non-conformity to dominant cultural values. In a society still regarded as Christian, conversion meant strengthened commitment to shared social norms, not adopting the counter-cultural values of God's kingdom. Evangelism was not politically, socially or economically disruptive. It was individualistic and inculcated personal spirituality, reinforcing the status quo.

This approach to mission within Christendom always had serious limitations – failure to differentiate gospel and culture, individualistic appeal, privatised approach to ethics and irrelevance to the urban poor – but it persisted into the late twentieth century. During the past forty years, however, it has become clear we need different approaches in post-Christendom. Assumptions, language, expectations, strategies and values need thorough overhaul.

Evangelism in Post-Christendom

Mission and evangelism are not identical, though the relationship between evangelism and engagement with political, economic, cultural and social issues has been debated widely. Nor were missionary activities between the sixteenth and twentieth centuries confined to evangelism. But the evangelistic aspect of mission demonstrates clearly the problematic Christendom legacy and the challenge of reconfiguring mission in post-Christendom.

Evangelism today is deeply unpopular, within and beyond the churches. Although the Decade of Evangelism, despite shortcomings, rekindled interest in evangelism, it did not remove the aversion many sensitive Christians feel. Despite the abandonment of inappropriate forms of evangelism and the adoption of humble, patient, holistic and contextual approaches, rooted in friendship, many still find evangelism problematic. Asking Christians to name images, techniques or attitudes associated with evangelism consistently uncovers strong antipathy and discomfort. They are:

- The antics, poor witness, publicity seeking and money grabbing of high-profile televangelists.
- Outdated and embarrassing evangelistic literature, events and programmes.
- Disempowerment caused by assuming only trained, eloquent and persuasive individuals can evangelise.
- Knowing churches are declining, reluctance to invite friends into a struggling institution.
- Distaste for strategies that involve conversations with strangers and attempts to evangelise without establishing prior relationships.
- Imperialistic mission activities that confuse conversion with proselytism and fail to respect other cultures.
- Ill-advised attempts to motivate congregations through guilt or warnings that they need new recruits to survive.
- Approaches that seem manipulative, where 'friendship' is merely an excuse for 'witnessing'.
- Disillusionment from past experiences of 'converts' not becoming disciples or integrated into congregations.
- Concern that verbal evangelism alone is inadequate for sceptical postmodern culture.

Many issues can be addressed by recognising their legitimacy, exploring alternative approaches and equipping individuals and churches more effectively.[14] Rehabilitating and reconfiguring evangelism are crucial but attainable tasks on the threshold of post-Christendom. Even where

---

[14] Graham Tomlin, *The Provocative Church* (London: SPCK, 2002); Brian McLaren, *More Ready than you Realize: Evangelism as Dance in the Postmodern Matrix* (Grand Rapids: Zondervan, 2002).

deep-rooted antipathy to evangelism means new language is needed, Christianity is at heart a missionary faith and the desire of most Christians to tell the story is deeper than our reluctance to engage in activities we associate with evangelism.

But the level of antipathy towards evangelism within the churches – to say nothing of the suspicion evangelism evokes outside them – requires further explanation than the above reasons. Could mission in Christendom have produced this deep-seated aversion to evangelism? Such aversion comes not from widespread familiarity with this story, although members of Jewish and Muslim communities are often well informed, but from deep suspicion that evangelism is neither pleasant nor honourable. When the story is told, many respond, 'Now I understand why I hate evangelism!' To reconfigure evangelism for post-Christendom, we must disavow some expressions of evangelism in Christendom. Disavowal involves recognising that once-effective strategies are no longer appropriate, repentance for attitudes and methods that were inconsistent with the gospel and rooting out vestiges that distort evangelism today.

Some doubt evangelism can be rehabilitated. Can this deeply compromised practice be purged and reconfigured? Why not declare a moratorium on it? Why not focus on being faithful communities and trust the attractive power of the gospel to draw others to Christ and these communities? Cannot we work for social transformation without telling the story that motivates us?

These questions should be pondered, not dismissed out of hand. If we do not feel their challenge, we have not understood the Christendom story. Might a 'decade of repentance' for the legacy of past centuries be more helpful than another decade of evangelism? Some Christians have chosen quieter incarnational witness over active evangelism. Some groups pioneering fresh expressions of church in contemporary culture have rejected evangelism in favour of exploring more authentic worship and community. And many churches have developed innovative and impressive forms of community service that are suspicious of evangelism.

But there are problems with this. In the context of sustained church decline, a decade of evangelistic inactivity is a luxury. Pursuing authentic worship and community without evangelism means driving a typical Christendom wedge between church and mission. Hoping passive and inwardly focused churches will attract others is to invest in Christendom expectations. And community engagement that excludes evangelism does not appreciate the fast-diminishing Christendom capital it relies on for workers. Ironically, this understandable reluctance to evangelise and the suggested alternatives are imbued with Christendom assumptions. Nevertheless, these concerns should be incorporated into any attempt to reconfigure evangelism for post-Christendom.

Three factors have influenced recent thinking about evangelism in Britain: lessons from the Decade of Evangelism; the impact of process-evangelism courses, including *Alpha*; and the challenge of postmodernity. 'Incarnation and explanation' evangelism is superseding 'exhortation and invitation'. Evangelism is being reconfigured in ways that are more congenial to those disenchanted with previous models. The Christendom legacy is a fourth factor, undergirding these developments and stimulating additional reflection. What might post-Christendom evangelism mean?

- Acknowledging the charge of hypocrisy that fourth-century Christians faced for the first time and that remains common – a miserable Christendom legacy.

- Confessing our failure to embody the gospel, now and previously, and inviting others to join imperfect pilgrims, not a perfect community. Brian McLaren suggests this approach: 'I'm sorry we Christians have so often put roadblocks up for spiritual seekers through our narrow-mindedness, our failure to bridge racial and cultural and class barriers, and our lack of acceptance ... Please don't blame Jesus for our failure to live up to his teaching and example. And be assured we'll try to do better, with God's help. Please pray for us, okay?'[15]
- Renouncing imperialistic language and cultural imposition, making truth claims with humility and respecting other viewpoints.
- Discovering evangelists who 'prepare God's people for works of service'[16] rather than eloquent performers in public events.
- Realising churchgoing is no longer a normal social activity; church buildings and culture are alien, and many searching for spiritual reality do not anticipate finding this in churches.
- Recognising post-Christendom's diversity and developing strategies for different audiences – secularists, spiritual seekers, traditionalists, neo-pagans and others.[17]
- Searching for multiple contact points with the gospel in a culture no longer dominated (as Christendom was) by guilt, employing the full range of New

---

[15] McLaren, *More Ready*, 48.
[16] Ephesians 4:12.
[17] John Drane, *The McDonaldization of the Church: Spirituality, Creativity, and the Future of the Church* (London: Darton, Longman & Todd, 2000), 55–84.

Testament imagery and learning to relate the story to
contemporary angst and yearnings.

- Starting further back than in Christendom, not
assuming our language and concepts are understood
by the first generation in centuries without
significant church connection through Sunday
schools.
- Rediscovering the 'go' in the Great Commission:
reducing over-busy church programmes and
equipping members to share faith at work, among
friends and in the local community.
- Appreciating this dispersed evangelism requires
accessible and welcoming, authentic and provocative
congregations, expressing faith through holistic
mission.
- Engaging in conversation rather than confrontation
– evangelism alongside others, not declaiming from
an authoritative height, through dialogue instead of
monologue, listening and speaking, receiving and
imparting.
- Concentrating on low profile contextual witness,
eschewing razzmatazz and large-scale monochrome
strategies (inappropriate in a plural society).
- Anticipating longer journeys towards Christ:
process-evangelism courses must assume less and last
longer than those currently available.
- Speaking consciously from the margins and inviting
people to a lifestyle that, properly understood (we
will need process-discipleship courses), contravenes
dominant social values.

Post-Christendom evangelism must be uncoupled from
'inviting people to church' and disabused of any lingering
feeling others should pay attention to what churches say.
Graham Cray writes:

All the major church traditions in this country have been shaped by Christendom – by an expectation that they have a special right to be heard and that people 'ought' to listen to them. Whole strategies of evangelism have been based on a residual guilt about not going to church.[18]

Some of these proposals relate particularly to the present transitional period; they may become less relevant. Some will be enduring features of evangelism from the margins. They do not primarily concern strategies and methods – though there are implications for these – but attitudes, expectations and contextual sensitivity. Evangelism is needed more than ever in post-Christendom and opportunities to tell an unfamiliar story will multiply; but old patterns and approaches will seriously hinder our ability to respond. Unpretentious long-term witness is our best hope. Gentle questioning must supersede domineering assertions. Bold humility must replace arrogant insecurity. The images of fellow travellers and conversation partners must usurp memories of inquisitors and crusaders.

But we should be under no illusions: evangelism in the overlap between Christendom and post-Christendom is difficult. Many assume Christianity has been tried and found wanting: we struggle to gain a hearing for something widely regarded as passé. The old Christendom familiarity with the story is disappearing (though enough remains to inoculate people) and the post-Christendom scenarios, with which this book began, where there is curiosity about an unfamiliar and intriguing story, are not yet common. Most assume that the gospel is a boring reaffirmation of establishment values; Christians are naïve, hypocritical, judgemental and intolerant; evangelism is an invitation to add a religious

---

[18] Graham Cray, *Youth Congregations and the Emerging Church* (Cambridge: Grove, 2002), 9.

veneer to life and guarantee preferential treatment beyond the grave; and those responding need make only small, usually negative, adjustments to their lives. Such 'good news' lacks newsworthiness and sounds unattractive.

Reconfiguring evangelism will also mean rediscovering the gospel of the kingdom: liberation rather than personal fulfilment, reconciliation rather than justification, transformation rather than stability; focusing on hope rather than faith; explaining the work of Christ in other ways than penal substitution; announcing good news to the poor and powerless but judgement to the rich and powerful; naming certain sins in some communities and different sins in others; addressing the sinned against as well as sinners. Who knows what good news a church on the margins might rediscover?

Mission in a Plural Society

Another Christendom legacy is uncertainty about relating to members of other faith communities and mission in a plural society. What is our mission in this unfamiliar context? Where do we agree with other faiths and where do we differ? Is evangelism appropriate? Are there forms of mission we can engage in together?

Christendom was an essentially unitary culture, encountering other faiths only as tiny minorities or through travellers' tales. Consequently, 'inherited theological traditions forged in the context of a Christian monopoly provide little help when encountering devout adherents of other religions'.[19] But post-Christendom is a plural culture with many religious traditions represented by growing faith communities. Churches across Europe are pondering how

---

[19] Smith, *Mission*, 62.

to build relationships with these communities. The answers found will impact profoundly not just the churches but a fragmented society uncertain what binds people together without shared values.

The Christendom legacy is unhelpful:

- Assuming Europe is Christian causes immense confusion. Members of other faiths who equate 'Christian' and 'Western' unsurprisingly dismiss Christianity as corrupt and uninspiring; conversion is perceived as cultural suicide.
- Identifying Christianity and European culture hinders cultural self-criticism and the development of expressions of Christianity that are more congenial to other faiths.
- Violence against Muslims and Jews has bequeathed a legacy of hostility and fear, and a distorted but entirely understandable perception of Christianity.
- European colonialism meant Christians encountered other faiths as conquerors and masters, not equals, resulting in arrogant religious superiority.
- The post-Reformation phenomenon of religious nationalism has encouraged some to interpret recent global conflicts as religious wars, with the Christian West confronting Islam.
- Proselytism, coercion and inducements to convert have discredited evangelism and jeopardised faith sharing across communities.
- The theological basis for religious liberty is underdeveloped in most churches, which apply or oppose secular ideas of tolerance to inter-community relations.
- Inter-faith dialogue suffers from assumptions that other religions lack spiritual value, that Christians can learn nothing from dialogue and that the

conversion of either conversation partner is illegitimate.

- Many Christians are warier of co-operating with other faith groups than with secular agencies, more worried about spiritual contamination than subversion by secularism.
- Arguing we should not evangelise other faith communities implies we should evangelise only 'latent Christians' and that evangelism is unpleasant – both concepts deeply rooted in Christendom thinking.

Evangelism is not, however, the starting point for mission in a plural society. Given the horrendous record of intolerance in Christendom and deep mutual suspicion, the priority is to build relationships of respect and friendship. If these are genuine and involve more than superficial communication, it is perfectly legitimate to share religious convictions and encourage conversion (in either direction). But listening to and learning from each other and seeking common ground represents disavowal of the Christendom legacy.

Churches in post-Christendom must invest time and energy learning about other faith communities, reflecting theologically on other religions and confronting deep-seated fears and negative attitudes. Many Christians have never taken seriously the spiritual experiences of Muslims or Hindus, or moved beyond superficial understanding and dismissive responses. In a plural society, where fragmentation and violence are ever-present dangers, and stereotyping and caricature fuel prejudice and anxiety, churches must model more hopeful ways of relating to those whose views dissent from the majority. This will mean disavowing the Christendom mindset.

But if the Christendom legacy is flawed, the favoured approach of secular societies is also deficient. 'Tolerance' has achieved almost unchallengeable status: who wants to be dubbed intolerant? But the philosophical basis for tolerance is not mutual respect for deeply held but divergent convictions, but relativism that does not treat religious beliefs seriously and imposes uniformity (all religions are the same and equally valid). Tolerance requires those with religious convictions to restrict their significance to their private lives, refrain from questioning the convictions of others and accept the denigration of all religious convictions as 'dispensable folkloric appendages that we shall not mind losing from view behind the pieties of the melting pot'.[20]

Developed by Enlightenment thinkers as an alternative to incessant religious conflict, tolerance is superficially attractive, but has major weaknesses and cannot achieve the peaceful plural society it envisages. Its apparent neutrality masks secular imperialism, imposing its views as powerfully as any religious tradition and intolerant towards any who challenge its assumptions. Marginalising and trivialising religious convictions and real differences between religions are as unacceptable to most other communities as to Christians. This represents a strategy of avoidance rather than engagement and has little prospect of success in a society where secularism is under serious threat. A more robust and coherent strategy is needed, rooted in a different approach to faith convictions.

Might the 'religious liberty' tradition developed within marginal movements like the Anabaptists, Quakers and English Baptists offer an alternative? These were passionate movements with strong convictions, which they eagerly shared with others, and this sometimes resulted in conflict. But they were deeply committed to religious liberty – not because their convictions were unimportant, but because

---

[20] Yoder, *Priestly*, 192.

they were too important to be imposed. Smith describes Anabaptists' dual commitment to evangelism and religious liberty: 'Anabaptist evangelists criss-crossed Europe seeking converts and paid a terrible price in suffering and death, yet modern Christianity acknowledges its debt to them for their courageous advocacy of the principle of religious liberty, and their awareness that mission is part of the nature of the church.'[21]

Secular 'tolerance' owes something to this tradition, but full-bloodied religious liberty is more attractive and potent than this anaemic derivative. Religious liberty treats convictions seriously, accepts faith communities hold divergent views, respects their freedom to make competing truth claims, encourages exchanges of views, identifies secularism as another faith position, rejects inducement and coercion and develops ways to protect minorities from oppression. It invites members of a plural society to be equally passionate about defending the freedom of others to hold religious views they disagree with as about sharing their own convictions.

Advocating religious liberty might be a key component of mission in a plural society. But this will mean renouncing the flawed Christendom legacy, rejecting the insipid tolerance of secular modernity and recovering the insights of the dissenting tradition. It will mean those who refrain from evangelising members of other faiths *and* those who harbour a latent persecuting mentality re-evaluating their positions. And it will mean developing a missiology that is passionate about the Christian story, passionate about sharing this with others, passionate about defending their freedom to reject it, passionate about resisting all attempts to impose religious views and passionate about friendship that is not jeopardised by divergent convictions.

---

[21] Smith, *Crying*, 4.

The foundation for this missiology is renewed reflection on how God in the person of Jesus of Nazareth operated through invitation rather than imposition. The repeated use of 'passionate' signals whole-heartedness, rooted in beliefs about God's character and activity, not grudging concessions in a plural society. Faith is a passionate matter – only a passionate approach to religious liberty will do.

Any discussion of religious liberty should consider disadvantages others experience in a society whose institutions developed during Christendom. The dominant position of Christianity resulted in legislation that was unremarkable in a unitary society but is anomalous and unjust in a plural society. It has also bequeathed attitudes that suggest this previously dominant position should be restored or its vestiges preserved. Surely we should advocate equality for other faith communities, perhaps by campaigning for Hindu, Muslim and other religious representatives in the House of Lords; advocating a more inclusive approach to blasphemy; or ensuring other communities enjoy similar rights in relation to charitable status or faith schools. Or we might advocate abolition, not extension, of Christendom vestiges. Different issues may elicit different strategies to remove discrimination and achieve justice for all communities.

But this approach will be strongly resisted in many churches, construed as denying the truth of the gospel or Christ's lordship, capitulation to secularism or cowardice in the face of demands from other communities. Some, grieving the demise of Christendom and fearing the influence of other religions, will label this defeatist. Others, claiming the religious high ground, will justify special treatment for Christianity and argue other religions should not be encouraged in their falsehood. An argument frequently encountered is that Christians in Muslim nations do not enjoy freedoms and privileges Muslims already have in

Britain: so we should not give further ground. This popular argument depends on two assumptions: that Britain is a Christian nation, comparable to Muslim sacral states; and that Jesus had things back-to-front when he instructed us to 'do to others as you would have them do to you'[22] rather than 'repay others for they way they treat you'.

If Christians campaigned for the rights of those with whom they profoundly disagree, how this might enhance other aspects of mission? Since historic inequalities are being eroded and will gradually disappear, supporting the rights of other faith communities is preferable strategically to resisting this development. It is also more Christian.

Another contentious possibility is that Christians and members of other faiths might develop partnerships, based on the recognition of sufficient common ground for co-operation. Three areas of agreement are recognition of a spiritual dimension to human existence, the value of community for human relationships and the importance of ethical guidelines for human behaviour. Some aspects of mission in a plural society might be pursued through such partnerships, where the convictions of all involved are respected. In a secular society, alliances between faith communities may be fruitful. Furthermore, adjusting to our new status as a religious minority, we may (if we are willing) learn from the past and present experiences of other religious minorities.

What about evangelism? Authentic post-Christendom evangelism engages equally with secular, nominal Christian or Muslim conversation-partners. There are additional historical and cultural factors, but the same principles apply. Members of some other faiths are not averse to evangelising and do not expect Christians to be, but we will more readily be heard if we refrain from speaking as representatives of

---

[22] Luke 6:31.

the dominant religion. Sharing faith in a plural society means roundtable dialogue where we have one seat at the table, rather than speeches from the head of the table. Inviting others to consider the person and work of Jesus, whom Christians believe to be unique, does not mean we discount or denigrate others' spiritual experiences.

Rather than being disempowered by the Christendom legacy or pretending we are still in control, then, we can disavow outdated attitudes and approaches and discover more appropriate – *and more Christian* – ways to evangelise. New theological foundations, and changes of attitude, are needed, together with confidence that the gospel does not need legal advantages and social privileges. Marginal churches can thrive in plural post-Christendom as they thrived in plural pre-Christendom.

Church and Society

Post-Christendom is not pre-Christendom. But the plural context and marginal status of the church in both eras allows us to learn from the experience of early Christians. Marginality is significant also for considering other ways than evangelism in which Christians engage with society. Mission includes many elements: creation care, social action, community development, peace and justice advocacy, political involvement, cultural renewal and much else. We cannot explore each in depth, but there are many parallels with the evangelistic dimension of mission, so the approach advocated above is more broadly applicable. But the marginality of post-Christendom churches is especially significant.

The church's involvement in all spheres of society is rightly regarded as an enormous advantage of Christendom. The church no longer operated on the edges of society but at its heart. The collapse of boundaries between church and world, whatever problems this caused, enabled Christian values to permeate culture, transform institutions, inspire caring and creative initiatives, and influence every aspect of human life. The Christendom legacy includes organisations, legal and judicial principles, voluntary agencies, charitable activities, cultural expressions, social and political developments and much else that can be celebrated as Christian contributions to human flourishing. None of these should be undervalued.

However, this should not be construed as legitimating Christendom. Already in pre-Christendom and from the margins, churches had pioneered initiatives that deeply affected their society. Their revolutionary approach to economic sharing and social care, rejection of violence, sacrificial service to plague victims and undermining of patriarchy and slavery in egalitarian communities impressed, challenged, outraged and attracted their contemporaries. The third-century expansion of the church and increasing official toleration derived from and resulted in growing social influence. So was partnership with the state, the Christendom shift and the church's dominant social role necessary? Might continued grass-roots influence have transformed society as effectively? Indeed, might this have accomplished as much and even more while avoiding many disfiguring and corrupting consequences of ecclesial coercion, wealth and status?

For the Christendom legacy in many areas of social and cultural engagement is deeply flawed: marginal churches in post-Christendom need to disavow this:

- If the Christendom shift offered opportunities for social transformation, it also lured churches away from creative and radical perspectives and ensured their thinking and practices became increasingly conventional.

- Nominal Christianity and the superficiality of Christendom church life meant pressure and penalties were required instead of moral influence and exemplary living.
- The church's enhanced social status generally precluded them from taking or endorsing initiatives that threatened the status quo and dulled their sensitivity to injustice.
- Churches often obstructed rather than pursuing greater social justice. Even when individual Christians promoted social transformation, official church policy and attitudes of church leaders delayed or frustrated progress.
- Controlling attitudes, patronising and demeaning forms of charity and conditions imposed on beneficiaries marred many social initiatives.
- Patronage of the arts and educational activities involved indoctrination and censorship as much as encouraging creativity and developing human potential.
- Church leaders often adopted a 'moral majority' stance in public debates and a tone of voice that conveyed this.

The demise of Christendom has dramatically circumscribed the church's involvement in society. Schools, universities, hospitals, voluntary societies, charities, aid agencies, campaigning organisations and other institutions with Christian foundations are now thoroughly secular and often under state control. Few cultural developments in the twentieth century (unlike previous centuries) were inspired by the Christian story or connected with the church. Some Christians supported twentieth-century campaigns against

the arms trade, nuclear weapons, environmental destruction, apartheid, racism and sexism, but churches often
seemed to be playing 'catch-up' or worse. Polarised debates
about evangelism and social action, rooted in Christendom
assumptions about the church's status and social role,
hindered churches from doing either effectively.

Rather than bemoaning what has been lost, clinging desperately to remaining vestiges of past social influence or
trying to galvanise the support of declining congregations
for multiple worthy causes, we need to develop a
post-Christendom strategy for social and cultural engagement. What might this mean?

- Accepting that our resources are limited (and
  diminishing); we cannot be involved in every issue.
  This is unnecessary now others are carrying
  responsibilities churches once carried – a cause for
  celebration, not regret – so we can use our resources
  strategically.
- Doing nothing rather than acting in ways that
  contravene our values. Marginal communities
  recognise there are things we cannot change or
  prevent without forsaking our principles. This does
  not mean condoning evil, but choosing not to
  endorse the myth of redemptive violence and other
  such counter-productive strategies.[23]
- Rejoicing we need no longer worry about ensuring
  history turns out how we think it should (a
  Christendom delusion). This frees to live 'out of
  control', acting faithfully and trusting outcomes to
  God.[24]

---

[23] Yoder, *Priestly*, 101.
[24] Stanley Hauerwas, *The Peaceable Kingdom: A Primer in
Christian Ethics* (Notre Dame: University of Notre Dame Press,
1983), 105.

- Acknowledging we can no longer expect to be consulted or demand a role on the basis of privilege or past status. Any contributions will be based on ability, expertise, imagination and commitment.
- Realising marginal churches can take risks and pioneer initiatives mainstream institutions cannot or will not. We can experiment with different ideas and strategies – especially on issues where conventional thinking is moribund.[25]
- Rediscovering the 'prophetic minority' stance and a tone of voice that befits marginal communities. Rather than pontificating or moralising, we can model alternatives to dominant cultural and social norms and commend these with integrity, grace and winsomeness.
- Offering a perspective that transcends 'right wing' and 'left wing' agendas, making connections between abortion, capital punishment and 'collateral damage' in warfare, or between racism, environmental destruction and pornography, and forging unpredictable and holistic alliances.
- Embracing realistic expectations that deliver us from pretensions and despair. Christendom believed God's kingdom could be built by human hands and was the church's gift to society. In post-Christendom we need a 'kingdom vision' that inspires action but awaits God's future.
- Choosing to believe God's mission can be effective from the bottom up rather than top down.

The church on the margins is not called into ghetto mode. Like the pre-Christendom churches and medieval dissidents there will be limits to our social engagement but also new freedoms. David Lyon writes: 'The demise of Christendom

---

[25] Yoder, *Priestly*, 96–9.

reduces radically the temptations of power, clearing space for the old story to be retold.'[26] Powerless churches need not wrangle over the relationship between evangelism and social action (this was always essentially about power), but can develop fresh perspectives on seemingly intractable social issues, because things look different from the margins. We can more easily identify with those main-stream society excludes. There are already encouraging signs, as churches develop initiatives for paedophiles who want to change, pioneer victim–offender reconciliation and seek alternatives to the failing strategy of prisons.

Social engagement in post-Christendom may be more modest than in Christendom. It may involve social respon-sibility and social *irresponsibility* if our primary vocation is to be Christian rather than effective. But it can also be cre-ative. Churches are still in many communities highly significant in terms of their human and physical resources, their connections within and beyond the local area and the trust placed in them. There will be no shortage of opportu-nities. But transformed attitudes, expectations, models and priorities are needed to incarnate the gospel in a world we no longer control.

Nigel Wright concludes:

> We are living after Christendom. But to have a Christian vision for the social and political orders was never wrong. The church at the time of Constantine was right to offer what it could for the good of the social order. Along the way it was drawn into ways of acting that eroded its witness and integrity. The chal-lenge is to find a true vision, and one that resonates with the Christ we follow, and to pursue it with intent.[27]

---

[26] David Lyon, *Jesus in Disneyland: Religion in Postmodern Times* (Cambridge: Polity Press, 2000), 147.
[27] Wright, *New Baptists*, 111.

Church and State

How might a Christian vision for the *political* order be cast and pursued in post-Christendom? If the alliance between church and state, which was at the heart of Christendom, is obsolete and illegitimate, what is the alternative? Christendom's defenders argue that, for all its flaws, Christendom represented a proper attempt to bring political authority under Christ's lordship. Winston Churchill once defended democracy as the worst form of government – except all others that had been tried; Christendom is similarly lauded as better than paganism, secularism or pluralism. What alternative do its critics offer?

Three initial responses can be made. First, those who acknowledge Christendom was flawed rarely examine the extent of these flaws and whether they were incidental or inherent in the system. But assumptions that an equivalent system largely free of such flaws might be introduced, or that these flaws are insufficient to abandon the whole arrangement, are open to challenge. The evidence may suggest the system itself is the problem, which no refinements or safeguards can make useable.

Second, criticisms of Christendom are not invalidated by the absence of fully formed and persuasive alternatives. After many centuries of partnership between the state and a powerful, wealthy and established church, when dissenting voices were quickly and often brutally silenced, developing an alternative Christian political vision may take time. Deconstruction that clears the ground, together with wholehearted disavowal of a flawed system and attentiveness to hints offered by dissenters, may be necessary starting points.

Third, churches on the margins (especially those adjusting to this unfamiliar location) may have other priorities than developing political philosophies or strategies they cannot implement and that may receive little support.

Whatever our ideal view of church–state relations, Christianity will be, soon and for the foreseeable future, one among many religious minorities in a society dominated by secular assumptions. In such a society, the state's responsibility is to be religiously neutral, ensuring the interests of all minorities are protected and that none exercises undue influence. Churches will receive no special treatment and will be subject to restrictions similar to those imposed on other minorities. Christians are complaining greater sensitivity is shown to the feelings of other communities than to Christians and that others are gaining ground at our expense, but this is understandable in light of our previous dominance.

Whether we welcome this prospect or not, as Christendom fades and churches lose or renounce remaining privileges, we will have a secular state governing a plural culture. Some welcome this enthusiastically, seeing the combination of plural context, level playing field and neutral state as the healthiest environment for mission. Here, faith can be exercised without pressure and churches can participate in the political arena on the basis of merit rather than patronage. Others regard 'principled pluralism' as denying the lordship of Christ and dismiss as naïve notions of neutrality. They argue that a secular state is guided by secularist ideology and cannot be regarded as neutral. Historical examples of secular states suggest restrictions on faith communities often evolve into persecution.

These are valid concerns, but we may be unconvinced Christ's lordship requires a dominant church or partnership with the state; indeed, if it is true not only that Jesus is *Lord* but that *Jesus* is Lord, our understanding of how his lordship is exercised may preclude this arrangement. Nor should we dismiss the possibility of a secular state respecting the rights of religious minorities and acting impartially.

A Christian vision for the political order might include a state committed to principled pluralism that values the contributions of faith communities, safeguards their liberties and restricts their ability to control or dominate others. Such a state cannot be guaranteed and, if it is achievable, vigilance will be needed lest secularist assumptions gradually erode religious liberties. But this is more feasible than the restoration of a Christian state – and more Christian.[28]

The most urgent questions, then, are not how the church should respond when invited into partnership with the state or when its numerical strength means it can exercise decisive influence. These questions faced fourth-century Christians and may face Christians in Europe again if our current decline is arrested and substantial growth occurs. They are legitimate questions (and live issues in other nations) and we may want to examine various responses or at least establish theological reference points within which to assess these. But reflection on this hypothetical issue must not distract us from discerning how to engage in politics as a minority community in the coming years. If we learn to do this faithfully, when the church's influence increases we will be able to draw on other memories than Christendom and be better placed to shape and pursue a vision for the political order that is consistent with the gospel.

What theological and ethical principles should inform a post-Christendom vision for the political order?[29]

- Understanding the state as one of the 'principalities and powers', created for human well-being, fallen and prone to idolatry and self-aggrandisement, but capable of at least partial redemption.

---

[28] See further Ramachandra, *Faith in Conflict?*, 158–65
[29] See further Nigel Wright, 'Reinventing Christendom', *Anabaptism Today* 33 (June 2003), 2–9.

- Recognising the state is only one such power – although it often claims greater significance. What it can achieve is limited, because of its own inadequacies and the influence of other (economic, social, cultural and political) powers.
- A principled commitment to the freedom of the church from the state and the state from the church, liberating both to fulfil their divine vocations and interact with each other in diverse and creative ways.
- A hermeneutic of justice, rather than order, that prioritises the powerless and poor, and a vision of shalom that inspires multi-faceted goals and action.
- Insisting Christians owe primary allegiance to God's kingdom and the global church community (and have obligations to our planet and global human community). National interest and party loyalty, though valid, are secondary. If Jesus is Lord, Caesar's authority is limited.
- Suspicion of top-down notions of political engagement and confidence in the subversive and creative potential of prophetic truth telling and grass-roots action. We may decide involvement in education, the arts, the media, business, industry, local government, symbolic protests or civil disobedience will have greater potential for effecting lasting change.
- Rejecting the philosophy that 'the end justifies the means' and adoption of 'speaking the truth in love'[30] as a political strategy: affirming what is good in opposing viewpoints or parties, avoiding name-calling or manoeuvring for position, choosing gentleness and integrity over efficacy.

---

[30] Ephesians 4:15.

- Modest expectation that neither dismisses political engagement as worthless nor accords this messianic significance (as in Christendom and many post-Enlightenment secular systems).

Rodney Clapp writes: 'Non-Constantinian Christians are in no position to overthrow the system. What we can hope to do, most often and over the long haul, is survive it and subvert it to its own good. What we are about might then be called sanctified subversion.'[31] We should also heed Kenneth Leech's warning that the nature of politics is changing, not least because of disillusionment with political processes. He writes:

> Much, probably most, political action occurs outside the party machines. Religious groups are increasingly involved with political issues. What seems to have occurred has been a shift in the centre of gravity of the political. It is therefore vital that churches in the future do not allow their approach to political action to be confined within dated conceptions.[32]

Leech identifies seven forms of political engagement – reinforcement, retreat, rescue, reform, radicalism, resistance and revolution[33] – arguing all (even reinforcement, which characterised Christendom) are appropriate in specific contexts. Flexibility is crucial. This befits a theology that places limited confidence in the state and maintains a critical distance, connects with political realignments in contemporary culture and is feasible for churches on the margins as it was not for a church at the centre, locked into

---

[31] Clapp, *Peculiar People*, 200. See further Bartley, *Subversive Manifesto*.
[32] Leech, *Long Exile*, 210–11.
[33] Leech, *Long Exile*, 214–18.

political structures. Post-Christendom churches may not have their accustomed access to political influence. They may redefine political engagement. But scope for such engagement will be greater than ever.

The development of a post-Christendom political praxis will take time, both because the nature of politics is changing and because churches are not yet familiar with their post-Christendom status and calling. This calling involves mission from the margins, not the centre, and requires new perspectives and skills. Electing more Christians to Parliament is inadequate – even dangerous – if they collude with the status quo and operate from old paradigms of church and state. Authentic political engagement will, above all, require churches to incarnate the good news they share and model political and social strategies they advocate.

9

Post-Christendom: Church

What Kind of Church?

What kind of church can incarnate the gospel in post-Christendom? However we answer, the question itself presupposes post-Christendom. In Christendom, questions about church involved neither culture nor mission. Engaging in mission and interacting with culture were secondary concerns that did not affect how churches were understood, governed or organised. There was a gulf between church and mission: ecclesiology and missiology were largely unrelated. Church was primary; culture was a hospitable environment shaped by the church's story; congregations delegated mission to other agencies. There were many discussions about church – doctrine, liturgy, authority, sacraments, ministry, architecture and pastoral theology – but cultural exegesis and reflection on mission did not shape developments in church life.

But the self-confidence of a dominant institution expecting culture to adapt to the church is waning. Christians in all traditions are asking searching questions about the shape and focus of church; most are thinking deeply about the cultural context and many are starting with mission. 'What is church?' Ancient creedal answers or internal denominational statements are insufficient. 'What is non-negotiable and what might be done differently?' Cultural analysis and mission perspectives challenge traditional structures and practices and spark experiments into alternatives. Talk of 'new ways of being church' or 'emerging church' indicates Christendom is fading.

Several related factors have prompted reflection:

- Recognition of a yawning cultural chasm between church and contemporary culture hindering movement in either direction. Church members struggle to bridge the gap at work or with friends; many know their friends will find church incomprehensible, irrelevant, archaic or twee.
- Realisation that Christendom has given way to plural sub-cultures in post-Christendom. Inherited forms of church attract certain sub-cultures (especially white, middle-class, educated and middle-aged conformists) but are ineffective in mission beyond these.
- Disappointment with the Decade of Evangelism and recent church planting initiatives. Many argue we gave inadequate attention to the kinds of churches we planted.[1]
- Alarm that we are losing many former members who retain their faith but find church uninspiring, disempowering and dehumanising. In post-Christendom, institutional loyalty no longer prevents this haemorrhage of disillusioned Christians.

Much has been written on these issues – cultural analysis, reflections by and with church leavers, proposals for

---

[1] George Lings and Stuart Murray, *Church Planting: Past, Present and Future* (Cambridge: Grove, 2003).

missional churches. Consultations and conferences ask: 'What is church?' New models of church – seeker-sensitive, purpose-driven and cell-church especially – are promoted as missionally effective. Others pioneer churches for particular sub-cultures, attempting to contextualise the gospel. Designing church for postmodernity is a popular quest. More extensive still are various ethnic minority churches, which are proliferating and represent a major additional presence in British Christianity.

As in the previous chapter, these developments will be examined through the lens of post-Christendom, asking 'what kind of church?' from this perspective.

Emerging Church

Deep yearnings for spiritually authentic, culturally attuned and attractive expressions of church are a hopeful feature of contemporary church life. This may mean planting churches that are not clones. It may mean transforming inherited modes of church.[2] On the fringes are some whose experiences make them reluctant to use the term 'church'. What is emerging is hard to track, classify or evaluate.

This might be a short-lived, typically postmodern, fragmentation of church that rejects institutional forms and celebrates plurality and diversity; or rearranging deckchairs on the sinking Titanic; or a navel-gazing distraction from mission. But it might constitute spontaneous grass-roots reactions to moribund churches that alienate members and non-members alike. It might indicate God is renewing us for mission in a time of cultural turbulence. It might herald a movement capable of bridging the gap between church and

---

[2] 'Inherited' is preferable to 'traditional' or 'mainstream', both loaded terms.

culture and encountering the 'double whammy' of postmodernity and post-Christendom.

Some emerging churches are *refocusing mission*. Purpose-driven churches review and streamline their programmes to pursue core purposes, rather than dissipating energy in secondary activities. Cell churches simplify church, focusing on small groups as their pastoral heart and missional cutting-edge. Seeker-targeted churches research their communities and design strategies and events that connect with local needs and aspirations. Those planting churches, not in geographical areas (the inherited parish/neighbourhood model), but in networks and sub-cultures, take targeting further. Churches are emerging among science-fiction buffs, surfers, Goths, homeless people, transvestites, many ethnic minorities and youth cultures. They are emerging in cafés, pubs, clubs, mosques, workplaces and on the Internet. Recognising that in urban society networks are often more significant than neighbourhoods for human relationships, churches are reinventing themselves to engage with a changing world.

Some emerging churches are *reconfiguring community*. In fragmented, individualistic postmodernity, many long for authentic community and friendship. Churches at their best offer rich experiences of community – some homogeneous, others spanning classes, generations, ethnicity and personalities – few groups can match this. But churches are not always at their best. They can be superficial, vicious, patronising, dysfunctional and parochial. Many church leavers express grief and anger over damage churches cause. Some emerging churches are places of refuge and recovery: table churches, some alt.worship groups, gatherings of post-evangelicals and post-charismatics, and post-church communities. Others are rediscovering human-scale churches: home church, household church, base church, cell church, intentional communities. Still others are finding involvement in social action and community development is provoking a radical overhaul of church – midweek congregations, churches developing accidentally around projects, organic and permeable churches without clearly defined boundaries.

Some emerging churches are *refreshing worship*. Many church leavers lament banal, uninspiring, repetitive, culturally dated forms of corporate worship, unrelated to life beyond the congregation. Charismatic worship promised much but has stalled: post-charismatics criticise its unrelenting joyfulness that discounts grief, anger and other emotions, limited content and musical range, and self-absorption. Some rediscover traditional liturgical forms, but many find these uncongenial. Emerging churches are exploring fresh possibilities: alt.worship draws eclectically on ancient worship forms and contemporary culture and technology; multi-congregational and 'menu' churches offer diverse worship without rekindling past 'worship wars'; contextual liturgies earth worship in local cultures; web-based exchanges and renewed interest in the arts are stimulating and resourcing innovation and creativity.

Mission, community and worship – three crucial components of church – are inspiring and energising emerging churches. The most hopeful stories involve the integration of all three elements, although most concentrate initially on one or other. This movement is young, small-scale, fragile, diffuse, evolving, liberating and provocative. There are counter-trends: cathedrals congregations are growing. In this transitional period, some inherited models will thrive. For this movement to achieve its potential, emerging and inherited churches must forge gracious and creative partnerships. Arrogant, impatient and dismissive attitudes are unhelpful. Emerging churches need the theological and historical insights, accumulated wisdom and traditions of inherited churches. Inherited churches need the stimulus, provocation, pioneering and creative cultural engagement of emerging churches.

The Post-Christendom Lens

What does this emerging church landscape look like through the post-Christendom lens?

Christendom meant enforced uniformity and contextual insensitivity. Constantine's search for unity and the willingness of fourth-century bishops to conform to social norms produced a centralised institution locked into particular cultural patterns that were baptised as orthodox. Liturgical, creedal and governmental responses to fourth-century issues ossified and were accorded inordinate authority. Theological emphases, worship patterns and authority structures were imposed on various European cultures (and later exported worldwide), discouraging indigenous theological reflection and creativity. Unity required uniformity: dissent was labelled heresy or schism. Although through the centuries there were developments, they were painfully slow and required top-down authorisation, limiting local or regional initiatives.

But emerging churches embody the diversity, flexibility and cultural sensitivity post-Christendom churches need. Few claim theirs is the best or only expression of church; many are configuring worship, community and mission for particular contexts. At their best, these represent genuine missionary engagement with post-Christendom. The humility, vulnerability and openness within many emerging churches contrasts markedly with the 'this- is-the-answer' strategies in late Christendom – such strategies offered desperate churches pre-packaged antidotes to decline but generally failed to deliver. Provisionality and contextualisation are vital in the turbulence of postmodernity and post-Christendom. Inherited churches should welcome and support these initiatives, rather than feeling threatened, erecting barriers or worrying unduly about implications for church order.

Many emerging churches are small – not just because they are young and have not yet grown numerically, but because they value human-scale community and regard small churches as more flexible, egalitarian and participatory. Anti-institutionalism thrives in postmodernity, so we could interpret this as either cultural sensitivity or captivity to cultural prejudice. The post-Christendom lens suggests size affects church dynamics. Small-scale churches may enable post-Christendom churches to rediscover essential aspects of church obscured or distorted by large Christendom congregations.

Some still champion mega-churches (usually with small-group structures to offset the disadvantages). Many, including cell-church enthusiasts, recognise that institutional models during Christendom marginalised small groups but advocate symbiotic larger and smaller gatherings. But retaining larger structures may preclude radical changes, locking emerging churches into traditional and hierarchical patterns. Smaller churches seem vulnerable, but in post-Christendom vulnerability may be advantageous; smaller churches may be better placed to flourish in post-Christendom and nurture Christian disciples in an alien culture. Steven Croft argues: 'In the twentieth century, such small communities were desirable but not essential. In the twenty-first century such communities are now a requirement if the church is both to maintain and develop its common life.'[3] And if we are mission oriented rather

---

[3] Steven Croft, *Transforming Communities: Re-imagining the Church for the 21st Century* (London: Darton, Longman & Todd, 2002), 101.

than maintenance oriented, we can deploy limited resources more effectively through simpler structures.

Emerging churches exhibit features found in the dissident tradition. Some replace the clergy–laity divide, patriarchy and hierarchical authority, with egalitarian communities. Some are exploring alternatives to sermons and emphasise multi-voiced participation in planning and conducting events. Some, appreciating the significance of ambience and architecture are designing worship spaces that discourage front-led performances and foster mutuality. Some are being church in accessible venues rather than hoping people will find them. Studying dissident movements, however, reveals the power of the Christendom mindset: experimental approaches readily revert to conventional patterns, especially when successful. George Orwell's *Animal Farm* remains essential reading for anyone involved in emerging churches!

There are encouraging examples in emerging churches of attempts to mine the riches of Christendom without endorsing the system. In alt.worship gatherings, worshippers blend icons, candles, labyrinths, rituals, gestures, incense, chants and ancient prayers with contemporary technology and iconography, re-contextualising them. Offering an alternative *both* to anaemic late-modern, late-Christendom worship *and* to inherited liturgical practices steeped in Christendom assumptions and values, this subverts the Christendom legacy.[4] Other emerging churches are also adapting historic resources – *lectio divina* over shared meals, daily offices with ancient and contemporary prayers and readings, and new monastic orders. These are intriguing attempts to differentiate between disposable baggage and life-giving provisions for post-Christendom church.

---

[4] See further Jonny Baker and Doug Gay, *Alternative Worship* (London: SPCK, 2003).

Reflecting on them through the post-Christendom lens, however, suggests they often unwittingly mediate the Christendom mindset. Some features of emerging churches are conducive to being church in post-Christendom, but there are also questions:

- Might emerging churches be better resourced if they knew more history and learned from earlier movements?
- Will they integrate cultural sensitivity and counter-cultural radicalism? Will they ponder past applications of the 'pilgrim' and 'indigenising' principles?[5]
- Is the demise of Christendom taken seriously? Do some emerging churches 'betray lurking assumptions that, if a surface-level hostility towards traditional religion can be overcome, contemporary people remain basically hospitable and friendly to the message of Christ'?[6]
- Are emerging churches developing inter-generational strategies to pass on the faith in a culture where the Christian story and its values are becoming alien?
- Many supposedly ancient Christian practices have pagan origins. Were they so thoroughly Christianised they can be used in emerging churches? Or should we be more discriminating?
- Are some emerging churches more concerned with style than core values? How are issues of power, gender, ethnicity, class and ability handled?
- Does emphasising 'church' – even emerging church – hinder missionary engagement with post-Christendom? Is preoccupation with ecclesiology a Christendom reflex?

---

[5] See Chapter 3.
[6] Smith, *Mission*, 123. Cf. Davie, *Europe*, 46.

- Are emerging churches parasitic on inherited church if they primarily recruit dissatisfied Christians? Can they evangelise non-churched as well as de-churched people?
- Can emerging churches incarnate the gospel beyond the church fringe rather than mainly attracting those (white, educated, middle class) who are already over-represented in inherited churches?
- Will emphasising networks rather than neighbourhoods further marginalise the poor? Will emerging churches disavow the Christendom bias to the powerful and be good news among those with limited networks?

Inherited Church

This chapter has investigated emerging churches as examples of the rethinking the demise of Christendom requires and stimulates. But most Christians are in inherited churches, which are also experiencing this transitional period. Some are oblivious to their changing context, busily participating in congregations large enough to cushion them from emerging realities and located where traditional models still seem to work. Some pin their hopes on yet another programme – or revival. Some church leaders know radical change is needed but are marking time, hoping familiar patterns will survive until they retire. Other churches, accepting things cannot continue as normal, are facing into the future, exploring new forms of worship, mission and community. The boundary between inherited and emerging church is permeable: Christendom's demise invites from us all courageous, creative and careful responses.

This means eschewing nostalgia and welcoming the challenges and opportunities of post-Christendom. Reconfiguring post-Enlightenment patterns for postmodernity is important; but the post-Christendom shift requires reappraising a longer period. What features of inherited church are Christendom distortions that will hinder us in post-Christendom? What practices need abandoning or revising? What neglected elements need reinstating?

Clergy/laity

The gradual but contested transition towards clericalism that predated Constantine progressed inexorably after Constantine towards a clerical caste and passive laity. Dissidents criticised this and explored alternatives, but clericalism survived the Reformation almost unscathed and re-established its hold on movements that initially rejected it. But what does the clergy/laity division help to perpetuate?

- The hierarchical structure and patriarchal ethos that compromises the church's witness in contemporary culture. Ordaining women is an inadequate response.
- Confusion between 'scattered' and 'gathered' church, hindering recognition of the ministry of the whole people of God in society.
- The myth that clergy are on the spiritual 'front line' and laity should support their ministry. The reverse is true.
- Performance-oriented and front-led services, discouraging transition towards multi-voiced communities.

- Different ethical standards for clergy and laity. Sometimes this is official and explicit.
- Unrealistic expectations, exacerbating the chronic shortage of church leaders.

We might make some progress by abolishing either clergy or laity, or designating all Christians as both: the New Testament calls all Christians the *laos* (people) of God[7] and applies *kleros* (appointed) – from which 'clergy' derives – to all.[8] This will mean changing our language. Karl Barth declared: 'The term "laity" is one of the worst in the vocabulary of religion and ought to be banished from Christian conversation.'[9] But changed terminology is inadequate: movements that explicitly reject clericalism revert to two-tier ecclesiology with discouraging regularity. We need a changed mindset, reinforced by structural arrangements and monitoring processes.

The vision of fully functioning communities using diverse gifts in pursuit of shared goals and growing towards maturity, described in Ephesians 4:1–16, has energised many renewal movements. Some people – apostles, prophets, evangelists, pastors, teachers – equip others to use their gifts effectively. There is no hint of clericalism and the thrust is outwards. The church is where God's people (those on the front line) are resourced for mission and ministry. The Christendom shift reversed the thrust: clergy manning an imaginary front line and laity expected to support their ministry. Faithful discipleship meant institutional mainte- nance. Some movements have restored apostles and prophets but have not addressed the Christendom thrust- reversal.

---

[7] Hebrews 4:9; 8:10; 1 Peter 2:9–10; Revelation 21:3.
[8] Galatians 3:29; Ephesians 1:11; Colossians 1:12. See Stevens, *Abolition*.
[9] Cited in Stevens, *Abolition*, 24.

Post-Christendom churches cannot justify this caste system or sustain a clergy/laity division that undergirds maintenance orientation, misconstrues their focus and drains gifted Christians by requiring them to support an institution that should be supporting them. Nor can we endorse a system that damages the spiritual, emotional and physical health of church leaders for so little benefit. This system is unsustainable. An agenda for change might include:

- Recovering the pre-Christendom practice of appointing leaders from within congregations. They may be trained and gain experience elsewhere, but are commissioned to serve their congregation, only transferring in exceptional circumstances – and then not immediately assuming leadership.
- Regarding bi-vocational team leadership as normal: this releases resources and scope for part-time leaders with different gifts, helps leaders connect with the world beyond the church and discourages clerical perceptions and expectations.
- Replacing the reductionist concept of 'ministry of word and sacrament' with 'equipping God's people for ministry': church leaders should not dominate or be exclusively responsible for any aspect of church life.
- Restoring the New Testament emphasis that Christians meet together to build each other up to participate in God's mission.[10] If worship, preaching or such ecclesial activities remain central, clerical control will be re-established.
- Recognising believers' baptism as ordination; affirming the ordination of all members (not only

---

[10] I. Howard Marshall, 'How far did the early Christians worship God?', *Churchman* 99 (1985), 216–29.

leaders and overseas missionaries) by laying hands on those called into new jobs, parenthood, retirement and other vocations; and reflecting prayerfully and theologically together on issues encountered in these vocations.

This does not mean churches without leaders, or that trained and accredited women and men should not be deployed in strategic roles within and among congregations. But it means determined and sustained action[11] to erode clericalism, redefine church leadership, empower the whole people of God for ministry and recalibrate churches as missionary communities.

Monologue sermons

Reviewing the role of church leaders encourages reflection on the place of monologue sermons. These became dominant in Christendom and remain so in many traditions, but there are drawbacks:

- The huge proportion of the working week conscientious church leaders devote to sermon preparation, deflecting them from other activities required in a post-Christendom context.
- The mediocrity of most preachers: the system depends on exceptionally gifted communicators, who are scarce.
- The ineffectiveness of monologues as modes of instruction and their tendency to de-skill audiences.

---

[11] Alan Kreider, 'Abolishing the Laity: An Anabaptist Perspective', in Paul Beasley-Murray (ed.): *Anyone for Ordination?: A Contribution to the Debate on Ordination* (Tunbridge Wells: MARC, 1993), 84–111.

- The limited impact on personal and community development of listening passively even to excellent monologues.
- The excessive frequency of sermons, allowing congregations no opportunity to work through their implications before hearing another.
- The unpopularity of monologue among those leaving churches, weary of dogmatism and rhetorical performances, of being spoon-fed and patronised.

Beleaguered preachers rebut these challenges by proclaiming the long and honourable history of preaching; they refuse to capitulate to cultural shifts, and argue that sermons are spiritual encounters rather than lectures. Many will also, if they are honest, admit their fear of straying from a known format into the insecurity of practices for which neither they nor the congregation has been trained. So preaching remains dominant, enhanced now by audiovisual technology, and deeper concerns are sidestepped.

But when viewed through the post-Christendom lens, other factors appear. Dismissing criticisms of preaching as culturally driven is inadequate: its dominance *resulted from* a cultural shift (as churches became big, left home and embraced classical norms).[12] The dominance of preaching is a Christendom vestige, related to clericalism, massive buildings, unchallengeable proclamation and nominal congregations. Can we learn from dissident groups, who explored other ways of learning together, which their adversaries grudgingly admitted produced biblically literate and passionate disciples?

What are some alternatives? Open-ended presentations, allowing people to reflect and investigate biblical teaching;

---

[12] See Chapter 5.

offering resources rather than rhetoric, posing questions rather than dispensing answers, inviting ownership rather than imposing conclusions; making room for comments, challenges, ideas and exploration; drawing congregations into sermons by eliciting responses and welcoming insights; having several speakers debating issues, with congregational participation; forming discussion groups during or after sermons; asking several people to construct sermons together; developing a culture where people can interrupt and interject comments; providing preparatory reading so congregations can contribute thoughtfully.[13]

This does not mean abandoning sermons but their integration into a more varied and holistic approach. Nor should we devalue theological training or rhetorical skill; but these are resources to equip, not dominate congregations. In post-Christendom we might:

- Designate congregations as participatory 'learning communities' and find diverse ways of stimulating such learning.
- Introduce forms of interactive learning, persisting until they become familiar.
- Welcome monologue presentations as helpful contributions, but probably no more frequently than monthly, and normally with feedback and questions.
- Regard sermons as invitations to conversation – exploring issues, clarifying questions, and identifying biblical and historical resources – not final statements. Ironically, *sermo* originally meant 'conversation'.

---

[13] See further Jeremy Thomson, *Preaching as Dialogue* (Cambridge: Grove, 1996); Tim Stratford, *Interactive Preaching* (Cambridge: Grove, 1998).

- Develop models of theological reflection that relate such biblical and historical resources to issues facing church members in daily life, moving from life to text and from text to life.
- Train preachers and congregations to participate creatively and responsibly in learning communities: otherwise familiar problems – such as the pooling of ignorance, domination by insistent voices, unimaginative questions and failure to move from theory to practice – will stymie such developments.

Christendom discouraged interactive and open-ended learning, treated congregations as audiences and relied too heavily on sermons. Bible study groups, cell groups, adult Sunday school and similar structures offer alternatives; but these peripheral and often disappointing activities have not transformed congregations into mature learning communities. More radical action is needed to equip churches for post-Christendom.

Similar action is needed for multi-voiced worship to replace performance-oriented services, dominated by 'worship leaders', disconnected from the concerns, interests and daily lives of most worshippers. Traditional liturgies and charismatic song-fests display similar inflexible and disincarnate tendencies. Post-Christendom churches must recover the meaning of liturgy ('the people's work'), developing approaches to worship that are contextually earthed, culturally relevant, aesthetically enriching and provoke growth in discipleship. 'Singing the Lord's song' in the strange land of post-Christendom will mean rediscovering the political implications of proclaiming 'Jesus is Lord', re-telling the Christian story (biblical and post-biblical) in our worship rather than assuming this is known, and blending traditional and contemporary resources. Alt.worship communities have pioneered in this area, but many forms of 'alternative' worship are needed in a plural culture. Some churches need a temporary moratorium on singing in order to explore other ways of worshipping together.

If post-Christendom churches become more participatory and multi-voiced, there will be implications for architectural design and seating arrangements. Churches will ask questions about the ethos of their buildings and how these affect what they can and cannot do together. Artists and designers within congregations may be invited to contribute neglected insights and skills in theologically informed discussions about the physical environment. Within the limitations of inherited or available buildings, this might at least mean changing seating arrangements to facilitate interaction. Some churches may decide to abandon buildings where visual heresies contradict verbal orthodoxy.[14] Where there is freedom to experiment, principles of simplicity, beauty, environmental gentleness, contextual coherence, theological congruity and flexibility might stimulate diverse and creative developments.

Church discipline

To interactive learning and worship can be added interactive pastoral care – multi-voiced church expressed through practices traditionally called 'church discipline'. Previous chapters examined the distorting and pernicious effects of Christendom on this and determined but flawed attempts of dissident movements to purge and restore this biblical practice. This troubled history offers little incentive to implement church discipline in post-Christendom churches. There are further disincentives: disciplinary language offends contemporary notions of tolerance and

---

[14] For this terminology and further reflections, see Drane, *McDonaldization*, 89–101.

individualism; the process is often poorly understood, unwisely practised and pastorally damaging; accountability is confused with judgmental attitudes; and in a shrinking church market, introducing measures that might provoke transfers or reduce numbers is unappealing.

However, post-Christendom churches may find the recovery of church discipline vital for sustaining Christian community and discipleship. In the alien environment of post-Christendom, many philosophies and value systems vie for our allegiance. Only the mutual accountability envisaged in Matthew 18 and other texts on church discipline will enable us to avoid assimilation and develop counter-cultural reflexes. Individual discipleship may have been feasible (though never ideal) in an environment where the Christian story and its implications were familiar: in post-Christendom we will need each other's help to resist the lure of consumerism, the reductionist perspectives of economism, the myth of redemptive violence and other destructive tendencies.

Like interactive worship and learning, mutual accountability must be modelled, taught and encouraged. Practising church discipline without developing congregational skills in handling conflict courts disaster. Matthew 18:15–17 summarises the process but we need to learn together, reflect on our experiences and refine our practices. Matthew 18 does not mention church leaders. Abolishing clericalism means church discipline can flourish without being perceived as hierarchical: leaders can equip congregations to practice mutual accountability, but this is not a system they impose.[15]

Matthew 18 assumes congregations will experience conflict and need strategies to resolve these. Eddie Gibbs comments:

---

[15] Stuart Murray, *Explaining Church Discipline* (Tonbridge: Sovereign World, 1995).

The potential for conflict is even greater in the church than elsewhere. This is due to the diversity of constituencies that make up many congregations, the fact that the church is not selective but welcomes all comers, and the fact that the matters of faith and life with which the church deals represent deeply held convictions.[16]

The realistic process Jesus teaches prevents backbiting, superficial relationships, simmering discontent, destructive arguments and church disintegration. It involves truth telling, courage, listening skills, persistence and grace. Mutual accountability is counter-cultural[17] but can sustain post-Christendom churches by fostering authentic community and discipleship. Dealing with conflict creatively and peacefully may also equip churches as reconciling agents in post-Christendom, which will be fragmented and riven by conflict. As Robert Warren writes: 'A church that has found a way to handle conflict creatively will be good news to all around and in it.'[18]

Peace church

Conflict transformation is one dimension of becoming a 'peace church'. This term has historically designated Anabaptists and Quakers, who espoused pacifism rather than 'just war'. Although not every member of churches in these traditions is pacifist, many are, and their churches

---

[16] Eddie Gibbs, *Church Next: Quantum Changes in Christian Ministry* (Leicester: Inter-Varsity Press, 2001), 112.

[17] Although there are parallels in processes many companies have established to address grievances.

[18] Robert Warren, *Being Human, Being Church: Spirituality and Mission in the Local Church* (London: Marshall Pickering, 1995), 17. For training and resources on conflict transformation, contact Bridgebuilders: < www.menno.org.uk >

have been front runners in initiatives to develop alternatives to violence: communities of reconciliation, peace tax campaigns, peace camps, protests against militarism and capital punishment, acts of worship on military bases, citizens' weapons' inspections, peace teams in conflict zones, victim–offender reconciliation programmes and other mediation work. Such creative, risky, confrontational forms of peacemaking counter accusations that pacifism implies passivity or idealism. Groups in other traditions have also pioneered peace initiatives,[19] but traditions that exclude the option of violence have access to opportunities others are denied.

The Enlightenment dream of uniting humanity through reason has foundered. Secular philosophies and national economic interests provoke conflict as readily as religious convictions inspired previous wars. Enlightenment values contributed to the demise of Christendom but appear powerless to curb global and local conflict. Peace movements in the 1960s (when Christendom and modernity started imploding) sought alternatives to war but could offer no stronger foundations for peace than the collapsing secular and religious systems. Christians in post-Christendom face the challenge of building peace churches that model alternatives to violence with enough integrity to offer these to a divided society.

Some proposed the Baptist Union of Great Britain should declare itself a peace church in 2000. This did not happen, but the suggestion was timely. The 'just war' approach has been ineffective historically and is palpably inapplicable to most current conflict scenarios. Furthermore, a Christian minority without access to information necessary to form a judgement

---

[19] Examples include Pax Christi and Catholic Worker groups, the Fellowship of Reconciliation and Baptists in the civil rights' movement.

cannot implement 'just war' theory, should it wish to. We should now jettison this well-intentioned but idealistic Christendom vestige, revisit the pre-Christendom and dissident tradition and consider becoming peace churches. This may mean examining pacifism biblically and theologically and learning from instances of non-violent regime change and active peacemaking that peaceful means are realistic and effective. For others, dissatisfied with traditional options but unsure of pacifism, it might mean studying the biblical vision of shalom and reviewing personal, political and church approaches to injustice, exploring alternatives to violence. Congregations might commit themselves to becoming peace churches, reflecting on the implications for their worship, witness and life together.[20]

Is commitment to peace culturally attuned or counter-cultural in post-Christendom? As with many issues in a diverse culture, it may be both, depending on the context. Church initiatives to ease community conflict and church statements opposing war are greeted warmly by many; although those who know the Christendom story are not easily persuaded churches are serious about peace. Peace churches that practise their convictions will have spiritual resources and theological insights to offer other peace groups but also much to learn from those who have long advocated peace.

However, a consistent church peace commitment that challenges efforts to defend the Western culture of 'military consumerism'[21] and maintain the present unjust world order will be less popular. Peace churches that refuse to

---

[20] See Alan and Eleanor Kreider, *Becoming a Peace Church* (Oxford: Anabaptist Network, 2003) and further resources available from < www.anabaptistnetwork.com >.

[21] Walter Brueggemann, *Interpretation and Obedience: From Faithful Reading to Faithful Living* (Minneapolis: Fortress Press, 1991), 113 and elsewhere.

place national interests over the needs of the global poor and the bonds of transnational Christian community may find opposition mounting. Consider a 'modest proposal' for peace: 'Let the Christians of the world agreed that they will not kill each other.'[22] What would be the impact if we agreed not to kill each other in any circumstances? This does not legitimise killing those who are not Christians: in impersonal modern warfare the status of the (often) unseen enemy is unknown, so no killing can be risked. But it envisions the creation of a global peace church modelling new ways of relating. Post-Christendom needs such creative and hopeful non-conformity. Churches rising to this challenge may encounter fresh interest in the story they tell.

Beyond tithing

If 'just war' thinking is inadequate for challenging Western militarism, tithing cannot subvert Western consumerism. If we would resist the lure of consumerism and build communities of justice, hospitality and generosity, we must abandon this Christendom vestige and explore the implications of more foundational biblical principles – jubilee, koinonia and contentment.

Tithing was a popular ancient practice incorporated into Old Testament economics. Within that system, of which jubilee was the keystone, it was useful. Extracted from that context and applied in different economic systems it is irrelevant or oppressive. Despite the lack of support for tithing in the New Testament and pre-Christendom, Augustine introduced this and gradually tithing evolved from a recommendation into a tax. Deeply resented by the poor, tithing was frequently opposed by dissident groups but persisted

---

[23] Made by Mennonite Central Committee worker, John Stoner, in 1984.

for centuries. Not until 1936 did tithing finally disappear from English law.

But tithing, like other Christendom vestiges, is resilient: as established churches were abandoning this practice, Baptists and Pentecostals rediscovered it and – apparently unaware of its troubled history – promoted it as an expression of radical discipleship! Tithing undoubtedly has attractions: it is simple, systematic, appears to be biblically endorsed and ensures a steady and substantial flow of funds into church coffers. But it derives from irresponsible biblical interpretation, truncates or trivialises discussion of economic and lifestyle issues, offers false security to those who assume it subverts consumerism and fails to address injustice and inequality.[23]

Post-Christendom presents an opportunity to disavow our historic association with the wealthy and powerful and relocate our churches – physically and spiritually – among the poor and powerless. This does not mean withdrawal from other parts of society but replacing trickle-down mission strategies with trickle-up policies. Churches that embrace what liberation theologians call a 'preferential option for the poor' many find fresh perspectives to empower and guide them on the margins. This changed angle of vision is crucial if we are to pursue economic justice and participate in Jesus' mission to bring 'good news to the poor'.[24]

Simple Church

Many other elements could be added to this agenda for post-Christendom churches, but we should beware of over

---

[23] Murray, *Beyond Tithing*.
[24] Luke 4:18–20.

complicating. The relative simplicity of the early churches was already giving way to more complex arrangements before Constantine, but during Christendom theologians were preoccupied with church structure, policy and practice rather than mission. Its demise invites us to focus on central issues rather than trivial or procedural matters most people inside and outside the church find irrelevant. Leith Anderson warns: 'The twenty-first century church must be less preoccupied with internal issues, petty conflicts and traditional divisions … luxuries of affluence and of a religious culture.'[25] Emerging churches, too, though currently creative and flexible, must beware becoming precious or prescriptive about shapes and styles, or confusing peripheral issues with core values and dynamics. Becoming peace churches, creating 'learning communities', practising mutual accountability and radical hospitality are more demanding than meeting in pubs, building labyrinths or mastering PowerPoint. Such developments are also missiologically and pastorally more significant.

Church is really quite simple! We carry unnecessary Christendom complications into post-Christendom at our peril. The transition from institution to movement, from the centre to the margins, means discarding baggage and retaining only what we need to sustain worshipping missionary communities. Simple church might mean:

- Recovering friendship (not insipid 'fellowship' or institutional 'membership') as our relational paradigm. Friendship is non-hierarchical, holistic, relaxed and dynamic. In mission-oriented churches it is inclusive, not exclusive, so people can belong before they believe.

---

[25] Leith Anderson, *A Church for the 21ˢᵗ Century* (Grand Rapids: Bethany House, 1992), 20.

- Eating together. The intimacy and informality of shared meals resonates with the gospel story. It builds community and hinders institutional and hierarchical retrenchment. Worshipping and sharing bread and wine around the meal table encourages multi-voiced participation and restores eucharistic celebration to its original domestic context.
- Laughter. Church in Christendom was serious and solemn. Post-Christendom churches should avoid pomposity and taking themselves too seriously. This does not mean flippancy or cynical postmodern humour, but joyful confidence in the God who does surprising things with unpromising people, irreverence towards the powers dominating our culture and demanding our loyalty, and hope in God's coming kingdom.

The search for simplicity is growing. Some churches have embarked on a process of deconstruction, paring back their activities to what seems essential. Many Christians have left church, weary of its demands, irrelevance and self-absorption. Discussions with them highlight unfulfilled longings from their church experience – encountering God in worship; authentic community; earthed spirituality; cultural relevance; and freedom to grow as human beings and followers of Jesus. This demanding but simple agenda means reinventing and re-imagining, rather than restructuring, church.

Re-imagining Church

Christendom made Christianity conventional, predictable, uninspiring and dull. Given the character of its founder, this was some achievement! Post-Christendom requires us to build communities that more creatively and faithfully incarnate the Christian story. Both postmodernity and post-Christendom encourage the use of our imagination. The reliance on logic, reason and technology that dominated modernity and the tendency of Christendom to enforce conformity and crush dissent discouraged this, but there is renewed emphasis now on intuition and imagination. Without over-complicating, can we re-imagine church in post-Christendom. For example:

Imagine a community stirred by poets and storytellers

For the church to understand itself as a movement, not an institution, it needs to know its history and destiny. Movements are dynamic, people sharing history and traditions and journeying together towards a longed-for future. Post-Christendom churches must be communities that hand down traditions and tell stories that challenge other stories in society.[26] These traditions and stories impart insights and reflexes to live faithfully and distinctively. We must also present the Christian story as a meta-narrative. This involves challenging the postmodern disdain for meta-narratives; uncovering hidden but influential postmodern meta-narratives; recognising most people are searching for a meta-narrative; facing accusations that the Christian story is just another oppressive meta-narrative; and telling this story in a winsome and authentic way.[27]

---

[26] Stanley Hauerwas, *A Community of Character: Toward a constructive Christian social ethic* (Notre Dame: University of Notre Dame Press, 1981), 13.

[27] See Richard Middleton and Brian Walsh, *Truth is stranger than it used to be: Biblical faith in a postmodern age* (London: SPCK, 1995); Andrew Walker, *Telling the Story* (London: SPCK, 1996).

The emphasis on doctrine and morality, rather than narrative, in most sermons and the minimal narrative element in contemporary hymnody offer little to help communities rediscover and rehearse their story. Walter Brueggemann advocates poetic ministry to help us understand our times and develop radical hope: 'The practice of ... poetic imagination is the most subversive, redemptive act that a leader of a faith community can undertake ... the work of poetic imagination holds the potential of unleashing a community of power and action that finally will not be contained by any imperial restrictions and definitions of reality.'[28]

Such poets are not mystical dreamers but exercise prophetic and apostolic roles. Post-Christendom, according to Alan Roxburgh, 'requires leaders whose identity is formed by the tradition rather than the culture. It also requires leaders who listen to the voices from the edge. This is where the apostle, the prophet, and the poet are found.'[29] We need neglected apostolic and prophetic roles restored to the church – men and women with poetic and storytelling gifts, stirring our memories of who we are and inspiring creative and adventurous discipleship. Poets and storytellers have a long history in European culture (and in postmodernity are making a comeback), but these have been unfamiliar roles in churches. Indeed, many with poetic and narrative gifts have left, marginalised and frustrated by prosaic and unimaginative leadership. Can we imagine churches where apostolic storytellers and prophetic poets are at work?

---

[28] Walter Brueggemann, *Hopeful Imagination: Prophetic Voices in Exile* (London: SCM, 1986), 96. See also *Finally Comes the Poet: Daring Speech for Proclamation* (Minneapolis: Augsburg Fortress Publishers, 1989).
[29] Roxburgh, *Missionary Congregation*, 57.

Imagine the church as a monastic missionary order

Anabaptism has been interpreted as a radical monastic movement.[30] The Reformers dismantled two-tier Christianity by abolishing monks; Anabaptists dismantled this by applying the monastic calling – and the task of mission – to all Christians. Monasticism is often perceived as withdrawal from society rather than mission into it, but monastic missionary orders combined prayer and social action, evangelism and contemplation. Some are advocating a new monasticism to sustain counter-cultural discipleship and enable mission. Andrew Walker writes: 'We will have to return to structures … akin to the monastery, the religious community and the sect … we will need to create sectarian plausibility structures in order for our story to take hold of our congregations and root them in the gospel.'[31] Tom Sine agrees: 'We will need to aggressively work for the re-monking of the church to enable followers of Jesus Christ to intentionally set the focus and rhythm of their lives out of biblical calling instead of cultural coercion.'[32]

What might 're-monking' mean? Church leavers persistently criticise the separation of church from daily work (problematic since Constantine designated Sunday a day free from work). Churches often fail to appreciate the demands and pressures of work; church leaders, often unable to reflect helpfully on work-related issues, preach mainly on personal spirituality or church-related issues; churches do little to equip members to address relational

---

[30] Kenneth Davis, *Anabaptism and Asceticism: A Study in Intellectual Origins* (Scottdale: Herald Press, 1974).

[31] Andrew Walker, *Telling the Story: Gospel, Mission and Culture* (London: SPCK, 1996), 190.

[32] Cited in Heather Wraight (ed.), *They call themselves Christians* (London: Christian Research/ LCWE, 1998), 109.

and ethical issues at work; and evangelistic strategies ignore the workplace despite the multiplicity of friendships there that could facilitate effective faith sharing.

Might these criticisms be met by re-imagining the church as a monastic missionary order, communities of encouragement, support and training from which we emerge to live as Christians in the workplace and to which we return for reflection and renewal? Some propose a model of 'church beyond the congregation' that emphasises our role in the created order and drastically reduces the role of the gathered church.[33] Although presented as radical, this is rooted in the Christendom mindset: in Christendom church was society wide; in this proposed model, too, church- as-gathered-community is relegated to a minor role and society remains central. This underestimates the need for gathered communities to sustain witness and nurture counter-cultural discipleship in post-Christendom. Re-monking (whatever this means in light of the ambivalent history of monasticism) may enable healthier interaction between 'gathered' and 'scattered' church.

Imagine churches as safe places to take risks

Inherited church culture is not characterised by enthusiasm about risks. Safety-first thinking dominates most congregations and denominations, inhibiting and frustrating those wanting to pioneer fresh initiatives and strategies. In some emerging churches, experiments can take place with less

---

[33] For example, James Thwaites, *The Church Beyond the Congregation: The strategic role of the church in the postmodern era* (Carlisle: Paternoster Press, 1999) and *Renegotiating the Church Contract: The Death and Life of the 21st Century Church* (Carlisle: Paternoster Press, 2001).

opposition from those concerned about proposed changes and the risks involved. But emerging churches are not always well equipped to evaluate outcomes. A more promising scenario involves inherited and emerging churches pooling their expertise, resources and insights. Risk taking and reflection are both required.

A criticism of emerging churches is that few are radical enough in their engagement with culture or ecclesiological creativity. Some have been labelled 'ecclesiastical re-engineering' and 'tactical attempts to breathe new life into old structures'.[34] Those involved may disagree, but we probably need riskier experiments to grapple with the challenges and opportunities of post-Christendom. Furthermore, John Drane, citing evidence of craving for excitement in contemporary culture, asks: 'is the church as we know it just too bland, dull and safely predictable for people who crave an experience of radical challenge?'[35] If so, churches will need to foster risky living. What would this require?

- A theological understanding of risk. As long as many see risk taking as averse to faith in God, prophetic direction, God's sovereignty or wise pastoral practice, experimentation will be limited.
- A mature and sensitive pastoral framework that values pioneers and balances freedom and accountability. The riskier the venture, the harder this balance is to maintain, but this is vital for pioneers to have confidence to experiment.
- An explicit recognition that experiments do not always succeed, so risk takers can fail with dignity. For example, an urban church-planting agency

---

[34] Gibbs, *Church Next*, 168–9, 213.
[35] Drane, *McDonaldization*, 28.

includes in its core values recognition that teams
working in risky environments are 'free to fail'.[36]

- Assessing 'success' and 'failure' by missiological, not
numerical, criteria and by long-term rather than
short-term effects.

Insights for post-Christendom church will emerge from
apparent failures as much as from so-called successes. Mike
Riddell writes:

> This is not a time of master plans or franchised churches. It is a
> time of groups who grapple with issues of the emerging culture
> and the living out of their faith as followers of Jesus in that cul-
> ture. This multiplicity of new models, their failures and their
> successes, their evolution and their demise will be what funds
> the movement of God into the future.[37]

Humility, rather than arrogance and intransigence, will
enable inherited and emerging churches to listen to each
other. Humility, acknowledging our chequered history and
complicity in oppression and injustice, will equip us to tell
the story of Jesus in post-Christendom in ways that attract
rather than repel people. Humility, recognising how little
we understand, will encourage us beyond insecure certainties into the adventure of risk taking. Humility will help us
keep church simple.

There are hopeful signs: re-imagining church is underway. Storytellers and poets are stirring the churches again; a
new missionary monasticism is emerging; risk-taking is
becoming fashionable! This is just a sample: much more
re-imagining lies ahead. And re-imagining church is one

---

[36] See < www.urbanexpression.org.uk >.

[37] Mike Riddell (et al), *The Prodigal Project: Journey into the
Emerging Church* (London: SPCK, 2000), 132.

small part of re-imagining the world as God's kingdom breaks in.

Revival or Survival?

How do we imagine the church's near future? There are surveys that paint a bleak picture, hints that continuing decline is not inevitable, dangers of clutching at straws in new programmes, prophecies of revival that may be wishful thinking and claims that post-Christendom means unprecedented opportunity. How can we weave these strands together? What are the prospects for the church in post-Christendom?

- The annihilation of the church in Western culture is unlikely. Even the most foreboding analyses suggest churches will survive. Callum Brown concludes: 'despite their dramatic decline, they will continue to exist in some skeletal form with increasing commitment from decreasing numbers of adherents'.[38]
- Institutional survival may mean congregations, mission agencies, theological colleges and denominations merging. Some denominations, no longer viable as national organisations, may evolve into networks.[39] Translocal leadership may be expressed in fresh ways.
- As decline continues and the church's influence wanes, some may despair. But signs of hope may appear – ways of sharing faith and incarnating our

---

[38] Brown, *Death*, 197.
[39] Pete Ward, *Liquid Church* (Carlisle: Paternoster Press, 2002).

story in viable and attractive communities.
Congregations may no longer be the dominant
expression of a kaleidoscopic Christian community.

- If we negotiate this turbulent period and emulate
previous generations who discovered the capacity of
Christian faith to survive cultural shifts (though we
face the greatest challenge since the fourth century),
we may discover fresh opportunities for witness and
service in whatever post-Christendom becomes.

In other words, we anticipate *survival*, not *revival*. We are
not expecting restoration of former glories, the renewal of
Christendom or rapid and painless transition to a new era
of triumphant progress. We are hoping to survive and incarnate the story of Jesus faithfully in whatever culture
emerges. If we accept this prognosis (or something like it),
our priorities might be to:

- Stop praying for revival. Stop encouraging
unrealistic expectations that foster disillusionment
and hinder contextual missionary engagement.
- Accept our status as marginal communities and
embrace the opportunity to rediscover neglected
aspects of our story and faith.
- Disavow Christendom, repenting of the suffering it
caused, and decide what to discard, what to retain
and how to handle Christendom vestiges and
reflexes.
- Eschew short-term perspectives in favour of lasting
transformation, aware we will not see the necessary
paradigm shift accomplished in our lifetime.
- Concentrate on modest, sustainable and provisional
initiatives; develop tactics, not grand strategies;
abandon goal setting as irrelevant in uncharted

territory; and create nimble structures able to respond flexibly to new challenges.

- Forge partnerships between inherited and emerging churches and mission agencies. A new ecumenism beckons: heterogeneous, grass roots, sectarian, informal, global, mission-oriented and messy.
- Pray and work for survival, listening for the Spirit's prompting, aware God may surprise us, and welcome the gradual emergence of post-Christendom Christianity.

10

Post-Christendom: Resources

A comprehensive vision of mission and church in post-Christendom has not emerged in the past three chapters. Investigation with the post-Christendom lens has stimulated reflection and prompted tentative proposals. But many Christendom vestiges were not examined. Many questions remain:

- Should we sing a *national anthem* that combines divine authentication of monarchy, militarism and religious nationalism?
- Should churches *reclaim income tax* on gifts spent on internal programmes rather than truly charitable causes?[1]
- Might we create *new Christian festivals* rather than whingeing about the secularising of Christmas and Easter?
- Are there better ways than 'keeping Sunday special' to observe the principle of Sabbath?
- Who will write *hymns and songs* that subvert Christendom attitudes in the churches?

---

[1] This contravenes the principle that donors should not benefit from donations and depends on the Christendom assumption that church activities are inherently charitable.

This is but a small selection: there are more questions than answers in this transitional period. But where will we find resources to reflect on such issues? How will we read the Bible in post-Christendom? What language will we use and avoid? What images will guide and inspire us? What impact will post-Christendom have on our theology and, especially, our understanding of Jesus?

Church

Post-Christendom is a new mission context. Callum Brown concludes: 'Britain is showing the world how religion as we have known it can die.'[2] Not just in Britain, but throughout Western culture, Christians are facing something we have not previously encountered. Christianity has been almost eradicated before by conquering armies or the influx of competing religious ideas, but not by internal erosion in a religious and ethical vacuum that disparate spiritual and philosophical ideas cannot fill. We have not been this way before. From dominant centrality to impotent marginality in a few decades has left the church reeling and uncertain.

But, though there are no exact parallels, there are resources in the global church, past and present, on which we can draw.

Pre-Christendom

Although post-Christendom is not pre-Christendom,[3] aspects of the early church's context resemble ours: *pax Romana* was a coercive peace and imperial culture not dissimilar from the world order envisaged by *pax*

---

[2] Brown, *Death*, 198.
[3] See Chapter 1.

Americana; toleration of multiple private religious and ethical views that did not threaten political, social or economic power structures was normal then as now; and we are acclimatising to the marginality churches experienced before Constantine. There were also significant differences: the early churches knew of no Christians in different contexts; they experienced the threat of persecution that seems remote in Western society; and they had no Christendom to celebrate or disavow. Two further cautions – the early churches were not uniform and, especially in the third century, developed in ways that made feasible the Christendom shift. Nevertheless, we can learn much from pre-Christendom.

We will find some parts of the story inspiring and easy to translate into our context. Other things we may discard; some we may initially find uncongenial but gradually appreciate their significance. We can learn from the early Christians' faithfulness and compromise, unwise syncretism and creative indigenising, unattractive legalism and courageous non-conformity. We must not idealise pre-Christendom or disassociate it entirely from the 'fallen' church that succumbed to Constantine, but on many issues we may grant 'the benefit of the doubt to over two centuries of fallible, divided, confused church life, during which nonetheless the vision of the major teachers was structurally sound'.[4] They were near in time to Jesus, inspired by his radical teaching and example: they show us ways of following Jesus obscured by Christendom. And Robert Webber's claim may encourage us: 'Throughout history a revived interest in the insights of the early church has usually been accompanied by significant renewal in the church.'[5]

---

[4] Yoder, *Priestly*, 129.
[5] Robert Webber, *Ancient-Future Faith: Rethinking Evangelicalism for a Postmodern World* (Grand Rapids: Baker, 1999), 34.

What might we investigate?

- The significance of conversion, baptism and catechesis. What does conversion mean on the margins? How do communities equip their members for counter-cultural discipleship in an alien environment?
- Their witness in a contested society, in which older and stronger communities commended different beliefs. How did Christianity penetrate society and result in such extraordinary church growth?
- Their internal dynamics. What can we learn from how they worshipped and prayed, which biblical texts and images inspired them, how they shared their resources and handled economic issues?
- Their resistance to imperial demands. How does their self-identity as a 'people of peace' who refused to swear oaths inform our engagement with issues of violence and truth telling?

We will want to compare pre-Christendom churches with churches in Christendom. Some developments we may consider appropriate ways of contextualising the gospel into a changed culture or regard as signs of maturity; other changes we may disavow as distortions and unwarranted innovations. We will also note that dissidents (many with limited knowledge of pre-Christendom) sometimes unwittingly recovered older practices.

Anti-Christendom

Previous chapters suggested the dissident tradition might inspire post-Christendom churches. Although little from earlier movements survived the Christendom censors, Anabaptist writings offer access to this anti-Christendom tradition. On the threshold of post-Christendom we may find helpful insights from a movement that 500 years ago rejected Christendom and has pioneered different approaches to discipleship, church and mission. When these approaches resonate with what we know of earlier dissidents and pre-Christendom churches, we may conclude that we are encountering an alternative tradition older than Christendom itself. We will not idealise this tradition any more than pre-Christendom: there is neither a golden age before Christendom nor a silver thread running through Christendom. But we will value learning from these marginal communities as they struggled to be Christians without the Christendom framework.[6] We are no longer at the centre of a Christianised society, so many aspects of Christendom seem irrelevant or problematic, whereas principles and practices that brought persecution on the dissidents now seem pertinent, even essential.

Christendom

Even if Christendom was illegitimate and disfigured Christianity, our European Christian forebears were mostly Christendom people. Some were passionately committed to what they regarded as 'Christian civilisation'; others were critical but remained within the system; most simply took it for granted. And they produced wonderful spiritual and cultural treasures we will value in post-Christendom. We will carefully scrutinise such treasures, wary of the Christendom legacy they represent, but will carry much with us into post-Christendom. However we assess the Christendom shift, we will not discount God's grace in the midst of corrupt systems and structures.

---

[6] And from Jewish communities as they struggled *not* to be Christian in Christendom and survived as non-conformists.

Valuing dissident movements does not mean assuming they were always right and mainstream churches always wrong. Dissidents were under pressure with limited time and resources to reach balanced perspectives. Some groups became perfectionist and legalistic, unnecessarily rejected mainstream practices and fell into errors common to those struggling to define their identity and survive. Some overreacted: although their protests were valid, they deprived themselves of valuable resources. A recurrent and regrettable feature of church history is the breakdown of communication between these traditions.

What kinds of fifth-century churches might have emerged if Augustine and Pelagius had learned from each other's teaching on God's grace and radical discipleship? How might the sixteenth century have been different if the friendly conversations between Martin Bucer and Pilgram Marpeck had been replicated between other Reformers and Anabaptists? Can mutual respect and readiness to learn from each other characterise relationships between those with divergent visions of mission and church in post-Christendom? Can inherited and emerging churches learn from the past and avoid polarisation?

Extra-Christendom

But Christendom is not the whole story. African, Asian and Latin American churches, though planted by Western missionaries, evolved in ways these missionaries could not have imagined. They were influenced by Christendom values and expectations, but indigenous theology, spirituality, ecclesiology, liturgy, ethics and missiology have all gradually emerged. The global church offers beleaguered and disheartened Western Christians resources for grappling with post-Christendom: a buoyant spirituality not drained by the secularity of Western culture; a sense of perspective, setting atypical Western decline in the context of worldwide expansion; a gift of imagination, offering fresh models of mission and church; and experience with other religious traditions. Andrew Walls insists: 'It will hardly be possible for the West to enter serious dialogue with Eastern religions without the help of Indian Christians.'[7]

But we must learn *how* to receive these resources, differentiating between transferable principles and practices that are appropriate and effective only in certain contexts. We should not perceive the reverse missionary movement as the arrival of the cavalry to lift the siege. Their energy, spirituality, faith and missionary commitment are very welcome. But many are re-importing Christendom patterns and outdated practices Western missionaries taught them. They have not yet discovered effective strategies for mission and church planting among westerners. But they are bringing theological insights, cross-cultural experience and spiritual disciplines we desperately need.

If we would develop partnerships for mutual learning, we must recognise we are a decreasing minority and not imply our perspectives are normative. Transnational denominations and organisations must ensure the numerical growth and spiritual vigour of churches in non-Western nations is reflected in representation at conferences and transnational leadership roles. We have much to learn, if we are willing. But this learning can be mutual: non-Western missionaries in post-Christendom may discover resources to help them grapple with nominality, imported Christendom vestiges and neo-Christendoms in their own societies.

---

[7] Walls, *Cross-Cultural Process*, 47. Cf. Vinoth Ramachandra, *The Recovery of Mission: Beyond the Pluralist Paradigm* (Carlisle: Paternoster Press, 1996) and *Faiths in Conflict?: Christian Integrity in a Multicultural World* (Downers Grove: InterVarsity Press, 1999).

Cross-cultural mission agencies that have abandoned outmoded paradigms (not all have) can act as interpreters and facilitators in forging these partnerships. Much closer integration is needed between denominations and their missionary societies, which can also offer their own experience of operating in extra-Christendom contexts. Walls summarises their mandate: 'to commend, demonstrate and illustrate the gospel; to persuade without the instruments to coerce'. He continues: 'To undertake this task implied a readiness to enter someone else's world instead of imposing the standards of one's own. It meant learning another's language, seeking a niche within another's society, perhaps accepting a situation of dependence.'[8] This description of missionary methods in Africa or Asia applies equally to mission in post-Christendom.

Bible

What biblical resources do we have for post-Christendom, and how do we read the Bible now?

Disavowing Christendom hermeneutics

Earlier chapters critiqued the ways Christendom interpreters read the Bible:

- They emphasised textual analysis and philosophical speculation rather than application and discipleship.
- They used biblical texts to legitimise practices based on other considerations.
- They relied on the Old Testament, uninformed by New Testament insights, for ethical and ecclesial judgements.

---

[8] Walls, *Cross-Cultural Process*, 220.

- Theologians, councils and politicians issued authoritative interpretations, disempowering individuals and communities.
- They employed a hermeneutics of order, not justice – confirming conventional norms and structures.
- They interpreted biblical passages from the perspective of the powerful rather than the powerless.
- They applied higher ethical standards to monks, nuns and clergy than to other Christians.
- Their interpretations were oriented towards maintenance rather than mission.

Biblical interpretation is always contextual. As interpreters we bring presuppositions from our political, economic, social, cultural and individual contexts, which influence questions we ask, stories that resonate, angles of vision from which we view texts and choices between possible interpretations. Naturally, the Christendom shift impacted interpreters and presuppositions. But presuppositions are not determinative: reading Scripture can cause us to critique our context and change our perspectives. Dissident movements found, as they read the Bible together, that it undermined the system they were familiar with and encouraged new ways of thinking.

Post-Christendom invites us, too, to question Christendom presuppositions and review longstanding interpretations. We do this conscious that we will import post-Christendom presuppositions and without claiming objectivity or finality. But we do it in dialogue with the dissidents and non-Western interpreters, who bring their own presuppositions and criticisms of the European hermeneutic tradition. The hegemony of Christendom marginalised other hermeneutical options – within and beyond Christendom – and claimed unwarranted status for its hermeneutics.

Dissident and extra-Christendom traditions have exposed this claim as imperialistic and illegitimate.

So we disavow Christendom hermeneutics, not dismissing all previous interpretations or devaluing centuries of biblical scholarship, but reflecting on the influence of the Christendom shift, adopting a hermeneutic of suspicion, scrutinising long-established readings and exploring Scripture from post-Christendom perspectives.

Angles of vision

Marginal churches, once they accept their location, discover fresh angles of vision from which to examine issues. Initially unsettling, this can become liberating, even exhilarating, as Scripture pulsates with new resources for discipleship, church and mission. What might this mean?

- Recognising different voices in the Old Testament and identifying with prophetic, poetic and marginal rather than imperial, prosaic and mainstream voices.[9]
- Identifying the subversive plot in the Song of Songs, which has an unknown lover as the hero, not Solomon.[10]
- Discovering how biblical authors subvert patriarchy and affirm the dignity of women and their participation in the story.[11]

---

[9] Walter Brueggemann's writings expound this approach to Old Testament interpretation.
[10] More medieval commentaries were written on this than any other Old Testament book, but most regard Solomon as the hero.
[11] See, for instance, Catherine Kroeger and Mary Evans (eds.), *The IVP Women's Bible Commentary* (Downers Grove: InterVarsity Press, 2002).

- Interpreting the Parable of the Weeds,[12] contrary
  to Augustine and others, as a kingdom parable,
  refuting the 'mixed church' Christendom
  interpretation.
- Reading the story of the rich young ruler[13] from the
  perspective of the poor recipient of his wealth rather
  than from the rich man's perspective.
- Being less impressed by the extraordinary
  generosity of the widow who gave her last mite to
  the Temple treasury[14] than outraged by the
  rapacious religious system that 'devoured widows'
  houses' in this way.
- Identifying the king in the Parable of the Pounds[15]
  not as Jesus but as a Roman collaborator, and the
  uncooperative servant as the hero, not the villain.
- Appreciating that, when Jesus said 'give Caesar what
  is Caesar's',[16] he was radically relativising Caesar's
  pretensions – and how unwittingly subversive this
  text is in coronation services.
- Regarding Revelation 13, not Romans 13, as
  definitive on the nature of the state, and reading
  Romans 13 not as divine endorsement of the status
  quo but a call to non-violent subversion.

However, we must beware unrealistic expectations.
Post-Christendom churches may be marginal within Western society, but Western Christians inhabit the dominant
economic and political culture and are complicit in an
exploitative and unjust global system. This context preju-
dices our biblical interpretation. We need the insights of

---

[12] Matthew 13:24–30, 36–43.
[13] Matthew 19:16–30.
[14] Mark 12:38–13:2.
[15] Luke 19:11–27.
[16] Matthew 22:21.

poor, persecuted and powerless brothers and sisters to help us out of Christendom.[17]

We may also find surprising new insights from reading Scripture with those in post-Christendom who have no church background and read the Bible without traditional assumptions and interpretations. Andrew Curtis investigated how 'ordinary real readers' read the Gospels, noting the amazement of prostitutes reading Jesus' words to religious leaders, 'the prostitutes are entering the kingdom of God ahead of you',[18] and discovering through further research how different groups heard different messages from the same texts.[19] In plural post-Christendom, authoritative interpretations that universalise their limited angle of vision are unhelpful: we will need to read Scripture with many fellow travellers.

Resonating texts

Post-Christendom also encourages us to identify biblical texts that especially resonate with our changing context. Texts that were marginal in Christendom may become increasingly significant in post-Christendom.

In the fourth and fifth centuries, searching for ways to interpret and resource imperial Christianity, theologians perceived the Israelite monarchy as analogous to the rule of Christian emperors. However, as Walter Brueggemann reminds us, 'the convergence of "state and church" holds

---

[17] See, for example, Rasiah Sugirtharajah, *Voices from the Margins* (London: SPCK, 1991) and Ernesto Cardenal (ed.), *The Gospel in Solentiname* (Maryknoll: Orbis, 1982).
[18] Matthew 21:31.
[19] Andrew Curtis, 'An Encounter with Ordinary Real Readers Reading the Gospels: Implications for Mission', in Teresa Okure (ed.), *To Cast Fire on the Earth* (Pietermaritzburg: Cluster, 2000).

true for only a small part of the Old Testament, but it is the part ... that dominates our interpretive imagination.'[20] In the twenty-first century, as Christendom and imperialism lose legitimacy, other Old Testament paradigms may instruct us. We may see analogies between the periods described in Joshua and Judges and the advancing but decentralised mission of pre-Christendom churches. If Israel's monarchy represents Christendom, exile to Babylon offers a poignant image of post-Christendom. While we will rightly be wary of pushing this analogy too far, it relativises the Christendom predilection for the monarchical period and suggests different ways of reading the Old Testament. These take us beyond the dissidents, who knew the Old Testament was being misused but were unsure how to redeem it.

Certainly, exilic literature (Second Isaiah, Jeremiah, Ezekiel, some Psalms, etc.) is popular with commentators searching for an interpretive lens for post-Christendom. Brueggemann writes: 'If we are indeed in exile in an alien culture, then we would do well to live in the presence of the great exilic texts that our mothers and fathers formed in the exile. If we learn to trust these texts, we will have important resources to rely on.'[21] Searching for resources for social and political engagement in post-Christendom, we may find the stories of Joseph in Egypt, Daniel in Babylon or Esther and Mordecai in Persia more pertinent than models drawn from the state–church monarchy era.

A rediscovered New Testament theme is 'principalities and powers' – structures of spiritual oppression that dehumanise and enslave. Although there are various ways of interpreting this language, it resonates in post-Christendom, where marginal churches no longer

---

[20]   Brueggemann, *Cadences*, 100.
[21]   Brueggemann, *Interpretation*, 206.

perceive themselves as powerful. The longstanding popularity of this theme in urban missiology undergirds the suggestion that post-Christendom is most apparent in urban communities. As the church's marginality increases, the Book of Revelation, interpreted as insights for powerless communities in an oppressive society (not a tour guide to near-future events), may also become an important resource, as it has often been in contexts of marginality.

We may also enquire which texts were *not* read in Christendom. Which texts had such subversive potential they were hard to interpret in politically innocuous ways and so were ignored? We might ponder the 'texts of terror' (Abraham's treatment of Hagar, the rape of Tamar, the sacrifice of Jephthah's daughter) with their dreadful accounts of oppression that unmask the capacity of biblical characters to become vindictive.[22] Another awkward text for Christendom is the conversation between God, Samuel and the Israelite elders that subverts the institution of monarchy.[23] Richard Middleton and Brian Walsh argue these texts play a subversive role 'as an inner-biblical critique of any totalizing or triumphalistic reading of the metanarrative'.[24] This counter-narrative is an important response to postmodern claims that the Bible presents just one more oppressive meta-narrative.

Marginal churches searching for biblical resources are spoiled for choice. As the story unfolds, a repeated theme emerges – God is at work on the margins through marginal individuals and communities. Several biblical authors seem determined to underline this perspective:

---

[22] Phyllis Trible, *Texts of Terror: Literary-Feminist Readings of Biblical Narratives* (Philadelphia: Fortress, 1984).
[23] 1 Samuel 8.
[24] Middleton and Walsh, *Truth*, 179.

- The author of Exodus reports the names of the feisty Israelite midwives, but not the name of the Pharaoh.[25]
- The choice of David (not even in the starting line-up) as king subverts normal hierarchical expectations.[26]
- Matthew's genealogy includes disreputable incidents and marginalised female ancestors.[27]
- Luke lists important historical figures and centres of power before noting wryly: 'the word of God came to John son of Zechariah in the desert.'[28]
- The Christmas narrative is shot through with marginality – unmarried peasant mother, little Bethlehem, no room in the inn, stable and manger, shepherds, foreigners, babies slaughtered, refugees in Egypt, despised Nazareth.

Viewed through the post-Christendom lens, the Bible offers abundant resources for marginal churches. But it has been used in slogans and propaganda, as an instrument of hierarchical control and to justify mutual animosity, oppression and slaughter. For it to be a resource for inspiration, liberation and conversation in post-Christendom, we will need to handle it more responsibly and more humbly.

Theology

If the Bible was misused and misinterpreted in Christendom, we cannot avoid nagging concerns about the impact on Christian theology. Did fourth-century capitulation to

---

[25] Exodus 1:15.
[26] 1 Samuel 16:11.
[27] Matthew 1:3, 5–6.
[28] Luke 3:1–2.

imperial culture and priorities affect not just ecclesiology, missiology and ethics but other aspects of doctrine?

- Were fourth- and fifth-century ecumenical creeds skewed by the influence of Greek philosophy, resulting in their abstruse metaphysical language that lacks drama or narrative?
- Do certain features of the doctrine of God owe more to classical theistic ideas than biblical revelation? Is the contested 'openness of God' position[29] more congruent with a Christian doctrine of God?
- In post-Christendom do we need a less imperialistic Christology?
- What influence did Christendom have on certain theories of atonement (such as penal substitution or ransom)? Should we revisit our soteriology (doctrine of salvation) in light of post-Christendom anxiety about meaninglessness rather than guilt?
- What impact did the coercive and punitive ethos of Christendom have on thinking about justice, retribution, capital punishment and hell?[30]
- If God's kingdom is no longer identified with a triumphant church in a Christianised society, how can we recover its subversive dynamism, and what eschatology is appropriate for post-Christendom?

---

[29] Clark Pinnock (et al), *The Openness of God: A Biblical Challenge to the Traditional Understanding of God* (Downers Grove/Carlisle: InterVarsity Press/Paternoster Press, 1994); Tony Gray and Christopher Sinkinson (eds.), *Reconstructing Theology: A Critical Assessment of the Theology of Clark Pinnock* (Carlisle: Paternoster Press, 2000).
[30] Chris Marshall, *Beyond Retribution: A New Testament Vision for Justice, Crime and Punishment* (Grand Rapids: Eerdmans, 2001).

- Have we appreciated the changed context for apologetics, in which we must engage not just with secularists but members of other religious traditions?

Raising such issues provokes alarm lest postmodern revisionism erodes fundamental Christian doctrines. But perhaps post-Christendom offers space to reconsider ways of formulating doctrine and recover authentically biblical perspectives.

We might also query if 'theology' – separated from discipleship, worship and mission – is a Christendom distortion (the term was rare before 325). Kenneth Leech criticises Christendom theologising as cerebral, elitist, individualistic and disconnected from prayer and the pursuit of holiness.[31] Post-Christendom theologising should be grass roots, communitarian, doxological, provisional, applied and contextual, rather than addressing questions that interest a theological guild. To their priesthood, prophet-hood and missionary-hood, we should add the 'theologian-hood' of all believers. 'Trickle-down' theology, disseminated by academic theologians via graduates from theological institutions to passive congregations, must be replaced by theological reflection on the frontiers of mission and partnerships between those who know what questions matter and those who can offer biblical, historical and theological resources.

Imagery

The mindset shift needed to escape Christendom presuppositions will also require interpretive and evocative imagery.

---

[31] Leech, *Long Exile*, 121–7. This may apply especially to post-Reformation theologising.

The previous chapter advocated re-imagining: what images of discipleship, church and mission will guide us in post-Christendom?

A recurrent image throughout this book has been *marginality*. The Christendom shift involved the church coming into the cultural centre from the margins, at the expense of marginalising aspects of its story. The expansion of Christendom meant movement out from the political centre to the margins. The dissident tradition was an expression of Christianity on the margins of Christendom. The post-Christendom shift implies the church returning to the social margins and learning to operate from this marginal perspective. It also means acknowledging that Western Christians are on the margins of the global church and should learn humbly from others.

Marginality is no reason for despair: biblically and historically God's kingdom has often – maybe normally – advanced from the margins, not the centre. Global mission was peripheral in Christendom, but this marginal perspective sparked a movement that eventually transcended Christendom itself.[32] Mary Grey asks about the church's situation in Western society: 'Could this be a *kairos* moment to re-root ourselves in a more profound theological vision and praxis for Christian community, and to rediscover this from the position of marginality?' She advocates 'creative boundary living':[33] the margins can stimulate pioneering, adventure and discovery.

Marginality is a helpful image, but it has limitations. Some argue postmodernity is a decentred culture that makes any notion of centre and margins obsolete. In a world of individualism and privatised values, the notion of

---

[32] Walls, *Cross-Cultural Process*, 32–3.
[33] Mary Grey, *Beyond the Dark Night: A Way Forward for the Church?* (London: Cassell, 1997), 9.

society has been marginalised.[34] Maybe the church is one more fragment of a cultural kaleidoscope constantly shifting around no detectable centre.[35] Alan Roxburgh offers an alternative image: *liminality*. Drawing on anthropologist Victor Turner, he defines liminality as 'the transition process accompanying a change of state or social position'.[36]

Liminality is a threshold state, a transition between the familiar and the unknown, an unsettling process creating anxiety and vulnerability, where reluctance to abandon past securities jeopardises future prospects. Roxburgh suggests that Western culture is in a liminal state and that churches share this experience of uncertainty. Liminality offers opportunities for new discoveries and personal and communal maturing. But it feels threatening and churches hanker for previous certainties. Roxburgh writes: 'Currently much of the shaping conversation is that of return. Beneath schemes of renewal and strategies of growth lie these liminal impulses of return and recovery.'[37] The image of liminality helps us interpret the mixed dread and excitement we feel on the threshold of post-Christendom.

Another image already encountered is *exile*. Parallels with Israelites in Babylon may be helpful, challenging us to settle down and not expect quick changes in our fortunes, unmasking over-optimistic prophecies of restoration as false, encouraging us to learn to sing the Lord's song in a strange land.[38] If we resist the temptation to push this too far – for example, by retaining hopes of eventual return to the place from which we were exiled (Christendom) – we may be stirred by remembering the exile was a time of cre-

[34] Walker, *Telling*, 168.
[35] Gibbs, *Church Next*, 167, 220.
[36] Roxburgh, *Missionary Congregation*, 23.
[37] Roxburgh, *Missionary Congregation*, 34.
[38] Psalm 137:4.

ativity and renewal for Israel. Similar images of our present status and vocation are *resident aliens* and *sojourners*. We do not feel at home in post-Christendom as we did in Christendom, nor should we expect the same rights. Our commitments to social policies, political parties, economic systems and national identity are provisional, for our ultimate loyalty is to another kingdom we no longer confuse with Christendom. This is not a call to inaction or disengagement, any more than it was for the Israelites (whom Jeremiah told to seek the shalom of the city where they were exiles[39]), but it gives us a realistic perspective.

A fourth image is *pilgrimage*. The language of journeying is popular for describing how people come to faith in Christ in postmodern, post-Christendom culture. But journeying or pilgrimage is helpful imagery also for the life of discipleship that flows from an initial commitment to Jesus. It recalls one of the earliest names for the church – 'the Way'[40] – and also the Anabaptist concept of discipleship as 'following Jesus', which challenged static Christendom church membership. Pilgrimage encourages us to follow Jesus onto the margins, across the threshold and into exile and learn to be his disciples in a new context. Leech combines several of these images:

> As Christians enter the twenty-first century, they do so as exiles, strangers and pilgrims, aliens in a strange land. They will need to learn strategies of survival, and to sing the songs of Zion in the midst of Babylon. The era of Christendom is over, and we need to develop post-Christendom theologies of liberation.[41]

---

[39] Jeremiah 29:4–7.
[40] Acts 9:2; 19:23. See John Driver, *Images of the Church in Mission* (Scottdale: Herald Press, 1997) for reflections on this and other images.
[41] Leech, *Long Exile*, 229.

Another image, embracing several of these elements, which can be interpreted in various ways, is *church on the edge* – on the edge of society, on the edge of a new era, on the edge of possible extinction, on the edge of new possibilities, on the cutting-edge of mission. But no image captures everything, and further images will challenge and inspire us in the years ahead.

One word of warning: this is a Eurocentric perspective – elsewhere church is thriving, moving from the margins towards the centre, growing in strength and influence. But, for Western Christians at the end of Christendom, such images must infuse our hopes, songs, prayers and conversations if we would 'learn strategies of survival' and find new ways of being church, engaging in mission and following Jesus.

Terminology

Images stir us, but we should also watch our language: words are powerful, endorsing or challenging the status quo. Christendom has left a linguistic legacy. Problems with terminology were noted in previous chapters, although familiar terms were generally retained to avoid confusion. Even some biblical terms are problematic because their subversive and dynamic meaning has been distorted by conventional and oppressive Christendom interpretations. 'Kingdom' has been popular in many circles, but this has been trivialised by overuse and often conveys static and imperialistic notions, rooted in Christendom rather than biblical usage. Orlando Costas warns of 'neo-Christendom hiding beneath a resurgent lordship and kingdom imagery'.[42] If we continue using such terms, we must recover their biblical cadence and ethos.

---

[42] Orlando Costas, in Gerald Anderson and Thomas Stransky, *Christ's Lordship and Religious Pluralism* (Maryknoll: Orbis, 1981), 165.

Other terminology we might remove from our vocabulary:

- Terms like 'house of God', 'church' and 'sanctuary' to designate buildings where Christians gather. These undergird 'come' rather than 'go' forms of mission and sanctify venues rather than communities.
- The language of 'clergy' and 'laity' to describe two classes of Christian. This is inconsistent with New Testament ecclesiology and hinders the emergence of full-orbed and egalitarian Christian community.
- Other terms ('reverend', 'father', 'my lord bishop', 'your holiness', etc.) that contravene Jesus' explicit ban on honorific titles.[43]
- Non-inclusive language that perpetuates patriarchal assumptions and alienates those offended by its insensitivity.
- Using 'mainstream' and 'church' to differentiate respectable churches from those designated 'margins' or 'sects': in post-Christendom we are all marginal and (sociologically) sectarian.[44]
- Concepts of 'home mission' and 'foreign missions' as if this distinction made any sense in the context of global mission.
- Descriptions of evangelistic activities as 'campaigns' and 'crusades', given their militaristic history and associations.
- The language of 'winning converts' and 'taking our cities', suggesting ideas of conquest, have not been renounced.

---

[43] Matthew 12:8-10.
[44] George Lindbeck, 'The Sectarian Future of the Church', in J.P. Whelan (ed.), *The God Experience* (New York: Newman Press, 1971), 226–43.

- Asking 'what did you think of the preacher ...?' This
  focuses attention on rhetorical performance rather
  than communities learning together.

Church

We might consider other changes, such as using 'church' as
a verb, not a noun. This signals transition from institution
to movement, sidesteps interminable discussions about
structures and makes obsolete the ungainly and inappropriate term 'parachurch' for creative and mission-oriented
aspects of church life.

In some contexts, more radical changes may be required.
Some urban church planters avoid 'church' and 'Christian',
because of what these words convey to members of other
faiths, describing themselves instead as communities of
Jesus' followers. Maybe the term 'Christian' is problematic
throughout post-Christendom: if Jacques Ellul is right that
'Christendom astutely abolished Christianity by making us
all Christians',[45] then perhaps we need a term that conveys
the distinctiveness of following Jesus. A tongue-in-cheek
article proposed Christians call themselves 'Mounties',
because 'Christian' was devalued: the reference is to 'Ser-
mon-on-the-Mounties' to designate those who take Jesus'
teaching seriously!

Membership

The institutional language of 'membership' is also problematic. This is unappealing to many who are deeply
committed to congregations, let alone those on the edge.

---

[45] Jacques Ellul, *The Subversion of Christianity* (Grand Rapids:
Eerdmans, 1986), 39.

Some resist being labelled or included in organisational statistics; others are reluctant to signal denominational allegiance; some feel membership implies total agreement with everything a church teaches; others again are wary of communicating exclusivity. These reactions may be symptomatic of a 'post-commitment' culture, but during the transition to post-Christendom we might consider if this terminology is still helpful.

There are various responses to 'post-commitment' culture. Some urge churches to resist this and place more, not fewer, demands on members, citing evidence that many respond better to high expectations than mediocre demands. Others criticise the way church attendance is equated with committed church membership. Some argue the idea of membership, when accompanied by institutional language and expectations, is alien to Christian community: belonging is relational and does not need undergirding with bureaucratic paraphernalia. Philip Richter and Leslie Francis suggest churches 'recognise different types or levels of membership ... People may be invited to sign up as "seekers", "friends of the church", "associates" or "kindred spirits".'[46] John Drane commends a

> stakeholder model, in which there could and would be a place for diverse groups of people, who might be at different stages in their journey of faith, but who would be bound together by their commitment to one another and to the reality of the spiritual search, rather than by inherited definitions of institutional membership.[47]

This is not an arcane and irrelevant discussion about internal bureaucracy. A feature of post-Christendom churches is

---

[46] Richter and Francis, *Gone*, 144.
[47] John Drane, *McDonaldization*, 159.

the complicated relationship between 'believing', 'belonging' and 'behaving' – terms used in earlier chapters to examine Constantine's claim to be Christian and the nature of Christendom. The fluidity and variety apparent in how individuals relate to congregations make static models cumbersome. In post-Christendom many churches, often despite their theology, are discovering people need to belong before they believe or have discovered new ways of behaving.

Post-Christendom churches should spend more time nurturing their core values and community life than maintaining boundaries. Churches will need to be welcoming and accessible to those who are exploring faith and searching for authenticity – relaxed, responsive and non-judgemental communities where questions, doubts, criticisms and fears can be expressed, and where lifestyle issues do not jeopardise friendship. They will also need to embody core values that are attractive, clear, demanding and deeply owned. The term 'centred set' (rather than 'bounded set') is now popular to describe communities that welcome people to belong before they believe; but it is not always clear that the 'centred set' has a centre! We can define the centre in relation to Jesus Christ, the Christian story, theological principles, missional purposes, core values or some combination of these, but there needs to be a centre. Churches without centres are unsustainable and unattractive. Using familiar imagery, nourishing the 'centre' means the 'margins' can be open and flexible.

Jesus at the Centre

To suggest Jesus should be at the centre of 'centred set' churches or the spirituality of post-Christendom risks introducing a conventional ending to this book. But the price paid by the fourth-century church for moving from the margins to the centre was that Jesus was moved from the centre to the margins. Christendom – Christianity without Jesus at the centre – became conventional and oppressive. The marginal twenty-first-century church has an opportunity to restore Jesus to the centre and become creative and liberating. What might this involve?

- Paying attention to Jesus' human life – his relationships, radical teaching and exemplary lifestyle – and the implications for discipleship.
- Recognising that the significance of Jesus' death and resurrection cannot be detached from his life: not only asking 'why did Jesus die?' but also 'why did they kill him?'
- Indwelling the Gospel narratives in ways that shape our priorities, stir our imagination and train our reflexes.
- Reading Scripture from a Jesus-centred perspective, regarding his life as the focal point of God's self-revelation.
- Refusing to allow systems of interpretation or texts read without reference to Jesus to muffle his call to discipleship.
- Recovering the emphasis in pre-Christendom and the dissident movements on following Jesus, rather than only worshipping him.

A sermon and a prayer

During Christendom the most troublesome aspect of Jesus' teaching was the Sermon on the Mount. This required ingenious reinterpreting in the fourth and fifth centuries; dissident groups frequently rediscovered it and used it to chastise the establishment; and it continues to undermine efforts to make Christianity safe and conventional. Its uncompromising approach to truth, sex, wealth, retaliation, anxiety, relationships, power, oppression, loyalty, prayer and suffering disturbs civil religion and lukewarm discipleship. It has survived numerous attempts to emasculate its teaching, dilute its challenge and transform its counter-cultural message into pious platitudes.

But Jesus warned in the Sermon on the Mount[48] that his teaching would be admired rather than obeyed, and the lingering influence of Christendom still affects us.[49] John Alexander writes:

> Christians spend a lot of time and energy explaining why Jesus couldn't have meant what he said. This is understandable; Jesus was an extremist and we are all moderates. What's worse, he was an extremist in his whole life – not just in the narrowly spiritual areas – but in everything, so we have to find ways to dilute his teachings.[50]

But this passage provides many resources we need in post-Christendom. It offers unpretentious spirituality, principles for subversive political engagement, a discipleship ethic for marginal churches, resistance strategies against consumerism and religious hypocrisy, hope for a more just and gentle world and, at its heart, a short but remarkably potent prayer.

The Lord's Prayer[51] needs rescuing from over-familiarity and privatisation. Praying it, we are pleading for the

[48] Matthew 7:21–27.
[49] There are undeniably issues of interpretation to examine, but we should heed the warnings of the dissident tradition that these can excuse action.
[50] Cited in Tom Sine, *Mustard Seed versus McWorld: Reinventing Christian Life and Mission for the New Millennium* (Crowborough: Monarch, 1999), 246.
[51] Matthew 6:9–13.

in-breaking of God's upside-down kingdom and yearning (in jubilee language) for God's justice to transform human relationships so the hungry are fed, debts are cancelled and forgiveness outflanks retaliation. We are conscious of evil forces, wary of being seduced by their temptations and seeking deliverance. Unlike the Christendom creeds, where conflict is absent and everything seems static, this is a prayer for pilgrims who sense the clash of kingdoms and values. In post-Christendom we might retain its raw ending. Instead of concluding with the triumphant but bland 'for yours is the kingdom, the power and the glory, for ever and ever, Amen', perhaps we should pause where Jesus does: in the midst of conflict as we await the kingdom for which we are praying.

The example of Jesus

Restoring Jesus to the centre means probing the significance of the incarnation and following Jesus' example. Debates about the incarnation in the early Christendom years, though important in some respects, missed the most important point. Darrell Guder contrasts the meaning of the incarnation in Christendom with its application in pre-Christendom:

> The formulation of the gospel records reveals how important for the early church's missionary witness were the reports of the life, words and actions of the man Jesus. The incarnation was significant precisely because of its emphasis upon Jesus' humanness and its demonstration of what faithful witness to God is to be as taught and demonstrated by Jesus ... The essential character of the incarnation as the definition of Christian existence was largely diluted for the majority of Christendom.[52]

---

[52] Darrell Guder, *The Continuing Conversion of the Church* (Grand Rapids: Eerdmans, 2000), 110.

Perhaps in post-Christendom we can recapture the pre-Christendom perspective and ask how Jesus' human life inspires and guides mission and discipleship.

There are few explicit New Testament references to Jesus as example. A poignant instance is Jesus telling his shocked and embarrassed disciples he had washed their feet as an example.[53] Both the Christendom and dissident traditions have attempted to follow this example, though the dissidents' foot-washing practices seem closer to the spirit of Jesus' actions than the symbolic Maundy Thursday ceremony.[54] But 'follow me' at the beginning of Jesus' ministry and 'as the Father has sent me, I am sending you'[55] towards its end encourage us to read Jesus' whole life as an example. This offers resources for post-Christendom discipleship, such as:

- Jesus, the unpredictable evangelist – whose encounters with individuals were impossible to turn into a programme or methodology, contextually sensitive, winsome and challenging, gentle and unsettling – encourages us to evangelise in ways that invite rather than pressurise and intrigue rather than overwhelm.
- Jesus, the storyteller and question-poser – whose disciples were amused and perplexed by his sayings, whose opponents were disturbed and threatened by his probing and provocative parables, and who pricked bubbles of pomposity and surprised outcasts with his acceptance – inspires us to renounce prosaic

---

[53] John 13:15.
[54] The interest created by Archbishop of Canterbury Rowan Williams literally washing feet in 2003 (for the first time in centuries) suggests this practice still has subversive significance.
[55] John 1:43; John 20:21.

arguments and easy answers for dialogue, joyful exploration and openness to new insights.

- Jesus, the unconventional political activist – who threatened the establishment with his powerless authority, disappointed zealots with his disbelief that peace could come through violence, questioned political agendas and gave political language new meaning and depth – challenges us to subvert the system for its own good and trust faithfulness rather than efficacy.

- Jesus, the awkward dinner guest – who so often ate with the wrong people he was accused of gluttony, drunkenness and being a friend of sinners,[56] and whose parables describe the kingdom as a feast with unexpected companions – calls us to inclusive table fellowship and cross-cultural hospitality.

The teachings and example of Jesus also reveal his priorities and challenge ours. This does not mean mechanically tabulating references to different subjects in the Gospels as if frequency determined importance. Nor does it mean assuming Jesus had views only on topics the writers record him addressing. But reflecting on his unconventional engagement with various issues (such as punishing adulterers, Sabbath observance, eating with tax collectors and welcoming children), we may question if our priorities square with his.

We are as liable in post-Christendom as before to interpret Jesus in ways that fit our presuppositions (though we have available in the global church diverse resources to challenge our parochial readings), but the dissident movements testify that marginal communities rediscover aspects of the Jesus story churches at the centre overlook or discard as too threatening.

---

[56] Matthew 11:19.

Jesus on the margins

Our greatest resource in post-Christendom is Jesus. In a
society that is heartily and understandably sick of institutional Christianity, Jesus still commands interest and
respect. However garbled his teachings have become, and
however little his story is known, many people suspect Jesus
is good news, despite the shortcomings they see in our
churches and the distaste with which they regard our evangelistic activities. We may agree that 'to become an
"admirer of Jesus" (Kierkegaard's term) is much easier than
to become a follower',[57] but admiration – or even the curiosity evident in the snapshots with which this book began –
offers us a starting point.

Our priority must be to rediscover how to tell the story of
Jesus and present his life, teaching, death and resurrection –
recognising past attempts have seriously missed the mark.
We cannot continue to present Jesus only as the saviour
from guilt few feel in post-Christendom. Nor can we invite
people to follow a Jesus who merely guarantees life after
death to those who are otherwise comfortable or a Jesus
whose lordship affects only a limited range of personal
moral decisions. We can no longer present a safe establishment Jesus who represents order and stability rather than
justice, who appeals to the powerful and privileged for all
the wrong reasons. Nor can we reduce Jesus to dogmatic
statements in simplistic evangelistic courses or perpetuate
the overemphasis on his divinity at the expense of his
humanity that Christendom required.

Instead, we must present Jesus as (among much else)
friend of sinners, good news to the poor, defender of the
powerless, reconciler of communities, pioneer of a new age,

---

[57] Gordon Cosby, *By Grace Transformed* (New York: Cross-
road, 1999), 9.

freedom fighter, breaker of chains, liberator and peace-maker, the one who unmasks systems of oppression, identifies with the vulnerable and bring hope.

But if we would present Jesus in such ways to others we must encounter Jesus afresh ourselves. Disavowing Christendom and discovering mission strategies and ways of being church in post-Christendom, though important, are secondary to recovering the centrality of Jesus. The future of the church in Western culture – and possibly even Western culture itself – may depend on a fresh encounter with Jesus. An encounter with his example and teaching that inspires creative and counter-cultural living, an encounter with the meaning of his death and resurrection that unmasks the powers and gives hope for a different world, and an encounter with his Spirit that empowers and energises hopeful discipleship. It would be strange, however, if this encounter did not take place on the margins of church and society, since that is where Jesus is so often found. It is there he invites us to rediscover him and follow him in post-Christendom.

Appendix 1

The Donatists

History

Origins (311–316)

Mensurius, the Bishop of Carthage, died in 311: Caecilian succeeded Mensurius, but many thought him unsuitable. His personality was suspect, but more significant was his pro-government stance and suspicion he was either a *traditor* (someone who handed over copies of the Scriptures during persecution) or ordained by a *traditor*. In Africa, this was inexcusable. A council of bishops declared the consecration invalid and appointed Majorinus. Caecilian appealed to Constantine, who vindicated him. Majorinus died and was succeeded by Donatus, whose further appeal failed. Many rejected this decision and a schism developed. Little is known about Donatus, who for forty years led a movement that vied for recognition as the true church of Africa, but he was known as 'Donatus the Great' and acknowledged as a man of learning, integrity, wisdom, passion and oratory. His opponents destroyed his extensive writings, but Augustine acknowledged their brilliance.

Repression (317–321)

Constantine ordered Donatist leaders into exile and their churches confiscated. Donatus refused to comply, so churches were attacked and one Donatist bishop killed. The use of military force took the alliance between church and state into new territory and resulted in permanent schism. Donatists regarded this as evidence that Catholics were schismatics and their own movement was the true church. Repression failed and Constantine issued another decree granting toleration.

Consolidation (321–346)

Donatist churches were established throughout Africa: in many places they were unchallenged. Converts came from all classes, including philosophers and civic leaders. They tried to establish congregations outside Africa, and for 100 years Rome had a Donatist bishop. The divergent concerns of educated urban and oppressed rural Donatists produced the *Circumcellions*, a peasant organisation involved in direct action against landowners. Regarded by opponents as terrorists and supporters as freedom fighters, their activities enhanced and discredited Donatism.

Repression (347–361)

Donatus petitioned Constans for recognition as Bishop of Carthage. Constans sent representatives to investigate but they were not impartial and favoured the Catholics. Donatists and *Circumcellions* defied the imperial delegates, who massacred them and proscribed Donatism. Donatus and other leaders were exiled and the movement collapsed. Some returned to Catholicism and Catholic churches were established in Donatist areas. But Catholicism lacked effective leaders and Donatism retained the loyalty of the population.

Recovery (361–391)

Julian allowed exiled Donatists to return home and Donatism under Parmenian (Donatus had died) recovered. Catholic leaders were deposed and congregations absorbed into Donatist churches. Parmenian focused on maintaining Donatism's intellectual vigour and providing instruction for congregations. Hostility between Catholics and Donatists faded; toleration and respect developed.

Repression- (391–402).

Donatism was flourishing, with 400 bishops, but Primian, a more extreme leader, succeeded Parmenian. Optatus, Donatist Bishop of Thamugadi, joined Gildo, the imperial appointee in Africa, in attempting to form a nationalist government. An invasion force routed Gildo's army and executed Optatus. Roman rule was restored and Catholics re-emerged under the leadership of Aurelius of Carthage and Augustine of Hippo. Able bishops were appointed in Donatist strongholds, who gradually converted local inhabitants; even some Donatist bishops defected. Donatism was proscribed and, though Donatism was not yet a heresy, laws against heretics were applied.

Repression and resistance (403–429)

Frustrated by continuing resistance, the Council of Carthage decided to apply economic pressure. Then Honorius issued an edict, proscribing Donatism as heresy, prohibiting services, confiscating property and exiling leaders. In 411, a conference met to settle the conflict. A single day of debate resolved a century of division. The decision proscribed Donatist meetings and confiscated their property. Augustine attempted to enforce this and reunite the church throughout Africa. But Donatism was far from defunct. In some cities, Catholics advanced, but even here success was limited. The countryside remained loyal to Donatism. The *Circumcellions* continued to operate freely and were never effectively suppressed.

Persistence and demise

In 429 the Vandals invaded. We know little about the next 150 years – whether Donatism lay dormant, was absorbed into Catholic churches or continued to thrive. Justinian's re-conquest of Africa in 534 re-established Catholicism and an edict proscribed Donatism, suggesting it was still perceived as a threat. Donatism enjoyed a period of revival late in the sixth century – baptising converts, taking over Catholic churches, and establishing new bishoprics. As long as Christianity survived in Africa, the schism remained unhealed.

Beliefs

Although anti-heresy laws were used against them, their adversaries recognised Donatists as orthodox Christians. But Donatists disagreed profoundly about:

Ecclesiology

Donatists regarded themselves as the legitimate church in Africa: catholicity flowed from purity, not legitimacy from catholicity. Donatists taught that the church was a 'mystical union of the righteous inspired by the Holy Spirit and instructed by the Bible';[1] everyone took discipleship seriously, so they rejected monasticism; repentance, readiness to suffer and biblical study were crucial; they celebrated the *agape* meal and encouraged feasting and fasting. Bishops were highly regarded and standards expected were high: exemplary lives and readiness to suffer.

Church and society

The schism resulted from different responses to the Christendom shift: accommodation or continuing separation. Donatists taught that the church was a suffering people, expecting persecution, whether from pagans or false Christians; it must be separate from the world and not rely on state power or patronage; though resistance was legitimate, it should not persecute opponents; it was a missionary community, spreading geographically through making converts.

Ethics

Donatist sermons deplored low moral standards in Catholic churches. Some Donatist churches were wealthy, some resorted to violence; but many advocated non-violence and voluntary poverty. They were sensitive to social injustices and the oppression of the poor and they urged social justice in light of the approaching judgement.

Sacraments

Maintaining the purity and authenticity of the sacraments was fundamentally important within Donatism. The true

---

[1] W.H.C. Frend, *Saints and Sinners in the Early Church.* (Wilmington: Michael Glazier, 1985), 318.

church was the church whose sacraments were untainted. Catholics taught sacraments remained valid and effective despite unworthiness in officiating church leaders; Donatists regarded celebrants' worthiness as critical. Any baptised in churches tainted by fellowship with *traditors* were re-baptised. Consecrations in such circumstances were null and void. They rejected the Catholic argument that sacraments were gifts of Christ and valid despite clerical shortcomings.

Appendix 2

The Waldensians

History

In 1174, a French businessman, Valdes, encountered Jesus' teaching and committed himself to voluntary poverty and preaching. He had the Bible translated into the vernacular and gathered followers, from different social classes, but sharing a life of poverty and preaching – the 'Poor in Spirit'. They formed missionary bands, wore rough clothes and went around preaching repentance.

They had no intention of separating from Catholicism. But their simple lifestyle, popularity and unauthorised preaching aroused opposition. They were breaking canon law restricting doctrinal preaching to clergy. Valdes sought permission to preach but was refused. Growing more convinced of the church's corruption, they continued. The Archbishop of Lyons excommunicated them and expelled them from his jurisdiction. In 1184, they were included in a papal decree against heretics and, without evidence of unorthodoxy, became subject to anti-heresy legislation. But repression was patchy.

Through missions and enforced expulsion, groups developed elsewhere. Converts came from all social classes, including wealthy citizens, priests, monks and nuns. Their egalitarian stance attracted women and provoked hostility. In 1198, some authorities executed those refusing to recant, though persecution remained sporadic. Waldensian missionaries reached Lombardy and joined another radical group, the Humiliati, establishing congregations and schools.

Gradually tensions appeared. Valdes sought reconciliation with the Catholic Church and dreamed of bringing reform. More radical groups were challenging many aspects of Catholic teaching and practice. Some decided to form new churches. In 1205, the French and Italian branches split. Attempts at reunion continued; representatives met in 1218, but the conference failed.

Ineffective attempts to repress Waldensians gave way to a more discerning approach. Innocent III, Pope from 1198, distinguished between the genuinely heretical and those whose discontent distanced them from Catholicism, pursuing the former vigorously and wooing the latter by making concessions and welcoming their participation within the church.

French Waldensians enjoyed widespread peace and freedom until 1230. Persecution then increased, driving them underground and detaching less committed members. Numbers fell and, after 1300, inquisitors found few traces of the movement in Lyons. Waldensians survived by retreating into the mountains. The Lombards, under pressure and unable to establish alternative churches, took refuge in southern Italy or Alpine valleys. These losses in the heartlands were compensated for by growth elsewhere, as the movement spread into Austria, Bohemia, Moravia, Hungary, Poland and Spain.

By the fifteenth century, French and Italian Waldensians seemed in terminal decline, beleaguered peasants in remote valleys and small communities scattered throughout France. Only in Piedmont did Waldensians experience significant growth. Persecution was less intense but there were periods of severe pressure. Usually, Waldensians hid to avoid confrontation; occasionally, they resorted to violence. In 1487, a determined campaign against them resulted in executions, emigration and some returning to the Catholic Church.

German Waldensians were also an underground movement, surviving by outward conformity and transmission of beliefs within families to subsequent generations. In Bohemia and Moravia, Hussites encouraged Waldensians who encountered them. During the sixteenth century, exhausted by centuries of repression, they were absorbed into the Reformation as the Waldensian church, which continues today.

Beliefs

Anti-clericalism

Waldensians preached repentance, individual responsibility and holy living. They criticised clerical corruption and endorsed Bible study. Waldensians were marked by passionate desire to understand and obey the Bible. They had a 'believers' church' ecclesiology, where the local congregation ordered its life and recognised biblical authority alone.

Church structure

Waldensians emphasised the priesthood of all believers, men and women. Preachers were crucial but were not ordained, regarded as a separate class of Christians, or ranked in a hierarchy. They were committed to celibacy, travelling and poverty, depending for support on gifts from local groups. Once trained, they went in pairs to visit scattered groups. Those who were not preachers remained in their homes and jobs, studying the Bible and nurturing their faith in secret. They collected support for the preachers, ran training schools in their homes and tried to draw others into the movement.

Ethics

Waldensians were not interested in speculative theology or doctrinal issues, but in spirituality and ethics. They called people to follow and obey Jesus, advocating personal integrity, simple lifestyle and rejection of greed and excess. They opposed all forms of lying and deception and generally also refused to swear oaths. And usually they practised what they preached.

Non-violence

Early Waldensians were committed to non-violence, deriving this from a literal reading of the Gospels. They opposed violence: crusades against infidels and warfare in general; killing Jews; execution of thieves caught stealing food for their families; capital punishment; and coercion in matters of faith. This instinctive non-violence persisted, though occasionally Waldensians resorted to violence. Generally, this was provoked by repression, or the threat from defectors who might betray them, and was regarded as necessary to defend homes and family.

Simplicity

Finding familiar Catholic practices lacked biblical authority, Waldensians removed them from their churches and conformed to the simpler pattern they found in the New Testament. They regarded indulgences as benefiting greedy priests and challenged the doctrine of purgatory. They rejected prayers for the dead and official fast days and refused to bow before altars, venerate crosses or treat as special holy bread or water. Surprisingly, many retained devotion to Mary, despite their leaders' teachings.

Sacraments

They regarded communion as a remembrance, not a sacrifice, and all received bread and wine. They rejected the theology of the mass and were dubious about transubstantiation. Initially, many continued to receive communion from priests, but increasingly communion was celebrated in homes without clerical involvement. They were not convinced infant baptism was biblical or appropriate but seem rarely to have abandoned it.

Appendix 3

The Lollards

History

John Wyclif was an Oxford philosopher and theologian, whose early writings investigated complex metaphysical issues, before he turned to ecclesiastical abuses and developed anticlerical views. An establishment figure, his writings were not intended to foment social unrest or birth a new movement. His criticisms were accompanied by calls for reform, not the development of alternative churches, and he remained a member of the established church throughout his life. But his ideas inspired the first significant dissident movement in England. His academic reputation and powerful writings concerned the church authorities, who attempted to convict him of heresy and silence him. But protected by the support of powerful friends Wyclif propagated increasingly radical views until his death.

A practical initiative Wyclif suggested was the training and commissioning of 'poor preachers' to fill a gap he perceived in the established churches. His preachers would work alongside parish priests, teaching and evangelising. He provided an English Bible for his preachers and their hearers, and some of his writings were also in the vernacular, not Latin, so that theological discussion was no longer restricted to priests and academics.

These writings inspired a grass-roots movement. Groups emerging during his final years were dubbed 'Lollards' – probably deriving from a word meaning 'mumble' and mocking their practice of reciting Scripture or their praying. Lollards owed much to Wyclif's ideas, even if they knew them only in simplified form. He provided them with ammunition for a powerful assault on the established churches: it was a small step from denouncing the clergy to the priesthood of all believers.

After Wyclif's death, Lollard groups proliferated rapidly. Nicholas Hereford, John Aston, Philip Repton, Robert Winston and John Ashwardby (Oxford leaders) travelled widely and wrote extensively, gaining a substantial following. Under their leadership radical ideas were translated from academic to popular circles and Lollardy emerged as a loose-knit but identifiable phenomenon.

Lay evangelists, often dressed in russet tunics and walking barefoot, joined academic and clerical leaders. Most were from poorer sections of society, their greatest strength being among urban and rural artisans, especially those newly literate and open to fresh ideas. Lollard beliefs spread through public preaching, distribution of Bibles and tracts, and invitations to 'reading circles' to study the Bible and discuss radical ideas.

Lollard preaching urged personal responsibility rather than passive acceptance of clerical authority and expressed doubts many felt about seemingly superstitious ecclesiastical beliefs and practices. Disseminating portions of the Bible in English enabled Lollards to demonstrate these lacked biblical support.

The spread of this movement alarmed the authorities, who tried to arrest it, but no co-ordinated strategy developed. Many bishops reacted slowly and found Lollards deeply rooted in their dioceses when they finally acted. Lollard leaders enjoyed widespread popular support – and protection from influential landowners – making ecclesiastical action difficult. Secular authorities, though concerned about peasant unrest and possible Lollard complicity, cared little about ecclesiastical disputes.

From 1401, Lollards' opponents were authorised to execute relapsed and impenitent heretics. But English authorities were reluctant to use torture and burning to eradicate heresies, and Lollards profited from this restraint. Those arrested were generally given time to recant: the authorities wanted to restore them to the church, not execute them.

But in 1413, Sir John Oldcastle, the most distinguished secular Lollard leader, began to recruit for armed rebellion, presumably to impose Lollard reforms on church and nation. He was betrayed to the authorities before this could be implemented. But this incident roused official and public opinion against Lollardy. Oldcastle and others involved in the rebellion were executed. Lollards were discovered and prosecuted; now the authorities could rely on outraged neighbours to betray them. Gradually repression became less severe, but Lollardy was now an underground movement.

In the 1450s, Lollards recommenced evangelism and established new groups. Reading circles attracted adherents, and the authorities failed to halt distribution of Lollard literature and English Bibles. Their beliefs spread within families and through trade contacts. Sermons were transcribed and distributed to adherents and enquirers. Most groups were in southern England, the main centres in the fifteenth century being Kent, London, the Chilterns, Essex, Bristol, Coventry and East Anglia.

Beliefs

Personal responsibility/biblical authority

Lollards encouraged personal Bible study and reliance on the Holy Spirit as guide, urging members to reach independent decisions on matters of faith rather than accepting ecclesiastical opinions and dogmas.

Rejection of superstition

Lollards contrasted the early church's simplicity with the formalism and complexity of contemporary church life. They rejected anything they perceived as superstitious, including purgatory, transubstantiation and prayers for the dead. They regarded pilgrimages as a moneymaking scheme for priests.

Priesthood of all believers

Lollards rejected the clergy/laity distinction, replacing institutional church authority with the authority of the Bible interpreted in community. Although Lollards occasionally ordained leaders, most involved all believers, men and women, in all aspects of church life.

Sacraments

Lollards stressed commonsense beliefs, regarding transubstantiation as a perverted recent development. Some believed infant baptism was as acceptable in a ditch as a font, or rejected this altogether, because Christ redeemed infants. They valued marriage but some rejected clerical involvement.

Ethics

Lollards criticised the low moral standards of parishioners and clergy (especially sexual misdemeanours and social insensitivity), preaching repentance, discipleship and concern for the poor. Some taught war might be justified but other means were preferable; others opposed participation in war, making weapons, capital punishment, and self-defence; some supported armed rebellion. Some taught tithing lacked New Testament support; others held tithing was voluntary but unworthy priests should not receive tithes. Some opposed oaths as contrary to Jesus' teaching; others taught oaths were legitimate to save lives.

Appendix 4

The Anabaptists

History

Anabaptism was a sixteenth-century radical renewal movement in territories that now comprise parts of Switzerland, Austria, the Czech Republic, Germany, Alsace and the Netherlands. Its distinguishing features included Christocentrism, emphasis on new birth and discipleship in the power of the Spirit, establishment of believers' churches free from state control, commitment to economic sharing, and a vision of restoring New Testament Christianity.

It drew adherents primarily from poorer sections of the community, though early leaders included university graduates, monks and priests. Assessing its numerical strength is difficult, because it was driven underground by persecution; it certainly influenced many more people than those baptised as members. Historians identify four main branches – Swiss Brethren, South German/Austrian Anabaptists, Dutch Mennonites and communitarian Hutterites – but these comprised numerous groups gathered around charismatic leaders with distinctive practices and emphases.

Though other factors (such as social discontent) stimulated its emergence, its leaders acknowledged that Anabaptism owed much to the Reformation. But several features differentiated Anabaptists:

Radicalism

Anabaptists criticised the Reformers for not following through biblical convictions. They were convinced Scripture was authoritative for ethics and church life as well as doctrine. Anabaptists reminded Reformers of their own more radical early views, which they had jettisoned, and championed immediate action rather than the Reformers' cautious approach.

Restitution

Anabaptists believed the church was fallen beyond reform. Thorough restoration of New Testament Christianity was necessary, which required freedom from state control and ecclesiastical traditions. Anabaptists urged separation of church and state and rejected the Christendom system, asserting that the church was in error on the question of its identity and relationship with society.

An alternative tradition

Anabaptist ideas resonated with earlier movements, such as the Unitas Fratrum, Waldensians and Lollards. Anabaptists were heirs of the 'old evangelical brotherhoods', an alternative tradition that had reappeared throughout the centuries, advocating beliefs and practices the established church ignored or marginalised.

A church of the poor

Like those earlier groups, Anabaptists were mostly poor and powerless, with few wealthy, academic or influential members. Though few were primarily politically or economically motivated, they were regarded as subversive.

Some Anabaptists emerged from the failed Peasants' Revolt (1524–1526), pursuing their agenda through the alternative strategy of establishing communities where just practices were fostered. Anabaptist views owe much to their powerless position: they were prepared to obey the Bible regardless of social consequences. Anabaptism, as a grass-roots revival with disturbing social implications, was vehemently opposed by those whose vested interests were threatened.

Anabaptists

Anabaptists called themselves Christians or brothers and sisters; their opponents called them enthusiasts, revolutionaries or 'Anabaptists'. This label, meaning 're-baptisers', had negative connotations. Anabaptists objected to this: they did not regard believers' baptism as rebaptism for they denied the validity of infant baptism. Baptism was not the main issue, though it symbolised their rejection of Christendom.

Catholics and Protestants both persecuted Anabaptists and the movement was nearly exterminated. Those who survived did so by finding refuge in tolerant cities, keeping on the move, meeting in secret and becoming quiet about their beliefs. Gradually Mennonites and Hutterites migrated into Eastern Europe and Russia. From all over Europe, further migration took many to Canada and America. But most Anabaptists now live in the southern continents. In the twentieth century, through extensive and creative mission activities (evangelism, church planting, disaster relief, development work, and action for peace and justice in divided communities) Anabaptism became a global movement.

Beliefs

The Bible

Anabaptists agreed with the Reformers about the Bible's authority but disagreed strongly about its interpretation. They focused particularly on Jesus' life and teachings: 'Christocentrism' guided their biblical interpretation. They regarded the Bible as an unfolding of God's purposes, with the New Testament providing normative guidelines for ethics and church life. They challenged the Reformers' use of Old Testament models and disagreed with them about baptism, war, tithing, church government and oaths.

Salvation

The Reformers emphasised justification by faith and forgiveness of past sins. Anabaptists emphasised new birth and discipleship. The Reformers feared Anabaptists were reverting to salvation by works; Anabaptists accused them of not addressing moral issues biblically and tolerating unchristian behaviour in their churches. Anabaptists stressed the Spirit's work in believers and insisted Jesus was to be followed and obeyed as well as trusted.

The church

Anabaptists formed churches of committed disciples, denying that all citizens should automatically be church members. They differentiated believers from unbelievers, so membership was voluntary and meaningful. They acknowledged the state's role in government but resisted state control of their churches. They rejected infant baptism as unbiblical, forcibly imposed on children and hindering development of believers' churches. They challenged clericalism, lack of church discipline and coercion in matters of faith. Early gatherings were sometimes charismatic and unstructured, concentrating on Bible study; many encouraged women to participate.

Evangelism

The Reformers did not generally practise evangelism. Assuming within Protestant territories that church and society were indistinct, they pastored people through the parish system, rather than evangelising them as unbelievers. Anabaptists rejected this interpretation of society and embarked on a mission to evangelise Europe. They travelled widely, preached in homes and fields, interrupted church services, baptised converts and planted churches. Such evangelism by untrained men and women, ignoring national and parish boundaries, was regarded as outrageous.

Ethics

Anabaptists were socially deviant, challenging contemporary norms and living in anticipation of God's kingdom. They relativised private property. Some groups practised community of goods. Most retained personal ownership but taught their possessions were available to any in need. Whenever they shared communion they confirmed this mutual commitment. They rejected violence, refusing to defend themselves and urging love for enemies and respect for human life. They accepted governments would use force but taught this was inappropriate for Christians. Many refused to swear oaths, citing Jesus' teaching and arguing they should always be truthful, not just under oath. Nor would they swear loyalty to secular authorities.

Suffering

Anabaptists were not surprised by persecution. They regarded suffering for obedience to Christ as unavoidable and biblical: suffering persecution was a mark of the true church, as Jesus had taught.

Select Bibliography

Bainton, Roland, *Christian Attitudes Towards War and Peace: A Historical Survey and Critical Re-evaluation* (Nashville: Abingdon Press, 1960)

Barnes, Timothy, *Constantine and Eusebius* (Cambridge: Harvard University Press, 1981)

Bartley, Jonathan, *The Subversive Manifesto: Lifting the Lid on God's Political Agenda* (Oxford: Bible Reading Fellowship, 2003)

Bosch, David, *Transforming Mission: Paradigm Shifts in the Theology of Mission* (Maryknoll: Orbis, 1991)

Bradstock, Andrew and Christopher Rowland (eds.), *Radical Christian Writings: A Reader* (Oxford: Blackwell, 2002)

Bredero, Adriaan, *Christendom and Christianity in the Middle Ages: The Relations Between Religion, Church, and Society* (Grand Rapids: Eerdmans, 1986)

Brown, Callum, *The Death of Christian Britain: Understanding Secularisation 1800–2000* (London: Routledge, 2001)

Brown, Peter, *The Rise of Western Christendom: Triumph and Diversity, AD 200–1000* (Oxford: Blackwell, 2003)

Brueggemann, Walter, *Cadences of Home: Preaching Among Exiles* (Louisville: Westminster John Knox Press, 1997)

Cameron, Euan, *The Reformation of the Heretics: The Waldenses of the Alps, 1480–1580* (Oxford: Clarendon Press 1984)

Clapp, Rodney, *A Peculiar People: The Church as Culture in a Post-Christian Society* (Downers Grove: InterVarsity Press, 1996)

Davie, Grace, *Europe: The Exceptional Case* (London: Darton, Longman & Todd, 2002)

Drake, H.A., *Constantine and the Bishops: The Politics of Intolerance* (Baltimore: John Hopkins University Press, 2000)

Drane, John, *The McDonaldization of the Church: Spirituality, Creativity, and the Future of the Church* (London: Darton, Longman & Todd, 2000)

Durnbaugh, Donald, *The Believers' Church: The History and Character of Radical Protestantism* (Scottdale: Herald Press, 1985)

Fletcher, Richard, *The Barbarian Conversion: From Paganism to Christianity* (Berkeley & Los Angeles: University of California Press, 1999)

Fox, Robin Lane, *Pagans and Christians* (Harmondsworth: Penguin, 1986)

Frend, W.H.C., *The Donatist Church: A Movement of Protest in Roman North Africa* (Oxford: Clarendon, 1985)

Greenslade, S.L., *Church and State from Constantine to Theodosius* (London: SCM Press, 1954)

Hall, Douglas, *The End of Christendom and the Future of Christianity* (Harrisburg: Trinity 1996)

Hauerwas, Stanley, *After Christendom?: How the church is to behave if freedom, justice, and a Christian nation are bad ideas* (Nashville: Abingdon, 1991)

Hauerwas, Stanley and William Willimon, *Resident Aliens: A provocative Christian assessment of culture and ministry for people who know that something is wrong* (Nashville: Abingdon, 1991)

Herrin, Judith, *The Formation of Christendom* (Princeton: Princeton University Press, 1997)

Hudson, Anne, *The Premature Reformation: Wycliffite Texts and Lollard History* (Oxford: Clarendon Press, 1988)

Jenkins, Philip, *The Next Christendom: The Coming of Global Christianity* (New York: Oxford University Press, 2002)

Jones, A.H.M., *Constantine and the Conversion of Europe* (Harmondsworth: Penguin, 1972)

Kee, Alister, *Constantine versus Christ: The Triumph of Ideology* (London: SCM, 1982)

Kreider, Alan, *The Change of Conversion and the Origin of Christendom* (Harrisburg: Trinity Press, 1999)

—— (ed.), *The Origins of Christendom in the West* (Edinburgh: T. & T. Clark, 2001)

Lambert, Malcolm, *Medieval Heresy: Popular Movements from the Gregorian Reform to the Reformation* (Oxford: Blackwell, 1992)

Lieu, Samuel and Dominic Montserrat, *From Constantine to Julian: Pagan and Byzantine Views* (London: Routledge, 1996)

MacMullen, Ramsay, *Christianizing the Roman Empire (AD 100–400)* (New Haven: Yale University Press, 1984)

——, *Christianity and Paganism in the Fourth to Eighth Centuries* (New Haven: Yale University Press, 1997)

Markus, R.A. *The End of Ancient Christianity* (Cambridge: Cambridge University Press, 1990)

Murray, Stuart, *Church Planting: Laying the Foundations* (Carlisle: Paternoster Press, 1998)

——, *Beyond Tithing* (Carlisle: Paternoster Press, 2000)

——, *Biblical Interpretation in the Anabaptist Tradition* (Kitchener: Pandora Press, 2000)

Pearse, Meic, *The Great Restoration: The Religious Radicals of the 16th and 17th Centuries* (Carlisle: Paternoster Press, 1998)

Roxburgh, Alan, *The Missionary Congregation, Leadership, and Liminality* (Harrisburg: Trinity Press, 1997)

Smith, David, *Mission After Christendom* (London: Darton, Longman & Todd, 2003)

Snyder, C. Arnold, *Anabaptist History and Theology: An Introduction* (Kitchener: Pandora Press, 1995)

Walls, Andrew *The Missionary Movement in Christian History: Studies in the Transmission of Faith* (Edinburgh: T. & T. Clark, 1996)

——, *The Cross-Cultural Process in Christian History: Studies in the Transmission and Appropriation of Faith* (Edinburgh: T. & T. Clark, 2002)

Waugh, Scott & Peter Diehl (eds.), *Christendom and its Discontents: Exclusion, Persecution, and Rebellion, 1000–1500* (Cambridge: Cambridge University Press, 1996)

Wessels, Anton, *Europe: Was it ever Really Christian?: The Interaction Between Gospel and Culture* (London: SCM Press, 1994)

Wright, Nigel, *Disavowing Constantine: Mission, Church and the Social Order in the Theologies of John Howard Yoder and Jürgen Moltmann* (Carlisle: Paternoster Press, 2000)

Yoder, John Howard, *The Priestly Kingdom: Social Ethics as Gospel* (Notre Dame: University of Notre Dame Press, 1984)